STUDY GUIDE AND CASEBOOK FOR MANAGERIAL ECONOMICS

THIRD EDITION

Study Guide and Casebook for Managerial Economics

THIRD EDITION

by

Edwin Mansfield
University of Pennsylvania

W. W. Norton & Company
New York London

ISBN 0–393-96776-X

W. W. Norton & Company, Inc., 500 Fifth Avenue, New York, NY 10110
W. W. Norton & Company Ltd., 10 Coptic Street, London WC1A 1PU

1 2 3 4 5 6 7 8 9 0

Contents

Preface

This *Study Guide and Casebook* is designed to supplement my text, *Managerial Economics*, third edition. A major feature of the third edition of this *Study Guide* is that it contains the following eight full-length classroom-tested cases: (1) How H-P Used Tactics of the Japanese to Beat Them at Their Game (*Wall Street Journal*), (2) K. M. Westelle and Associates, Inc. (by Rhonda Aull), (3) Production Functions and Cost Functions in Oil Pipelines (by Leslie Cookenboo), (4) A Managerial Application of Cost Functions by a Railroad (by Edwin Mansfield and Harold Wein), (5) Applied CAD Knowledge, Inc. (by John Seeger and Raymond Kinnunen), (6) CATCO Electronics Corporation (USA) (by Patrick Schul, William Cunningham, and Lynn Gill), (7) The Carriage House Inn: A Family Corporation (by Michael Everett), (8) Revving Up for Relief: Harley-Davidson at the ITC (by Dorothy Robyn with assistance from Don Lippincott). I am grateful to these authors and publications for permission to reprint their cases here. Each chapter of this book parallels closely the contents of the corresponding chapter of my text. In order to provide comprehensive and varied exercises and problems, a four-pronged approach has been adopted:

1. *Chapter profiles* highlight and summarize the principal points of the chapter in the text.
2. Limbering-up exercises in the form of *completion questions* open the way to systematic review of each chapter.
3. Self-tests in the form of *true or false* and *multiple choice* questions are provided.
4. A considerable number of *problems* are taken up. These problems often simulate real-world situations and require the student to work with actual data in tabular and diagrammatic form.

Answers to all the questions and problems are contained at the end of each chapter.

This book contains over 500 questions and problems, enough to provide the student with a thorough review. Since a study guide should be a flexible learning tool, I have sought to supply not only a large number of questions but also a wide range in terms of difficulty. Each chapter begins at a relatively easy level, increasing gradually in rigor as students build confidence along with competence. The more demanding an economic concept, the more extensive the amount of review material given to it. Some of the problems at the end of chapters are hard enough so that the typical student should not expect to answer them all. Even the best students should be challenged by some of them.

E.M.

September 1995

Part One
INTRODUCTION

CHAPTER 1

Introduction to Managerial Economics

Chapter Profile

Managerial economics draws heavily on economics (particularly microeconomics) and the decision sciences. In contrast to microeconomics, which is largely descriptive, managerial economics is prescriptive. Courses in managerial economics provide fundamental analytical tools, as well as play a major integrating role. Managerial economics is at the core of the management of nonbusiness organizations like government agencies, as well as the management of firms.

Both for nonbusiness organizations and firms, the process of decision making can be divided into the following five basic steps. (1) Establish or identify the organization's objectives. (2) Define the problem. (3) Identify possible solutions. (4) Select the best possible solution. (5) Implement the decision.

To apply managerial economics to business management, we need a theory of the firm. According to the theory accepted by most managerial economists, the firm tries to maximize its value, defined as the present value of its expected future cash flows (which for now are equated with profits). However, this maximization occurs subject to constraints, since the firm has limited inputs, particularly in the very short run, and must act in accord with a variety of laws and contracts.

Managerial economists define profits somewhat differently than do accountants. When economists speak of profit, they mean profit over and above what the owners' labor and capital employed in the business could earn elsewhere. To a considerable extent, the differences between the concept of profit used by the accountant and that used by the economist reflect the difference in their functions.

Three important reasons for the existence of profits are innovation, risk, and monopoly power. Profits and losses are the mainsprings of a free-enterprise economy. They are signals that indicate where resources are needed and where they are too abundant. They are important incentives for innovation and risk taking. They are society's reward for efficiency.

Although managerial economists generally assume that firms want to maximize profit (and hence their value), this assumption is not universally adopted. Some have suggested that the firm "satisfices" rather than maximizes profit. That is, firms aim at a satisfactory rate of profit rather than the maximum figure. Others have pointed out that a principal-agent problem arises if managers pursue their own interests, even though this decreases the profits of the owners. These models can be useful, but profit maximization remains the standard assumption in managerial economics.

Every market has a demand side and a supply side. The market demand curve shows the amount of a product that buyers would like to purchase at various prices. The market supply curve shows the amount of a product that sellers would offer at various prices. The equilibrium price is the price where the quantity demanded equals the quantity supplied.

The field of managerial economics is intimately related to a prominent problem facing the United States and Canada (and a number of other countries)—the fact that many of our firms are being challenged more seriously by foreign rivals. In the business environment of the 1990s, there is little room for managers who fail to understand the principles and techniques of managerial economics.

Questions

Wool: An Opening Example

Because this is an introductory chapter, we do not present the full range of questions that will be included in subsequent chapters of this study guide. We begin by considering an interesting and important example—the case of wool.

(a) During the late 1980s, wool prices increased considerably due in part to increased demand by China and the former Soviet Union. From 1977 to 1988, the price of wool for worsted clothing rose from $3.67 to $5.81 per pound. Expecting that wool prices would remain high, wool producers raised a lot more sheep. Did this result in a shift to the right in the supply curve for wool? Why or why not?

(b) At the same time, the Chinese and Russians cut back on their purchases of wool because of lack of foreign currency (and in the case of China, because of organizational problems). Did this shift the demand curve for wool to the left? Why or why not?

(c) Australia is the world's largest producer of wool, and for a time the Australian Wool Corporation propped up the price of wool by buying up any unsold Australian wool. Why was this necessary to prevent the price from falling?

(d) The Australian Wool Corporation had to buy up so much wool that it exhausted its cash reserves and its credit. The firm turned for help to the Australian government, but its parliament refused to guarantee further loans to buy up even more surplus wool. In March 1991, the actual price of wool fell to about $2.50 per pound. Why?

True or False

_____ 1. No equilibrium price nor equilibrium quantity exists if a good's demand curve is a vertical line and its supply curve is a horizontal line.

_____ 2. The demand curve for a free good (a good with a zero price) must be a horizontal line.

_____ 3. If actual price exceeds equilibrium price, there is a tendency for actual price to rise.

_____ 4. A shift to the right of the market supply curve tends to increase the equilibrium price.

_____ 5. In any market, the seller alone determines the price of the product that is bought and sold. Since the seller has the product, while the buyer does not have it, the buyer must pay what the seller asks.

Multiple Choice

1. Suppose that the market demand curve and the market supply curve for broccoli are as shown in the graph below.

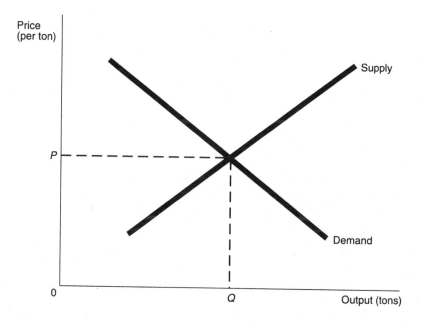

If the government sets a price equal to $2P$ per ton, the result will be

   a.   a reduction in the quantity of broccoli supplied.
   b.   an excess supply of broccoli.
   c.   a shift to the right of the market supply curve for broccoli.
   d.   all of the above.
   e.   none of the above.

2. In the previous question, if a university report indicates that broccoli contains important, hitherto-unrecognized ingredients that can help stave off cancer (as in fact was indicated in 1992)[1] the result is likely to be

   a.   a shift to the right in the market supply curve for broccoli.
   b.   a shift to the left in the market supply curve for broccoli.
   c.   a shift to the right in the market demand curve for broccoli.
   d.   all of the above.
   e.   none of the above.

---

[1]*New York Times*, March 25, 1992, p. C1.

3. If the government imposes a tax of $1 per ton on broccoli, the equilibrium price of broccoli will

   a. fall.
   b. increase by $10.
   c. increase by $2.
   d. increase.
   e. be unaffected.

4. If the price of asparagus falls considerably, the result is likely to be

   a. a shift to the right in the market demand curve for broccoli.
   b. a shift to the left in the market supply curve for broccoli.
   c. a shift to the left in the market demand curve for broccoli.
   d. an increase in the equilibrium price of broccoli.
   e. none of the above.

5. If the price of asparagus falls considerably and if the government freezes the price of broccoli at the level prevailing before the fall in the price of asparagus, the result is likely to be

   a. a surplus of broccoli.
   b. a shortage of broccoli.
   c. a shift to the left in the market supply curve for broccoli.
   d. a shift to the right in the market supply curve for broccoli.
   e. none of the above.

Problems

1. Based on unofficial estimates by economists at the U.S. Department of Agriculture, the market demand curve for wheat in the American market in the early 1960s was (roughly) as follows:

Farm price of wheat (dollars per bushel)	Quantity of wheat demanded (millions of bushels)
1.00	1,500
1.20	1,300
1.40	1,100
1.60	900
1.80	800
2.00	700

In the middle 1970s, the market demand and supply curves for wheat in the American market were (roughly) as follows:

Farm price of wheat (dollars per bushel)	Quantity of wheat demanded (millions of bushels)	Quantity of wheat supplied (millions of bushels)
3.00	1,850	1,600
3.50	1,750	1,750
4.00	1,650	1,900
5.00	1,500	2,200

a. If the market demand curve in the middle 1970s had remained as it was in the early 1960s, can you tell whether the farm price of wheat in the middle 1970s would have been greater or less than $2? Explain.

b. Did a shift occur between the early 1960s and the middle 1970s in the market demand curve for wheat? If so, was it a shift to the right or the left, and what factors were responsible for this shift?

c. Suppose that the government had supported the price of wheat at $4 in the middle 1970s. How big would have been the excess supply? What would have been some of the objections to such a policy?

2. a. The supply curve for a particular kind of cheese is

$$Q_S = 100 + 3P$$

where Q_S is the quantity supplied of this cheese (in millions of pounds per year) and P is the price of this cheese (in dollars per pound). If the demand curve for this cheese is a vertical line at $Q_D = 106$ millions of pounds per year, and if the government imposes a price floor of $1 per pound on this cheese, will there be an excess supply or excess demand of this cheese, and how big will it be?

b. If the government's price floor is set at $3 per pound, will there be an excess supply or excess demand of this cheese, and how big will it be?

Answers

Wool: An Opening Example
(a) Yes, because at each price more wool would be supplied than before.
(b) Yes, because at each price less wool would be demanded than before.

(c) To keep the price above its equilibrium level, the Australian Wool Corporation had to buy up the difference between the quantity supplied and quantity demanded.

(d) When the Australian Wool Corporation no longer propped up the price, it fell to its equilibrium level, which was about $2.50 per pound.

True or False

1. False   2. False   3. False   4. False   5. False

Multiple Choice

1. b   2. c   3. d   4. c   5. a

Problems

1. a. It is impossible to tell. At $2, the quantity demanded would have been 700 million bushels, but we are not given the quantity supplied at $2. If it were greater than 700 million bushels, the equilibrium price would have been less than $2; if it were less than 700 million bushels, the equilibrium price would have been greater than $2.

    b. Yes. At $3, the quantity of wheat demanded during the 1960s would have been less than 700 million bushels, if the demand curve was downward sloping to the right. During the 1970s, 1,850 million bushels were demanded at $3. Thus the demand curve seemed to shift to the right. The reason was increased foreign demand due partly to poor harvests in the Soviet Union, Australia, and Argentina, as well as devaluation of the dollar.

    c. 250 million bushels. Such surpluses have been an embarrassment, both economically and politically. They suggest that society's scarce resources are being utilized to produce products that consumers do not want at existing prices. Also, the cost of storing these surpluses can be large.

2. a. In equilibrium, $Q_S = Q_D$, so

$$100 + 3P = 106$$
$$3P = 6$$
$$P = 2$$

Thus the equilibrium price is $2 per pound. Since this exceeds the government's price floor, there will be no excess supply or excess demand of this cheese.

    b. If $P = 3$, the quantity supplied equals $100 + 3(3) = 109$, and the quantity demanded equals 106, so the excess supply equals $109 - 106$, or 3; that is, it equals 3 million pounds per year.

CHAPTER 2

Optimization Techniques

Chapter Profile

Functional relationships can be represented by tables, graphs, or equations. The marginal value of a dependent variable is defined as the change in this variable associated with a one-unit change in a particular independent variable. The dependent variable achieves a maximum when its marginal value shifts from positive to negative.

The derivative of Y with respect to X, denoted by dY/dX, is the limit of the ratio $\Delta Y/\Delta X$ as ΔX approaches zero. Geometrically, it is the slope of the curve showing Y (on the vertical axis) as a function of X (on the horizontal axis). We have provided rules that enable us to find the value of this derivative.

To find the value of X that maximizes or minimizes Y, we determine the value of X where dY/dX equals zero. To tell whether this is a maximum or a minimum, we find the second derivative of Y with respect to X, denoted by d^2Y/dX^2, which is the derivative of dY/dX. If this second derivative is negative, we have found a maximum; if it is positive, we have found a minimum.

A dependent variable often depends on a number of independent variables, not just one. To find the value of each of the independent variables that maximizes the dependent variable, we determine the partial derivative of Y with respect to each of the independent variables, denoted by $\partial Y/\partial X$, and set it equal to zero. To obtain the partial derivative of Y with respect to X, we apply the ordinary rules for finding a derivative; however, all independent variables other than X are treated as constants.

Managers of firms and other organizations generally face constraints that limit the options available to them. In relatively simple cases where there is only one constraint, we can use this constraint to express one of the decision variables as a function of the other decision variables, and we can apply the techniques for unconstrained optimization.

In more complex cases, constrained optimization problems can be solved by the method of Lagrangian multipliers. The Lagrangian function combines the function to be maximized or minimized with the constraints. To solve the constrained optimization problem, we optimize the Lagrangian function.

Questions

Completion

1. The derivative of Y with respect to X is defined as the limit of _____ as ΔX approaches _____.

2. If Y equals a constant, $\dfrac{dY}{dX}$ equals _____.

3. If Y equals AX^b, $\dfrac{dY}{dX}$ equals _____.

4. If $Y = U + W$, $\dfrac{dY}{dX}$ equals _____.

5. In the graph below, the slope of the curve equals _____ when Y is a maximum.

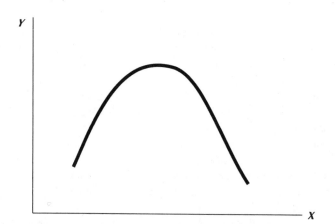

6. In the previous question, the value of d^2Y/dX^2 is (positive, negative, zero) _____ at the point where Y is a maximum.

7. If TR equals total revenue and Q equals output, $\dfrac{dTR}{dQ}$ equals _____.

8. The partial derivative of Y with respect to X_1 shows the effect of X_1 on _____ when other independent variables are

    _____ _____.

9. The Lagrangian multiplier λ, measures the change in the variable to be maximized or minimized if the constraint is relaxed by _____ unit(s).

True or False

_____   1. The marginal value of a dependent variable is always positive or zero.

_____   2. At any point where $\dfrac{d^2Y}{dX^2}$ is negative, Y is a maximum.

_____ 3. To find the value of $\partial Y/\partial X_1$, all independent variable other than X_1 are treated as constants.

_____ 4. If $Y = 3X^4$, $\dfrac{dY}{dX} = 12X^2$.

_____ 5. If $Y = 2X + X^3$, $\dfrac{dY}{dX} = 2 + 3X^2$.

_____ 6. If $Y = 3X_1 + 4X_2$, $\dfrac{\partial Y}{\partial X_1} = 4$.

_____ 7. If $Y = 3X_1 + 6X_2$, it is impossible to find a value of X_1 and X_2 where $\dfrac{\partial Y}{\partial X_1}$ and $\dfrac{\partial Y}{\partial X_2}$ equal zero.

_____ 8. If $Y = 4X(2 - X^2)$, $\dfrac{dY}{dX} = 8 - 12X^2$.

_____ 9. If $Y = 5X_1^{.2} X_2^{.8}$, $\dfrac{\partial Y}{\partial X_1} = .2(5X_1^{-.8} X_2^{.8})$.

_____ 10. If $Y = f(W)$ and $W = g(X)$, $\dfrac{dY}{dX} = \dfrac{dY}{dW} \cdot \dfrac{dW}{dX}$.

Multiple Choice

1. If $Y = -30 + 20X - 10X^2$, the value of X that maximizes Y equals

   a. 1.
   b. 2.
   c. 3.
   d. 4.
   e. none of the above.

2. In question 1, the maximum value of Y equals

   a. −20.
   b. −30.
   c. −10.
   d. 20.
   e. none of the above.

3. If $Y = 40 - 5X + 10X^2$, the value of X that minimizes Y equals

   a. .15.
   b. .20.
   c. .25.
   d. .30.
   e. none of the above.

4. In question 3, the minimum value of Y equals

    a. $39^{5}/_{8}$.
    b. $40^{3}/_{8}$.
    c. $40^{5}/_{8}$.
    d. $39^{3}/_{8}$.
    e. none of the above.

5. In question 3, the value of d^2Y/dX^2 at the minimum value of Y is

    a. 5.
    b. −5.
    c. 20.
    d. 10.
    e. none of the above.

6. If $Y = 100 + 2X - \dfrac{3}{2}X^2 + \dfrac{X^3}{3}$, the values of X that result in $\dfrac{dY}{dX}$ equaling zero are

    a. 1 and 2.
    b. 1 and 3.
    c. 2 and 3.
    d. 2 and 4.
    e. none of the above.

7. In question 6, if $X = 1$, the value of $\dfrac{d^2Y}{dX^2}$ is

    a. −8.
    b. −6.
    c. −4.
    d. −1.
    e. none of the above.

8. In question 6, Y is a maximum when X equals

    a. 0.
    b. 1.
    c. 2.
    d. 3.
    e. none of the above.

9. If $Y = 100 + 20X_1 + 14X_2 - 2X_2^2$, the value of $\dfrac{\partial Y}{\partial X_1}$

    a. does not vary with the value of X_1.
    b. does not vary with the value of X_2.
    c. equals 20.
    d. all of the above.
    e. none of the above.

10. In question 9, the value of $\dfrac{\partial Y}{\partial X_2}$

    a. equals $14 - 4X_2$.
    b. equals zero when $X_2 = 3.5$.
    c. decreases as X_2 increases.
    d. all of the above.
    e. none of the above.

Problems

1. The total cost function at the Tate Company is $TC = 200 + 3Q + 7Q^2$, where TC is total cost, and Q is output.

    a. What is marginal cost when $Q = 1$?
    b. What is marginal cost when $Q = 5$?
    c. What is marginal cost when $Q = 10$?

2. For the Algonquin Company, the relationship between profit and output is as follows:

Output (number of units per day)	Profit (thousands of dollars per day)
0	−8
1	−4
2	0
3	4
4	8
5	11
6	13
7	12
8	11

    a. What is the marginal profit when output is between 1 and 2 units per day? When output is between 4 and 5 units per day?
    b. At what output is profit a maximum?
    c. At what output is average profit a maximum? Should the Algonquin Company produce this output? Why or why not?

3. Determine the first derivative of the following functions:

    a. $Y = 4$.
    b. $Y = 4X$.
    c. $Y = 4X^2 + 6$.
    d. $Y = 4X^3 + 6X$.
    e. $Y = 4X^3 + 6X + 10$.

4. The Phoenix Corporation's chief executive officer believes that the relationship between its profit (π) and its output (Q) is as follows:

$$\pi = -20 - 5Q + 10Q^2 - 2Q^3.$$

   a. Should this firm set $Q = 5$? Why or why not?
   b. Should it set $Q = 10$? Why or why not?
   c. Should it set $Q = 20$? Why or why not?

5. Find the partial derivative of Y with respect to X in each of the following cases:

   a. $Y = 8 + 4X + 6Z$.
   b. $Y = 8X + 4X^2 + 6Z$.
   c. $Y = 8X + 4X^3 + 6Z + 2Z^2$.
   d. $Y = X \div Z$.

6. At the Peoria Company, the relationship between profit (π) and output (Q) is as follows:

$$\pi = -40 + 20Q - 2Q^2.$$

   a. At what value of Q does $\dfrac{d\pi}{dQ} = 0$?
   b. Is π minimized or maximized at this value of Q?
   c. What is the second derivative of π with respect to Q at this value of Q?

7. Determine the second derivative of Y with respect to X in each of the following cases:

   a. $Y = 7X$.
   b. $Y = 7 \div X$.
   c. $Y = 7X^2$.
   d. $Y = 7X(2 + X^2)$.

8. The Cornell Corporation makes two products, chairs and tables. The relationship between π, the firm's annual profit (in thousands of dollars), and its output of each good is

$$\pi = -80 + 30Q_1 + 25Q_2 - 4Q_1^2 - 3Q_2^2 - 2Q_1Q_2,$$

where Q_1 is the firm's hourly output of chairs, and Q_2 is the firm's hourly output of tables. (Neither Q_1 nor Q_2 needs to be an integer.)

   a. Find the output of chairs and the output of tables that will maximize the firm's profit.
   b. What is the maximum profit that the firm can earn per year?

9. For the Knowland Corporation, the relationship between profit and output is the following:

Output (number of units per day)	Profit (thousands of dollars per day)
0	−30
1	−24
2	−15
3	0
4	6
5	21
6	36
7	63
8	66
9	69
10	60

a. What is the marginal profit when output is between 3 and 4 units per day? When output is between 8 and 9 units per day?
b. At what output is average profit a maximum?
c. Should the Knowland Corporation produce 7 units per day? Why or why not?

10. The total cost function at the Driftwood Company is $TC = 300 + 2Q + 3Q^2$, where TC is total cost and Q is output.

a. What is marginal cost when output is 8?
b. What is marginal cost when output is 10?
c. What is marginal cost when output is 12?

11. The Secane Company's profit is related in the following way to its output:

$$\pi = -80 + 30Q - 4Q^2,$$ where π is total profit and Q is output.

a. If the firm's output equals 5, what is its marginal profit?
b. Derive an equation relating the firm's marginal profit to its output.
c. What output will maximize the firm's profit?

12. The Lone Star Corporation makes two products, lumber and paper. The relationship between π, the firm's annual profit (in thousands of dollars), and its output of each good is

$$\pi = -100 + 80Q_1 + 60Q_2 - 10Q_1^2 - 8Q_2^2 - 5Q_1Q_2,$$

where Q_1 is the firm's annual output of lumber (in tons), and Q_2 is the firm's annual output of paper (in tons). Find the output of each good that the Lone Star Corporation should produce if it wants to maximize profit.

13. A firm produces two goods. Its total cost per day (in dollars) equals

$$TC = 14X_1^2 + 18X_2^2 - 3X_1X_2,$$

where X_1 is the number of units of the first good produced per day, and X_2 is the number of units of the second good produced per day. Because of commitments to customers, the firm must produce a total of 20 units of the two goods per day. If the firm's managers want to minimize its costs (without violating the commitment to its customers), how many units of each good should it produce per day?

Answers

Completion

1. $\Delta Y/\Delta X$, zero   2. zero   3. bAX^{b-1} 4. $\dfrac{dU}{dX} + \dfrac{dW}{dX}$ 5. zero   6. negative

7. marginal revenue   8. Y, held constant   9. one

True or False

1. False   2. False   3. True   4. False   5. True   6. False   7. True   8. True
9. True   10. True

Multiple Choice

1. a   2. a   3. c   4. d   5. c   6. a   7. d   8. b   9. d   10. d

Problems

1. Marginal cost equals dTC/dQ.
   a. $3 + 14(1) = 17$.
   b. $3 + 14(5) = 73$.
   c. $3 + 14(10) = 143$.

2. a. 4 thousand dollars, 3 thousand dollars.
   b. 6 units per day.
   c. 5 units per day. If the firm wants to maximize profit, it obviously should not produce this output.

3. a. Zero.
   b. 4.
   c. $8X$.
   d. $12X^2 + 6$.
   e. $12X^2 + 6$.

4. a. No. Since $d\pi/dQ$ is not equal to zero when $Q = 5$, π is not a maximum.
   b. No. Since $d\pi/dQ$ is not equal to zero when $Q = 10$, π is not a maximum.
   c. No. Since $d\pi/dQ$ is not equal to zero when $Q = 20$, π is not a maximum.

5. a. 4.
   b. $8 + 8X$.
   c. $8 + 12X^2$.
   d. $\dfrac{1}{Z}$.

6. a. 5.
   b. Q is maximized.
   c. -4.

7. a. Zero.
   b. $14/X^3$.
   c. 14.
   d. $42X$.

8. a. $\dfrac{\partial \pi}{\partial Q_1} = 30 - 8Q_1 - 2Q_2 = 0$

   $\dfrac{\partial \pi}{\partial Q_2} = 25 - 6Q_2 - 2Q_1 = 0.$

   Since $Q_2 = 15 - 4Q_1$, it follows that
   $$25 - 6(15 - 4Q_1) - 2Q_1 = 0$$
   $$22Q_1 = 65$$
   $$Q_1 = 65/22.$$
   Thus, $Q_2 = 15 - 4(65/22) = 15 - 4(2.95) = 15 - 11.8 = 3.2$.

   b. $\pi = -80 + 30(2.95) + 25(3.2) - 4(2.95)^2 - 3(3.2)^2 - 2(2.95)(3.2)$
   $= -80 + 88.5 + 80 - 34.81 - 30.72 - 18.88$
   $= 4.09$.

9. a. 6 thousand dollars, 3 thousand dollars.
   b. 7 units per day.
   c. Not if it wants to maximize profit.

10. Marginal cost equals dTC/dQ.
    a. $2 + 6(8) = 50$.
    b. $2 + 6(10) = 62$.
    c. $2 + 6(12) = 74$.

11. a. $\dfrac{d\pi}{dQ} = 30 - 8Q = 30 - 8(5) = -10$.
    b. Marginal profit $= 30 - 8Q$.
    c. $Q = 30/8$.

12. $\dfrac{\partial \pi}{\partial Q_1} = 80 - 20Q_1 - 5Q_2 = 0$

    $\dfrac{\partial \pi}{\partial Q_2} = 60 - 16Q_2 - 5Q_1 = 0.$

Since $Q_2 = 16 - 4Q_1$,

$$60 - 16(16 - 4Q_1) - 5Q_1 = 0$$
$$59Q_1 = 196$$
$$Q_1 = 3.32.$$

Thus, $Q_2 = 16 - 4(3.32) = 2.72$. In other words, Lone Star should produce 3.32 tons of lumber and 2.72 tons of paper.

13. Because $X_1 = 20 - X_2$,

$$TC = 14(20 - X_2)^2 + 18X_2^2 - 3(20 - X_2)(X_2)$$

$$= 5,600 - 560X_2 + 14X_2^2 + 18X_2^2 - 60X_2 + 3X_2^2$$

$$= 5,600 - 620X_2 + 35X_2^2$$

$$\frac{dTC}{dX_2} = -620 + 70X_2 = 0$$

$$X_2 = \frac{620}{70} = 8.86.$$

Since $X_1 = 20 - X_2$, it follows that $X_1 = 11.14$. In other words, the firm should produce 11.14 units of the first good and 8.86 units of the second good per day.

Part Two

DEMAND AND FORECASTING

CHAPTER 3

Demand Theory

Chapter Profile

The market demand curve for a good shows how much of the good will be demanded at each price. The market demand curve shifts in response to changes in tastes, incomes, and the prices of other goods, as well as a host of other factors.

The market demand function for a good is an equation showing how the quantity demanded depends on the good's price, the incomes of consumers, the prices of other goods, advertising expenditure, and other factors. Holding all factors other than the good's price constant, one can derive the market demand curve for the good from the market demand function. Market demand functions can be formulated for individual firms as well as for entire industries.

The price elasticity of demand is the percentage change in quantity demanded resulting from a 1 percent change in price; more precisely, it equals $-(\partial Q_D/\partial P)(P/Q_D)$. Whether a price increase (or decrease) results in an increase in the total amount spent by consumers on a product depends on the price elasticity of demand.

Marginal revenue is the change in total revenue resulting from a 1-unit increase in quantity; that is, it equals the derivative of total revenue with respect to quantity. Marginal revenue equals $P\left(1 - \dfrac{1}{\eta}\right)$, where P is price, and η is the price elasticity of demand.

The price elasticity of demand for a good tends to be high if it has a large number of close substitutes. Also, for non-durable goods, it tends to be higher in the long run than in the short run. It is sometimes asserted that the demand for a product is relatively price inelastic if the product accounts for a very small percentage of the typical consumer's budget, but this need not be the case.

The income elasticity of demand is the percentage change in quantity demanded resulting from a 1 percent increase in consumer income; that is, it equals $(\partial Q/\partial I)(I/Q)$, where I is the aggregate money income of consumers. The income elasticity of demand may be positive or negative. Like the price elasticity of demand, it is of major importance in forecasting the long-term growth of the quantity demanded for many major products.

The cross elasticity of demand is the percentage change in the quantity demanded of product X resulting from a 1 percent increase in the price of product Y; in other words, it equals $(\partial Q_X/\partial P_Y)(P_Y/Q_X)$. If X and Y are substitutes, it is positive; if they are complements, it is negative. This elasticity is important to managers because they must try to understand and forecast the effects of changes in other firms' prices on their own firm's sales.

The optimal price for a product depends on its price elasticity of demand as well as on its marginal cost. To maximize profit, a firm should set its price equal to $MC\left(\dfrac{1}{1 - 1/\eta}\right)$, where MC is marginal cost, and η is the price elasticity of demand.

Questions

Completion

1. If the cross elasticity of demand between goods X and Y is positive, these goods are classified as _____.

2. The income elasticity of demand is the percentage change in quantity demanded resulting from a _____ change in money income.

3. Luxury goods are generally assumed to have a _____ income elasticity of demand.

4. If a commodity has many close substitutes, its demand is likely to be _____.

5. The price elasticity of demand equals _____ .

6. The demand curve for the individual firm under perfect competition is _____.

7. The price elasticity of demand is generally _____ in the long run than in the short run (for non-durable goods).

8. The total amount of money spent by consumers on a commodity equals the industry's _____ .

9. The _____ curve shows marginal revenue at various quantities of output.

10. If the industry is not perfectly competitive, the firm's demand curve will not be _____ .

True or False

_____ 1. The demand for open-heart surgery is likely to be less price elastic than the demand for aspirin.

_____ 2. If a good's income elasticity exceeds 1, a decrease in the price of the good will increase the total amount spent on it.

_____ 3. The demand curve for an individual firm under perfect competition is downward sloping, its slope being -1.

_____ 4. The market demand curve for a product under perfect competition is horizontal.

_____ 5. The demand for salt and pepper is likely to be price elastic.

_____ 6. In general, demand is likely to be more inelastic in the long run than in the short run (for non-durable goods).

_____ 7. The income elasticity of demand for food is very high.

_____ 8. It is always true that $\eta_{xy} = \eta_{yx}$.

_____ 9. The direct approach of simply asking people how much they would buy of a particular commodity is the best way to estimate the demand curve.

_____ 10. The income elasticity of demand will always have the same sign regardless of the level of income at which it is measured.

_____ 11. Marginal revenue is the ratio of the value of sales to the amount sold.

_____ 12. When the demand curve is linear, the slope of the marginal revenue curve is twice (in absolute value) the slope of the demand curve.

Multiple Choice

1. The president of a leading producer of tantalum says that an increase in the price of tantalum would have no effect on the total amount spent on tantalum. if this is true, the price elasticity of demand for tantalum is

   a. less than zero.
   b. 1.
   c. 2.
   d. more than 1.
   e. none of the above.

2. The demand for a good is price inelastic if

   a. the price elasticity is 1.
   b. the price elasticity is less than 1.
   c. the price elasticity is greater than 1.
   d. all of the above.
   e. none of the above.

3. The relationship between marginal revenue and the price elasticity of demand is

   a. $MR = P\left(1 - \dfrac{1}{\eta}\right)$.
   b. $P = MR\left(1 - \dfrac{1}{\eta}\right)$.
   c. $P = MR(1 + \eta)$.
   d. $MR = P(1 + \eta)$.
   e. none of the above.

4. A demand curve with unitary elasticity at all points is

    a. a straight line.
    b. a parabola.
    c. a hyperbola.
    d. all of the above.
    e. none of the above.

5. Suppose we are concerned with the relationship between the quantity of food demanded and aggregate income. It seems most likely that this relationship will look like

    a. curve *A* below.
    b. curve *B* below.
    c. curve *C* below.
    d. the vertical axis.
    e. the horizontal axis.

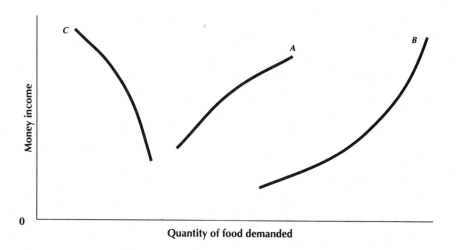

6. If goods *X* and *Y* are substitutes, the relationship between the quantity demanded of good *X* and the price of good *Y* should be like

    a. curve *A* below.
    b. curve *B* below.
    c. the vertical axis.
    d. the horizontal axis.
    e. none of the above.

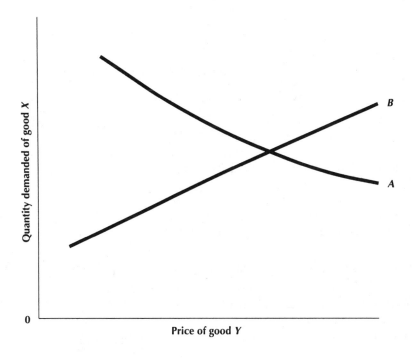

Problems

1. The Economic Research Service of the U.S. Department of Agriculture has reported the results of a study of the effects of the price of various types of oranges on the rate at which they were purchased.[2] In particular, three types of oranges were studied: (1) Florida Indian River, (2) Florida Interior, and (3) California. In nine test stores in Grand Rapids, Michigan, the researchers varied the price of each of these types of oranges for a month. The effect of a 1 percent increase in the price of each type of orange on the rate of purchase of this and each of the other types of oranges is shown below. For example, a 1 percent increase in the price of Florida Indian River oranges (holding other prices constant) seemed to result in a 3.1 percent decrease in the rate of purchase of Florida Indian River oranges, a 1.6 percent increase in the rate of purchase of Florida Interior oranges, and a 0.01 increase in the rate of purchase of California oranges.

[2]M. Godwin, W. Chapman, and W. Manley, *Competition between Florida and California Valencia Oranges in the Fresh Market* (U.S. Department of Agriculture, December 1965). This paper is also summarized in G. Stokes, *Managerial Economics: A Casebook* (New York: Random House, 1969). I have changed the numbers slightly.

A 1 percent increase in the price of:	Results in the following percentage change in the rate of purchase of:		
	Florida Indian River	Florida Interior	California
Florida Indian River	−3.1	+1.6	+0.01
Florida Interior	+1.2	−3.0	+0.1
California	+0.2	+0.1	−2.8

   a. What seems to be the price elasticity of demand for each type of orange?

   b. What seems to be the cross elasticity of demand for each pair of types of oranges?

   c. Which types of oranges seem to be the closest substitutes?

   d. Of what use might these results be to orange producers?

   e. How accurate do you think this study was? What improvements would you make in it?

2. a. The price elasticity of demand for a particular kind of screwdriver is 2, and marginal revenue is $2. What is the price of this screwdriver?

   b. The demand curve for screwdrivers shifts from D_1 in 1996 to D_2 in 1997. Use calculus to prove that the price elasticity of demand at any price less than $10 will be the same as it was before the shift in the demand curve.

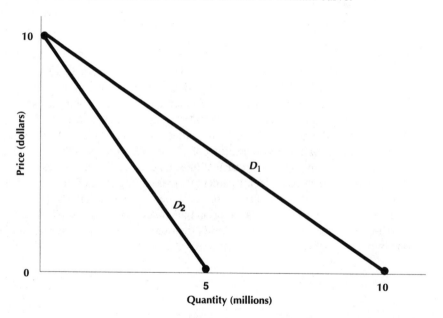

3. The president of your firm claims that the price elasticity of demand is the same as the slope of the demand curve. You (quite correctly) argue that this is not true. To buttress your point, you draw a linear demand curve (from B to A on the following grid) and point out that, although the slope is the same at all points along the demand curve, the price elasticity of demand differs from point to point. (Thus, the

slope and the price elasticity of demand cannot be the same.) The president of your firm asks you to identify those points (on the demand curve you have drawn) where the demand for the product is price elastic, those points where it is price inelastic, and those points where it is of unitary elasticity. Respond to his request.

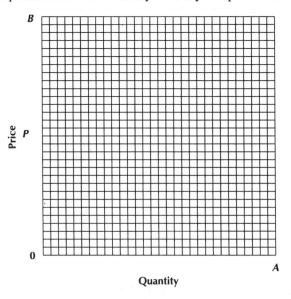

4. a. According to the president of Bethlehem Steel, the demand for steel is price inelastic because steel generally constitutes a very small percentage of the total cost of the product that includes it as a raw material. If this is the case, will a price increase result in an increase or decrease in the amount of money spent on steel?

   b. Suppose you are a business consultant and you become convinced that the U.S. steel industry underestimates the price elasticity of demand for steel. In what way might this information be useful to the steel companies? To the public?

5. a. According to Gregory Chow of Princeton University, the price elasticity of demand for automobiles in the United States is 1.2, and the income elasticity of demand for automobiles is 3. What would be the effect of a 3 percent decline in auto prices on the quantity of autos demanded, assuming Chow's estimates are right?

   b. What would be the effect of a 2 percent increase in income?

6. a. According to the Swedish economist Herman Wold's estimates, the income elasticity of demand for liquor is about 1. If you were an executive for a liquor firm, of what use might this fact be to you in forecasting sales?

   b. According to Rex Daly of the U.S. Department of Agriculture, the price elasticity of demand for coffee is about 0.25 to 0.30, and the income elasticity of demand is about 0.23. Suppose you were an economist for the coffee industry. How could you use this information to help forecast coffee sales in the United States?

7. The Rosenberg Corporation, a maker of machine tools, determines that the demand curve for its product is as follows:

$$P = 1,000 - 40Q,$$

where P is the price (in dollars) of a machine tool, and Q is the number of machine tools sold per month.

  a. What is the price elasticity of demand if price equals $500?
  b. At what price, if any, will the demand for Rosenberg's product be of unitary elasticity?

8. The David Company's demand curve for the company's product is

$$P = 2,000 - 20Q,$$

where P is the price, and Q is the number sold per month.

  a. Derive the marginal revenue curve for the firm.
  b. At what outputs is the demand for the firm's product price elastic?
  c. If the firm wants to maximize its dollar sales volume, what price should it charge?

9. The Byron Company's marketing vice president concludes that the demand function for its product is

$$Q = 50P^{-1.3}I^{0.9}A^{0.2},$$

where Q is the quantity demanded per month, P is the product's price (in dollars), I is disposable income (in dollars), and A is the firm's advertising expenditures (in thousands of dollars).

  a. What is the price elasticity of demand?
  b. Will increases in price result in increases or decreases in the amount spent on Byron's product?
  c. What is the income elasticity of demand?
  d. What is the advertising elasticity of demand?

10. The Keats Corporation estimates that its demand function is as follows:

$$Q = 200 - 2P + 3I + .5A,$$

where Q is the quantity demanded per month, P is the product's price (in dollars), I is per capita disposable income (in thousands of dollars), and A is the firm's advertising expenditures (in thousands of dollars per month). (In all parts of this problem, population is assumed to remain constant.)

  a. During the next decade, per capita disposable income is expected to increase by about $3,000. What effect will this have on the firm's sales?
  b. If Keats wants to raise its price enough to offset the effect of the increase in per capita disposable income, by how much must it raise its price?
  c. If Keats raises its price by this amount, will it increase or decrease the price elasticity of demand? Explain.

11. The president of the Malibu Corporation estimates that the demand function for the firm's product is

$$Q = 30P^{-2.5}I^{0.8},$$

where Q is the quantity demanded, P is the product's price, and I is disposable income. The marginal cost of the firm's product is estimated to be $40.

a. Malibu's price for its product is $60. Is this the optimal price? Why or why not?

b. If it is not the optimal price, write a brief memorandum indicating what price might be better, and why.

12. Harnischfeger, a leading machinery producer, tried to make major changes in the rough-terrain crane industry. It redesigned its cranes for easy manufacture and service through the use of modularized components and reduced material content. It established a conveyorized assembly line and ordered parts in large volumes. The firm's strategy was to become a low-cost producer in the industry. Based on its cost reductions, the firm was able to offer a product of acceptable quality and cut price by 15 percent, the result being that its market share increased from 15 to 25 percent.[3] Did the demand for its product seem to be price elastic? Explain. (Assume that the total quantity demanded in the market was the same before and after this price cut.)

Answers

Completion

1. substitutes 2. 1 percent 3. high 4. price elastic 5. $-\dfrac{\partial Q_D}{\partial P} \cdot \dfrac{P}{Q_D}$

6. horizontal 7. higher 8. total revenue 9. marginal revenue

10. horizontal

True or False

1. True 2. False 3. False 4. False 5. False 6. False 7. False

8. False 9. False 10. False 11. False 12. True

Multiple Choice

1. b 2. b 3. a 4. c 5. b 6. b

Problems

1. a. The price elasticity of demand for Florida Indian River oranges seems to be 3.1, the price elasticity of demand for Florida Interior oranges seems to be 3.0, and the price elasticity of demand for California oranges seems to be 2.8.

---

[3] M. Porter, *Competitive Strategy* (New York: Free Press, 1980), p. 37.

b. The cross elasticities (η_{xy}) are as follows:

Y	Florida Indian River	X Florida Interior	California
Florida Indian River	—	1.6	0.01
Florida Interior	1.2	—	0.1
California	0.2	0.1	—

c. Clearly, Florida Indian River and Florida Interior oranges are closer substitutes than the Florida and California oranges.

d. The fact presented in part c is of obvious use to orange growers in both parts of the country.

e. The study is limited, of course, by the fact that it pertains to only one city during only one relatively short period of time.

2. a. Since $MR = P\left(1 - \dfrac{1}{\eta}\right)$, it follows that $P = MR \div \left(1 - \dfrac{1}{\eta}\right)$. In this

case, $MR = \$2$ and $\eta = 2$; thus, $P = \$2 \div \left(1 - \dfrac{1}{2}\right)$, or $\$4$. ($MR$ equals

marginal revenue, P equals price, and η equals the price elasticity of demand.)

b. The price elasticity of demand is $-\dfrac{dQ}{dP} \cdot \dfrac{P}{Q}$. If the demand curve is D_1,

$\dfrac{dQ}{dP} = -1$; thus, $-\dfrac{dQ}{dP} \cdot \dfrac{P}{Q} = \dfrac{P}{Q} = \dfrac{P}{10 - P}$. If the demand curve is D_2,

$\dfrac{dQ}{dP} = \dfrac{-1}{2}$; thus, $-\dfrac{dQ}{dP} \cdot \dfrac{P}{Q} = \dfrac{P}{2Q} = \dfrac{P}{10 - P}$. Since the price elasticity of

demand equals $\dfrac{P}{10 - P}$ in each case, it must be the same for both demand

curves if the price is the same. (Note that if the demand curve is D_1,

$Q = 10 - P$, and if it is D_2, $Q = 5 - \dfrac{1}{2}P$. This is clear from the diagram in

the problem.)

3. The demand curve you have drawn is *BA*.

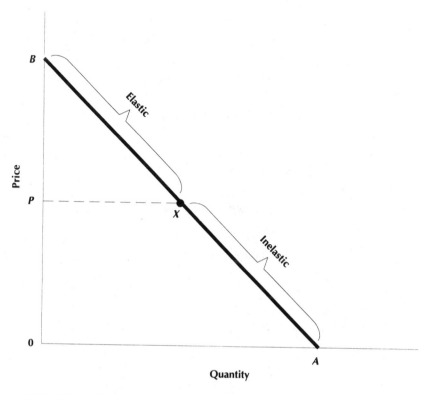

Point *X* is midway between points *B* and *A*.

4. a. It will result in an increase in the amount of money spent on steel.
   b. It might indicate that both the companies and the public might be better off if steel prices were lowered somewhat, since the quantity demanded might expand more than heretofore expected.

5. a. There would be about a 3.6 percent increase in quantity demanded.
   b. There would be about a 6 percent increase in quantity demanded.

6. a. All other things equal, you could expect that a 1 percent increase in income would result in about a 1 percent increase in the total quantity of liquor demanded.
   b. A 1 percent change in price would be expected to result in about a 0.28 percent change in quantity demanded. A 1 percent increase in income would be expected to increase the quantity demanded by about 0.23 percent.

7. a. Since $P = 1{,}000 - 40Q$, it follows that

$$Q = 25 - .025P.$$

Thus, $\dfrac{dQ}{dP} = -.025$. If $P = 500$, $Q = 12.5$. Therefore,

$$-\frac{dQ}{dP} \cdot \frac{P}{Q} = \frac{.025(500)}{12.5} = 1.$$

Thus, the price elasticity of demand equals one.
    b. $500.

8. a. $MR = 2{,}000 - 40Q$.
    b. If the demand is price elastic, marginal revenue is positive. Thus, the demand is price elastic if

$$MR = 2{,}000 - 40Q > 0,$$

which is true if $Q < 50$.
    c. To maximize its dollar sales volume, the firm should set $\dfrac{dTR}{dQ} = 0$, where TR equals total revenue. Since $\dfrac{dTR}{dQ}$ equals marginal revenue, this means that it should set marginal revenue equal to zero. Since $MR = 0$ when $Q = 50$, it follows that the price should be set at $1{,}000.

9. a. 1.3.
    b. Decreases.
    c. 0.9.
    d. 0.2.

10. a. It will increase the quantity demanded per month by about 9.
    b. $4.50.
    c. It will increase it.

11. a. To maximize profit, price should equal

$$\$40\left(\frac{1}{1 - 1/2.5}\right),$$

since the price elasticity of demand equals 2.5. Thus, price should be $40 \div 0.6 = \$66.67$.
    b. See part a.

12. Yes. Let Q be the total quantity demanded in the market (which we assume to be constant), and let P be the original price charged by the firm. The arc price elasticity of demand equals

$$-\left(\frac{.25Q - .15Q}{.20Q}\right) \div \left(\frac{.85P - P}{.925P}\right) = 3.1.$$

CHAPTER 4

Consumer Behavior and Rational Choice

Chapter Profile

An indifference curve contains points representing market baskets among which the consumer is indifferent. If the consumer prefers more (not less) of both commodities, an indifference curve must have a negative slope. Market baskets on higher indifference curves provide more satisfaction than those on lower indifference curves. Utility is a number that indexes the level of satisfaction derived from a particular market basket. Market baskets with higher utilities are preferred over market baskets with lower utilities. The marginal rate of substitution shows how many units of one good must be given up if the consumer, after getting an extra unit of another good, is to maintain a constant level of satisfaction. To obtain the marginal rate of substitution, multiply the slope of the indifference curve by minus one.

The budget line contains all of the market baskets that the consumer can buy, given his or her money income and the level of each price. Increases in income push the budget line upward; changes in the price ratio alter the budget line's slope. To attain the highest level of satisfaction that is compatible with the budget line, the consumer must choose the market basket on the budget line that is on the highest indifference curve. This market basket is at a point where the budget line is tangent to an indifference curve (unless there is a corner solution). If the consumer maximizes utility, he or she will choose in equilibrium to allocate his or her income so that the marginal rate of substitution of one good for another good equals the ratio of the prices of the two goods (unless there is a corner solution).

The theory of consumer behavior is often used to represent the process of rational choice. Frequently, a person or an organization has a certain amount of money to spend and must decide how much to allocate to a number of different uses. This theory indicates how such decisions should be made.

A consumer's demand curve shows how much the consumer will purchase of the good in question at various prices of the good, when other prices and the consumer's income are held constant. The theory of consumer behavior can be used to derive the consumer's demand curve, and the market demand curve can be obtained by summing the individual demand curves horizontally.

Questions

Completion

1. All other things being equal, it is assumed that the consumer always prefers _____ of a commodity to _____ of a commodity.

2. Economists assume that the consumer attempts to _____ utility.

3. The consumer, when confronted with two alternative _____ , can decide which he prefers or whether he or she is _____ between them.

4. If one market basket has more of one commodity than a second market basket, it must have (less, more) _____ of the other commodity than the second market basket—assuming that the two market baskets are to yield equal _____ to the consumer.

5. Besides knowing the consumer's preferences, we must also know his or her _____ and the _____ of commodities to predict which market basket he or she will buy.

6. Every indifference curve must slope (downward, upward) _____ and to the right to reflect the fact that commodities are defined so that (less, more) _____ of them are preferred to (less, more) _____ .

7. Since market baskets on higher indifference curves are given (higher, lower) _____ utilities, and since market baskets on higher indifference curves are always (preferred, not preferred) _____ to market baskets on lower indifference curves, the consumer will always choose a market basket with a (higher, lower) _____ utility over a market basket with a (higher, lower) _____ utility.

8. The consumer's _____ show what he or she wants, and the consumer's _____ shows which market baskets his or her income and prices permit him or her to buy.

9. An increase in money income means that the budget line (falls, rises) _____ , and a decrease in money income means that the budget line (falls, rises) _____ .

10. Commodity prices affect the budget line: a decrease in a commodity's price causes the budget line to cut this commodity's axis at a point (closer to, farther from) _____ the origin.

True or False

_____ 1. If the consumer's tastes were transitive, the consumer would have inconsistent or contradictory preferences.

_____ 2. According to the theory of consumer behavior, the consumer's equilibrium market basket is the one which yields maximum utility, given the constraints imposed on the consumer by his or her income and by prices.

_____ 3. The best way to allocate the military budget is to spend it all on the highest priority item of each service.

_____ 4. A utility is a number that represents the level of satisfaction the consumer derives from a particular market basket.

_____ 5. Indifference curves cannot intersect.

_____ 6. Market baskets on higher indifference curves must have lower utilities than market baskets on lower indifference curves.

_____ 7. The consumer's budget line shows the market baskets that can be purchased, given the consumer's income and prevailing commodity prices.

_____ 8. The higher the consumer's money income, the lower the budget line.

_____ 9. A consumer buys two goods, U and V. If the price of a unit of U is equal to the price of a unit of V, the slope of the consumer's budget line is −1.

_____ 10. Two consumers buy two goods, U and V. The first consumer is located in a region where the price of U is higher than in the region where the second consumer is located. The price of V is the same in both regions. Nonetheless, if the first consumer's income is higher than the second consumer's, it is possible for the two consumers' budget lines to be parallel.

Multiple Choice

1. An increase in the consumer's income will

   a. shift the budget line outward from the origin but not affect its slope.
   b. shift the budget line outward from the origin and increase its slope.
   c. shift the budget line outward from the origin and decrease its slope.
   d. not shift the budget line.
   e. none of the above.

2. In equilibrium, the rate at which the consumer is willing to substitute one commodity for another (holding satisfaction constant) must equal

   a. the consumer's income.
   b. the price of the good on the horizontal axis.
   c. the price of the good on the vertical axis.
   d. the rate at which the consumer is able to substitute one good for the other.
   e. none of the above.

3. The marginal rate of substitution is

   a. the slope of the consumer's indifference curve.
   b. the slope of the consumer's indifference curve multiplied by minus one.
   c. always equal to the price ratio.
   d. never equal to the price ratio.
   e. none of the above.

4. Indifference curves can intersect if

   a. the consumer is poorly educated.
   b. the two goods are high-priced.
   c. the consumer's income is very low.
   d. all of the above.
   e. none of the above.

5. If the expected return from an investment is plotted along the vertical axis and the riskiness of the investment is plotted along the horizontal axis, the indifference curve of the investor will be positively sloped if

   a. the investor doesn't care what rate of return he or she receives.
   b. the investor doesn't care how risky an investment is.
   c. the investor prefers a more risky to a less risky investment, when the expected rate of return is held constant.
   d. all of the above.
   e. none of the above.

Problems

1. Suppose Sandy gets the same utility from each of the 6 combinations of goods Z and W shown below. Good Z costs $10 per unit and good W costs $4 per unit.

	Commodity combination					
	1	2	3	4	5	6
Amount of good W (units)	1	2	4	7	11	16
Amount of good Z (units)	10	9	8	7	6	5

   a. What is the minimum income she must have to achieve the level of utility associated with these commodity combinations?
   b. If she has the income you found in part a, draw her budget line.

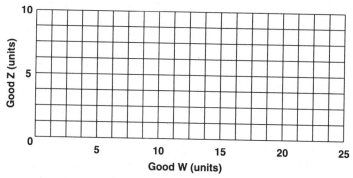

c. Draw her indifference curve.

2. Draw the indifference curve that includes the following market baskets in the following graph. Each of these market baskets gives the consumer equal satisfaction.

Market basket	Meat (pounds)	Potatoes (pounds)
A	1	9
B	2	8
C	3	7
D	4	6
E	5	5
F	6	4
G	7	3
H	8	2

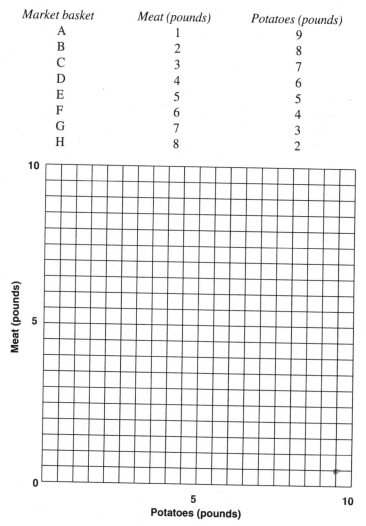

3. a. Suppose that the consumer has an income of $10 per period and that he or she must spend it all on meat or potatoes. If meat is $1 a pound and potatoes are 10 cents a pound, draw the consumer's budget line.

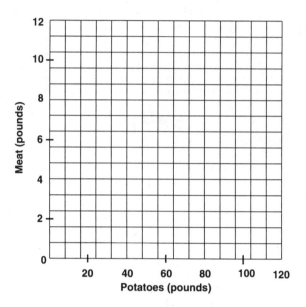

b. What will be the budget line if the consumer's income increases to $12? What will be the budget line if the consumer's income is $10, but the price of meat increases to $2 per pound? What will be the budget line if the consumer's income is $10, and the price of meat is $1 per pound, but the price of potatoes increases to 20 cents per pound?

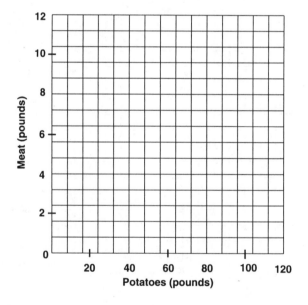

4. a. Suppose that John Jones has a money income of $100 per week and that he spends it all on nails and fertilizer. Suppose fertilizer is $2.50 per pound and nails are $1.00 per pound. Draw John Jones's budget line on the graph below:

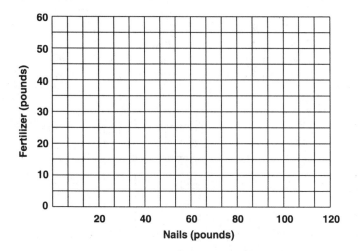

b. Suppose that John Jones has the following set of indifference curves:

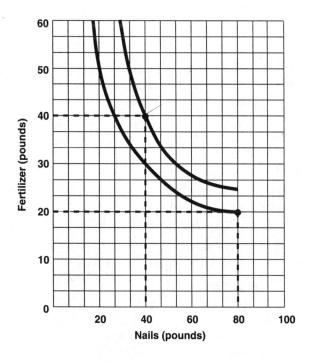

Does John Jones prefer 40 pounds of fertilizer and 40 pounds of nails to 20 pounds of fertilizer and 80 pounds of nails? Why or why not?

    c. Suppose that John Jones's money income is $100 per week and that fertilizer is $1.67 per pound and nails are $1.25 per pound. Based on the information in part b, what (approximately) is his equilibrium market basket?

5. Sally spends all her income of $3,000 per month on two goods, X and Z, whose prices are $30 and $60 respectively. She is currently spending half her income on each good and is maximizing her utility.
    a. How much of each good is she consuming?
    b. Represent Sally's utility-maximizing consumption of each good, given her tastes, income, and the price of each good in the graph below.

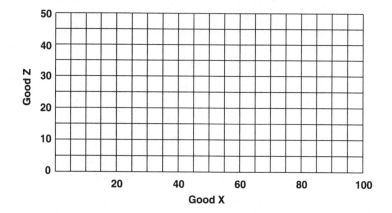

    c. Draw her budget line in the graph above.
    d. Using your diagram, show that, if she is now offered a choice of 10 additional units of good X for free or $300 extra income, she cannot be worse off, and may be better off, by taking the $300. Explain why this is true.

6. The straight lines shown below are budget lines. The curved lines are indifference curves of Mr. William White. The budget lines assume that Mr. White's income is $500 per week.

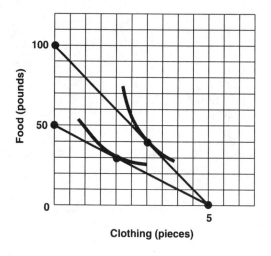

a. What is the price of a piece of clothing? Explain your reasoning.

b. Specify two points on Mr. White's demand curve for food.

Answers

Completion
1. more, less   2. maximize   3. market baskets, indifferent   4. less, satisfaction
5. income, prices   6. downward, more, less   7. higher, preferred, higher, lower
8. indifference curves, budget line   9. rises, falls   10. farther from

True or False
1. False   2. True   3. False   4. True   5. True   6. False   7. True   8. False
9. True   10. False

Multiple Choice
1. a   2. d   3. b   4. e   5. e

Problems
1. a. $96
    b. and c.

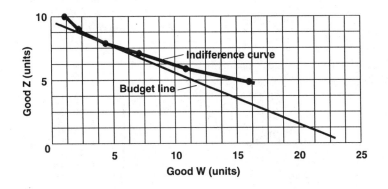

2.

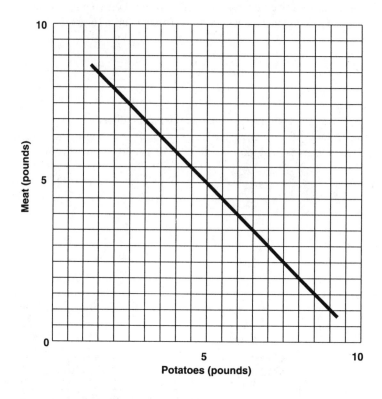

3. a. The consumer's budget line is drawn below.

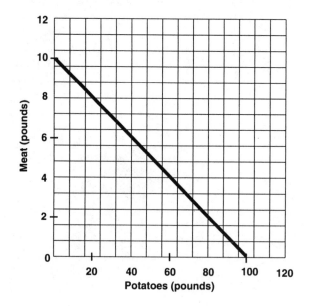

b.   Under the first set of circumstances the budget line is *A*. Under the second set of circumstances it is *B*. And under the third set of circumstances it is *C*.

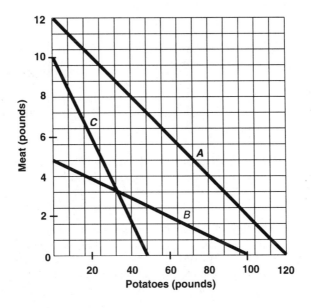

4. a.

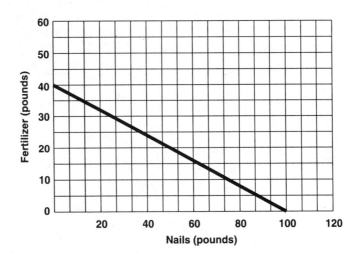

b.   Yes. Because it is on the higher indifference curve.

c.   It is difficult to tell from the diagram exactly what the equilibrium market basket will be, but it will contain about 25 to 40 pounds of nails and about 30 to 40 pounds of fertilizer.

5. a.   Quantity of $X = 50$, quantity of $Z = 25$.
    b. and c.

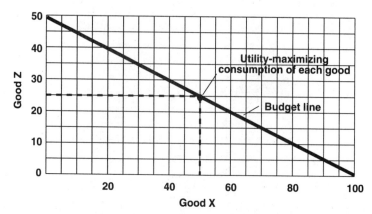

    d.   If she takes $300 extra income, her budget line shifts to the right and goes
         through the point corresponding to her consuming the same amount of Z
         and 10 additional units of X. Thus, she can consume 10 extra units of X if
         she likes. However, she may be able to attain a higher indifference curve by
         spending some of the extra $300 on Z.

6. a.   The price must be $100 per piece since the budget line (which pertains to an
         income of $500) intersects the horizontal axis at 5 pieces.
    b.   At $10 per pound he consumes 30 pounds of food. At $5 per pound he
         consumes 40 pounds of food.

CHAPTER 5

Estimating Demand Functions

Chapter Profile

An identification problem is likely to occur if price in various periods is plotted against quantity, and the resulting relationship is used to estimate the demand curve. Because nonprice variables are not held constant, the demand curve is likely to have shifted from one period to another. Sophisticated econometric methods often permit the estimation of the demand curve under these circumstances.

Market experiments and consumer interviews frequently are used to obtain information concerning the demand curve for products. For example, firms vary price from one city or region to another and see what the effects are on quantity demanded. An actual illustration in the textbook was the evaluation of the four promotion alternatives by L'eggs Products.

Regression analysis is useful in estimating demand functions and other economic relationships. The **regression line** shows the average relationship between the dependent variable and the independent variable. The method of least squares is the standard technique used to fit a regression line to a set of data. If the regression line is $\hat{Y} = a + bX$, and if a and b are calculated by least squares,

$$b = \frac{\sum_{i=1}^{n} (X_i - \bar{X})(Y_i - \bar{Y})}{\sum_{i=1}^{n} (X_i - \bar{X})^2}$$

$$a = \bar{Y} - b\bar{X}.$$

This value of b is often called the **estimated regression coefficient**.

Whereas a **simple regression** includes only one independent variable, a **multiple regression** includes more than one independent variable. An advantage of multiple regression over simple regression is that one frequently can predict the dependent variable more accurately if more than one independent variable is used. Also, if the dependent variable is influenced by more than one independent variable, a simple regression of the dependent variable on a single independent variable may result in a biased estimate of the effect of this independent variable on the dependent variable.

The first step in **multiple regression analysis** is to identify the independent variables, and then to specify the mathematical form of the equation relating the mean value of the dependent variable to the independent variables. For example, if Y is the dependent variable and X and Z are identified as the independent variables, one might specify that

$$Y_i = A + B_1 X_i + B_2 Z_i + e_i,$$

where e_i is the difference between Y_i and the mean value of Y (given the values of X_i and Z_i). To estimate B_1 and B_2 (called the **true regression coefficients** of X and Z) as well as A (the intercept of this true regression equation), we use the values that minimize the sum of squared deviations of Y_i from $\hat{Y}_i$, the value of the dependent variable predicted by the estimated regression equation.

In a simple regression, the coefficient of determination is used to measure the closeness of fit of the regression line. (As pointed out in the chapter appendix, the coefficient of determination equals the proportion of the total variation in the dependent variable that is explained by the regression line.) In a multiple regression, the multiple coefficient of determination, R^2, plays the same role. The closer R^2 is to zero, the poorer the fit; the closer it is to 1, the better the fit.

The F-statistic can be used to test whether any of the independent variables has any effect on the dependent variable. The standard error of estimate can help to indicate how well a regression model can predict the dependent variable. The t-statistic for the regression coefficient of each independent variable can be used to test whether this independent variable has any effect on the dependent variable.

A difficult problem that can occur in multiple regression is multicollinearity, a situation where two or more of the independent variables are highly correlated. If multicollinearity exists, it may be impossible to estimate accurately the effect of particular independent variables on the dependent variable. Another frequently encountered problem arises when the error terms in a regression are serially correlated. The Durbin-Watson test can be carried out to determine whether this problem exists.

In performing and interpreting regression and correlation analyses, it is important to bear in mind that a high correlation between two variables does not necessarily mean that the variables are causally related. (And even if they are causally related, the direction of causation may be different from that presumed in the analysis.)

Questions

Completion

1. Regression analysis assumes that the mean value of Y, given the value of X, is a linear function of _____ .

2. Regression analysis assumes that the mean value of Y, given the value of X, falls on the population _____ line.

3. The _____ regression line is an estimate of the population regression line.

4. The estimated regression coefficient is an estimate of the _____ of the population regression line.

5. The correlation coefficient is the _____ of the coefficient of determination.

6. Whereas a simple regression includes one independent variable, a multiple regression includes _____ independent variables.

7. The unknown constants in the true regression equation are estimated by the method of _____.

8. If the value of F is (large, small) _____ , this tends to imply that at least one of the independent variables has an effect on the dependent variable.

9. _____ is a situation where two or more independent variables are very highly correlated.

True or False

_____ 1. If each error term is correlated with the subsequent error term, this is a case of serial correlation.

_____ 2. Even if an observed correlation is due to a causal relationship, the direction of causation may be the reverse of that implied by the regression.

_____ 3. The Y intercept of the regression line measures the change in the predicted value of Y associated with a 1-unit increase in X.

_____ 4. The higher the coefficient of determination, the worse the fit of the regression line.

_____ 5. The standard error of estimate is a measure of the amount of scatter of individual observations about the regression line.

Multiple Choice

1. Suppose that $Y = 1$ when $X = 0$, that $Y = 2$ when $X = 1$, and that $Y = 3$ when $X = 2$. In this case, the least-squares estimate of B is

   a. 0.
   b. .05.
   c. 1.
   d. 1.5.
   e. none of the above.

2. Based on the data in the previous question, the least-squares estimate of A is

   a. −1.
   b. 0.
   c. 1.
   d. 2.
   e. none of the above.

3. Based on the data in question 1, the standard error of estimate is

    a. 0.
    b. 1.
    c. 2.
    d. 3.
    e. none of the above.

4. Based on the data in question 1, the sample correlation coefficient is

    a. −1.
    b. 0.
    c. .5.
    d. 1.
    e. none of the above.

* 5. If the sample coefficient of determination is 0.25, this means that

    a. none of the variation in the dependent variable is explained by the regression.
    b. 25 percent of the variation in the dependent variable is explained by the regression.
    c. 50 percent of the variation in the dependent variable is explained by the regression.
    d. 75 percent of the variation in the dependent variable is explained by the regression.
    e. none of the above is true.

* 6. If the sample coefficient of determination is 0.16, this means that

    a. the dependent variable is inversely related to the independent variable.
    b. the dependent variable increases at an increasing rate with increases in the independent variable.
    c. the dependent variable increases at a decreasing rate with increases in the independent variable.
    d. about 5/6 of the variation in the dependent variable cannot be explained by the regression.
    e. the dependent variable is directly related (in the population) to the independent variable.

7. A multiple regression is calculated with output of wheat (in tons per year) as the dependent variable, and with input of land (in acres) and of labor (in years) as the independent variables. If the regression coefficient of the labor variable is 10.1, this indicates that

    a. the annual output of wheat per year of labor equals 10.1.
    b. the number of years of labor required, on the average, to produce a ton of wheat is 10.1.
    c. an extra year of labor is associated with an extra 10.1 tons of wheat per year.
    d. an extra ton of wheat per month is associated with an extra input of 10.1 years of labor.
    e. none of the above is true.

---

* Question pertains to chapter appendix in the text.

Problems

1. Robert Klitgaard, in his book *Data Analysis for Development* (Oxford: Oxford University Press, 1985), estimated the following correlation coefficients, based on data for 71 countries:

	Per capita output	Calories	Population density	Urban population (percentage)
Life expectancy	0.71	0.55	0.32	0.76
Per capita output		0.53	0.25	0.74
Calories			0.18	0.61
Population density				0.47

Interpret his results.

2. According to the *Statistical Abstract of the United States*, the retail value of shipments of major kitchen appliances in the United States in 1983 and 1984 (in millions of dollars) was:

Appliances	1983	1984
Refrigerators	3,607	4,001
Microwave ovens	2,586	3,362
Ranges, electric	1,299	1,477
Dishwashers	1,205	1,368
Freezers	568	545
Ranges, gas	695	785
Disposers	395	466

Regress the 1984 value of shipments of an appliance on its 1983 value of shipments. Interpret your results.

3. A manager is interested in the relationship between a firm's expenditure on typewriters and its expenditure on paper clips. To correct for the fact that some firms are much bigger than others, he divides both a firm's expenditure on typewriters and its expenditure on paper clips by its sales. Having done this, he finds that there is a fairly close direct relationship between a firm's expenditure on typewriters (divided by its sales) and its expenditure on paper clips (divided by its sales). Comment on this procedure.

4. A retail outlet for air conditioners believes that its weekly sales are dependent upon the average temperature during the week. It picks at random 12 weeks in 1996 and finds that its sales are related to the average temperature in these weeks as follows:

Mean temperature (degrees)	Sales (number of air conditioners)
72	3
77	4
82	7
43	1
31	0
28	0
81	8
83	5
76	5
60	4
50	4
55	5

a. Plot these data in the graph below.

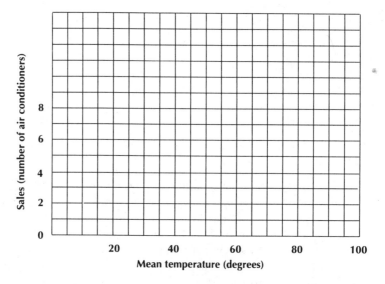

b. Calculate the intercept and slope of the sample regression line, where sales is the dependent variable and temperature is the independent variable.

c. Weather forecasts indicate that next week's mean temperature will be 80°; the retail outlet uses the regression to forecast its sales next week. What will be its forecast?

5. Suppose that a firm calculates a multiple regression where the dependent variable is the firm's monthly sales (in millions of dollars) and the independent variables are (1) the firm's expenditures on advertising during the relevant month (in millions of

dollars) and (2) the amount spent by its competitor on advertising during that month (in millions of dollars). The firm's marketing manager, when she receives the computer printout of the results of the multiple regression, finds that the value of the Durbin-Watson statistic is 1.25.

a. If the regression is based on 50 observations, what are the implications of this result?

b. The computer printout shows that the coefficient of determination between this firm's monthly advertising expenditures and its competitor's monthly advertising expenditures equals .96. What are the implications of this result?

c. The marketing manager instructs the people on her staff to obtain data concerning each variable that they think may be correlated with the firm's sales and includes all the suggested variables in a regression, regardless of whether there is any theoretical justification for their inclusion. What dangers may exist in this procedure?

* 6. Suppose the retail outlet in problem 4 suspects that its sales depend on the price of its air conditoners as well as on the mean temperature. For the randomly chosen 12 weeks, it obtains data regarding the price of an air conditioner as well as the mean temperature and the outlet's sales. The results are as follows:

Mean temperature (degrees)	Price of air conditioner (hundreds of dollars)	Sales (number of air conditioners)
72	2	3
77	2	4
82	1	7
43	2	1
31	2	0
28	2	0
81	1	8
83	2	5
76	2	5
60	1	4
50	1	4
55	1	5

a. Estimate the constants in the population regression equation, where temperature and price are both independent variables.

b. How much of an increase in weekly sales can be expected if the mean temperature goes up by 1° and the price of an air conditioner is held constant?

c. How much of an increase in weekly sales can be expected if the price of an air conditioner goes down by $1 and the mean temperature remains constant?

d. Suppose the retail outlet is convinced that the price elasticity of demand for its air conditioners is constant when the price of an air conditioner is between $100 and $300. If this is true, is this regression equation of the right mathematical form? If not, what alternative form would you suggest?

---

* This problem is for students who have experience in calculating multiple regressions.

7. The Crown Corporation's marketing department, using regression analysis, estimates the firm's demand function, the result being

$$Q = -51 - 1.4P + 2.9I + 1.2\,A + 1.3Z,$$

where Q is the quantity demanded of the firm's product (in tons), P is the price of the firm's product (in dollars per ton), I is per capita income (in dollars), A is the firm's advertising expenditure (in thousands of dollars), and Z is the price (in dollars) of a competing product. The regression is based on 100 observations. The value of R^2 is .70. (Population is constant.)

   a. According to the computer printout, the probability, if the true value of the regression coefficient of P is zero, that the t-statistic of P will be as large (in absolute terms) as we observe is .012. Can we be reasonably sure that the coefficient of P is less than zero?
   b. According to the computer printout, the probability, if the true value of the regression coefficient of A is zero, that the t-statistic of A will be as large (in absolute terms) as we observe is .389.Can we be reasonably sure that the coefficient of A exceeds zero?

8. The Strunk Company hires a consultant to estimate the demand function for its product. Using regression analysis, the consultant estimates the demand function to be

$$\log Q = 1.48 - 0.16 \log P + 0.43 \log Z,$$

where Q is the quantity demanded (in tons) of Strunk's product, P is the price (in dollars per ton) of Strunk's product, and Z is the price (in dollars per ton) of a rival product.

   a. Calculate the price elasticity of demand for Strunk's product.
   b. Calculate the cross elasticity of demand between Strunk's product and the rival product.
   c. According to the consultant, $\bar{R}^2 = .95$, and the standard error of estimate is .001. If the number of observations is 89, comment on the goodness of fit of the regression.

9. Barbetta's Pizza conducts an experiment in which it raises price by 45 percent during May 1996. This large price increase results in a decrease in the firm's revenues.

   a. What problems exist in carrying out an experiment of this sort?
   b. Taken at face value, does the price elasticity of demand seem to be greater than or less than 1?

10. Because of a shift in consumer tastes, the market demand curve for tortellini has shifted steadily to the right. If one were to plot price against quantity sold, would the resulting relationship approximate the market demand curve?

11. The Fenton Company uses regression analysis to obtain the following estimate of the demand function for its product:

$$\log Q = 3 - 2.6 \log P + 2.7 \log I,$$

where Q is the quantity demanded, P is price, and I is disposable income.

a. Fenton's president is considering a 2 percent price reduction. He argues that these results indicate that it will result in a 9 percent increase in the number of units sold by the firm. Do you agree? Why or why not?

b. The firm's chairman points out that, according to the computer printout, the probability that the observed value of the F-statistic could have arisen by chance, given that none of the independent variables has any effect on the dependent variable, is .359. He says that this regression provides little or no evidence that $\log P$ and $\log I$ really affect $\log Q$. Do you agree? Why or why not?

Answers

Completion
1. X 2. regression   3. sample   4. slope   5. square root   6. 2 or more
7. least squares   8. large   9. Multicollinearity

True or False
1. True   2. True   3. False   4. False   5. True

Multiple Choice
1. c   2. c   3. a   4. d   5. b   6. d   7. c

Problems
1. There seems to be a direct relationship between all pairs of these variables. The highest correlation (about .75) is between life expectancy and per capita output, life expectancy and percentage of population that is urban, and per capita output and percent of population that is urban. Of course, correlations of this sort do not indicate the lines of causation.

2. The regression equation is $\hat{Y} = -25 + 1.18X$, where Y is the 1984 sales of an appliance, and X is its 1983 sales. To estimate an appliance's sales, one can use this equation. Since r^2 is about 0.985, this equation seems to fit very well.

3. One possible problem with this procedure is that one can create a spurious correlation by dividing both the independent and dependent variables by the same quantity (in this case, the firm's sales).

4. a.

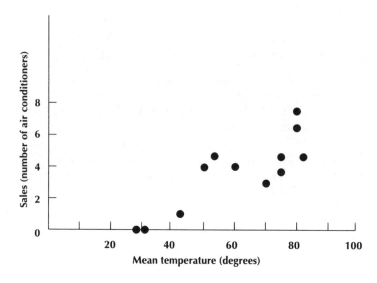

b.

	X	Y	X^2	Y^2	X Y
	72	3	5,184	9	216
	77	4	5,929	16	308
	82	7	6,724	49	574
	43	1	1,849	1	43
	31	0	961	0	0
	28	0	784	0	0
	81	8	6,561	64	648
	83	5	6,889	25	415
	76	5	5,776	25	380
	60	4	3,600	16	240
	50	4	2,500	16	200
	55	5	3,025	25	275
Sum	738	46	49,782	246	3,299
Mean	61.5	3.8333			

$$b = \frac{12(3,299) - (738)(46)}{12(49,782) - 738^2} = \frac{39,588 - 33,948}{597,384 - 544,644} = \frac{5,640}{52,740} = 0.1069$$

$a = 3.8333 - (.1069)(61.5) = 3.8333 - 6.5743 = -2.741.$

Thus, the sample regression is $\hat{Y} = -2.741 + .1069X$.

c. Its forecast is

$$-2.741 + .1069(80) = -2.741 + 8.552 = 5.811.$$

5. a. Since there are 50 observations and 2 independent variables, $n = 50$ and $k = 2$. If we set $\alpha = .05$ and use a two-tailed test, we should reject the

hypothesis of zero serial correlation of the error terms in the regression if the Durbin-Watson statistic is less than 1.38 or greater than 2.62. (See Appendix Table 7 of the text.) Since the observed value of this statistic is 1.25, there is evidence of serial correlation in the error terms.

b. This result indicates that there exists considerable multicollinearity, and that it may be difficult to sort out the effects of the individual independent variables.

c. It is important that the manager have good *a priori* reasons for including each of the independent variables. With enough trial and error, it is not very difficult to find some set of independent variables that "explain" much of the variation in practically any dependent variable, even if these independent variables really have little or no effect on the dependent variable—but only happen to be correlated with it in the sample.

6. a. Let X_1 be temperature and X_2 be price. From problem 4, we know that

$$\Sigma(X_{1i} - \bar{X})^2 = 49{,}782 - (738)(61.5) = 4{,}395$$

$$\Sigma(Y_i - \bar{Y})^2 = 246 - (46)(3.8333) = 69.6682$$

$$\Sigma(X_{1i} - \bar{X})(Y_i - \bar{Y}) = 3{,}299 - (46)(61.5) = 470.$$

If the calculations are to be done by hand, the following additional computations must be made:

	X_1	X_2	Y	$X_1 X_2$	X_2^2	$X_2 Y$
	72	2	3	144	4	6
	77	2	4	154	4	8
	82	1	7	82	1	7
	43	2	1	86	4	2
	31	2	0	62	4	0
	28	2	0	56	4	0
	81	1	8	81	1	8
	83	2	5	166	4	10
	76	2	5	152	4	10
	60	1	4	60	1	4
	50	1	4	50	1	4
	55	1	5	55	1	5
Sum	738	19	46	1,148	33	64
Mean	61.5	1.5833	3.8333			

Thus,

$$\Sigma(X_{2i} - \bar{X}_2)^2 = 33 - 19(1.5838) = 33 - 30.0827 = 2.9173$$

$$\Sigma(X_{2i} - \bar{X}_2)(Y_i - \bar{Y}) = 64 - 46(1.5833) = 64 - 72.8318 = -8.8318$$

$$\Sigma(X_{1i} - \bar{X}_1)(X_{2i} - \bar{X}_2) = 1{,}148 - 19(61.5) = 1{,}148 - 1{,}168.5 = -20.5.$$

$$b_1 = \frac{(2.9173)(470) - (-20.5)(-8.8318)}{(4,395)(2.9173) - (-20.5)^2} = \frac{1,371.131 - 181.052}{12,821.53 - 420.25}$$

$$= \frac{1,190.079}{12,401.28} = 0.0960.$$

$$b_2 = \frac{4,395(-8.8318) - (-20.5)(470)}{(4,395)(2.9173) - (-20.5)^2} = \frac{-38,815.76 + 9,635}{12,821.53 - 420.25}$$

$$= \frac{-29,180.76}{12,401.28} = -2.353.$$

$$a = 3.8333 - .096(61.5) - (-2.353)(1.5833)$$

$$= 3.833 - 5.9040 + 3.7255 = 1.6548.$$

Consequently, the multiple regression equation is

$$\hat{Y} = 1.655 + 0.096\, X_1 - 2.353\, X_2.$$

As pointed out in the textbook, multiple regressions ordinarily are calculated on a computer, which prints out this equation. The foregoing calculations are provided here for those readers who are interested in seeing how this equation can be calculated by hand. The general formulas used to obtain b_1, b_2, and a are provided in most statistics books. Students with access to computers should be encouraged to calculate this multiple regression on the computer.

    b.   A sales increase of 0.096 air conditioners.
    c.   A sales increase of 0.0235 air conditioners. (Recall that X_2 is measured in hundreds of dollars.)
    d.   No. If the price elasticity of demand is constant, it may be better to assume that

$$\log Y_i = A + B_1 \log X_{1i} + B_2 \log X_{2i} + e_i.$$

7. a.   Yes.
   b.   No.

8. a.   .16.
   b.   +.43.
   c.   The regression seems to fit well.

9. a.   For one thing, such a big price increase may drive away customers.
   b.   Greater than one.

10. Not necessarily. In fact, if the supply curve has remained fixed, the resulting relationship would approximate the supply curve, not the demand curve.

11. a.   Since the price elasticity of demand is estimated to be 2.6, it will result in about a 5.2 percent increase in the number of units sold.
   b.   Certainly, the probability is high (.359) that the observed results could have been obtained if neither independent variable had any effect on the dependent variable.

CHAPTER 6

Business and Economic Forecasting

Chapter Profile

Although surveys are of considerable use, most major firms seem to base their forecasts in large part on the quantitative analysis of economic time series. The classical approach to business forecasting assumes that an economic time series can be decomposed into four components: trend, seasonal variation, cyclical variation, and irregular movements. If the trend in a time series is **linear**, simple regression may be used to estimate an equation representing the trend. If it seems to be **nonlinear**, a quadratic equation may be estimated by multiple regression, or an exponential trend may be fitted.

The seasonal variation in a particular time series is described by a figure for each month (the seasonal index) that shows the extent to which that month's value typically departs from what would be expected on the basis of trend and cyclical variation. Such seasonal indexes can be used to **deseasonalize** a time series, that is, to remove the seasonal element from the data.

Many business and economic time series go up and down with the fluctuations of the economy as a whole. This cyclical variation, as well as trend and seasonal variation, is reflected in many time series. It is customary to divide business fluctuations into four phases: **trough**, **expansion**, **peak**, and **recession**. Variables that go down before the peak and up before the trough are called **leading series**. Some important leading series are new orders for durable goods, average work week, building contracts, stock prices, certain wholesale prices, and claims for unemployment insurance.

Economists sometimes use leading series, which are often called **leading indicators**, to forecast whether a turning point is about to occur. If a large number of leading indicators turn downward, this is viewed as a sign of a coming peak. If a large number turn upward, this is thought to signal an impending trough. Although these indicators are not very reliable, they are watched closely and are used to supplement other, more sophisticated forecasting techniques.

The simplest kind of forecasting method is a straightforward extrapolation of a trend. To allow for seasonal variation, such an extrapolation can be multiplied by the seasonal index (divided by 100) for the month to which the forecast applies. This entire procedure is simply a mechanical extrapolation of the time series into the future.

In recent years, managerial economists have tended to base their forecasts less on simple extrapolations and more on equations (or systems of equations) showing the effects of various independent variables on the variable (or variables) one wants to forecast. These equations (or systems of equations) are called **econometric models**.

Questions

Completion

1. A trend is a relatively smooth _____ movement of a time series.

2. Besides a linear trend, one can estimate a _____ or _____ trend.

*3. _____ smoothing is one way to calculate a trend.

4. The _____ index shows the way in which a particular month tends to depart from what would be expected on the basis of the trend and cyclical variation in the time series.

5. The _____ is the point where national output is lowest relative to its full-employment level.

6. One simple way to forecast the annual sales of a firm is an _____ of the trend in sales into the future.

7. _____ are economic series that typically go down or up before gross domestic product does.

*8. When used for forecasting, the basic equation for _____ _____ is $F_t = \theta A(t-1) + (1 - \theta)F_{t-1}$.

*9. In the previous question if θ is close to 1, past values of the time series are given relatively (little, large) _____ weight (compared with recent values) in determining the forecast.

10. The trend value of a time series is the value of the variable that would result if only the _____ were at work.

True or False

_____ 1. An exponential trend seems to fit many business and economic time series, including the capital-labor ratio and the savings-income ratio of the American economy.

_____ *2. Using exponential smoothing, the trend value at time t is a weighted average of all available previous values where the weights decline geometrically as one goes backward in time.

_____ *3. To calculate the value of an exponentially smoothed time series at time t, all we need is the value of the smoothed time series at time $t-1$.

_____ 4. If a peak occurs in October 1998, a recession must begin then.

_____ 5. Coincident series like employment and industrial production are useful in forecasting peaks and troughs.

---

* This question pertains to the appendix of Chapter 6.

_____ 6. Leading indicators have sometimes turned down when the economy has not turned down subsequently.

Multiple Choice

1. A market researcher calculates a least-squares linear trend based on data for 1964 to 1996. He lets $t' = -16$ for 1964, . . . , $t' = 0$ for 1980, . . . , $t' = 16$ for 1996. He computes the mean value of the time series (for 1964 to 1996) and finds that it is 12. For 1980, the trend value of the time series is

   a. 0.
   b. −16.
   c. 16.
   d. 12.
   e. none of the above.

2. The White Corporation calculates a seasonal index for its sales. For September, this index equals 90. If the firm's actual sales for September of this year are $90 million, the "deseasonalized" value of its sales—the value when the seasonal element is removed—is

   a. $81 million.
   b. $100 million.
   c. $90 million.
   d. $109 million.
   e. none of the above.

3. In the case of the White Corporation, the sum of the 12 seasonal indexes for the months of the year is

   a. 100.
   b. 120.
   c. 1,000.
   d. 1,200.
   e. none of the above.

4. The Blue Corporation's marketing vice president estimates a least-squares regression of the firm's annual sales on time, the result being $S = 25 + 3t$, where S is the firm's sales (in millions of dollars), and t is the year minus 1991.

   Based on the extrapolation of this regression, the firm's sales (in millions of dollars) in 2001 are forecasted to be

   a. 30.
   b. 25.
   c. 55.
   d. 60.
   e. none of the above.

5. Leading indicators

    a. include stock prices.
    b. include the average work week.
    c. turn downward in some cases, whereas the economy does not do so subsequently.
    d. do both a and b.
    e. do all of the above.

6. A firm extrapolates a quadratic trend of its sales to October 1999, the result being $80 million. The firm knows from past experience that its sales are subject to seasonal variations, and that the seasonal index for October is 104. The firm's forecast of its October 1999 sales is

    a. $80 million ÷ 104.
    b. $80 million × 104.
    c. $80 million ÷ 1.04.
    d. $80 million × 1.04.
    e. none of the above.

Problems

1. A retail store has sales of $2.8 million in November and $3.1 million in December. For this firm's sales, the seasonal index is 95 in November and 110 in December. A local newspaper runs a story saying that the store's sales were depressed in November because of a recession, but that they bounced back in December, thus indicating that a recovery was under way. Do you agree? Why or why not?

2. The Morse Corporation, a hypothetical producer of landing gear, had the following monthly sales:

	Sales (millions of dollars)		
Month	1993	1994	1995
January	2	3	3
February	3	4	5
March	4	5	4
April	5	6	6
May	6	7	7
June	7	8	8
July	8	8	9
August	7	7	8
September	6	6	7
October	5	5	6
November	4	3	5
December	3	4	3

    a. Is there evidence of seasonal variation in this firm's sales?
    b. How would you characterize this seasonal variation, if it exists?
    c. In 1996, the Morse Corporation's sales increased from $7 million in April to $8 million in May. The seasonal index is 123.0 for May and 106.3 for April.

Allowing for the seasonal variation, do you think that sales increased from April to May? Why or why not?

3. Suppose the Acme Corporation finds that a linear trend for its sales is

$$S = 5 + 0.1t,$$

where S is the firm's monthly sales (in millions of dollars), and t is measured in months from January 1990.

a. Based on this trend alone, what are the forecasted sales for the firm in February 1998?

b. Using past experience, the Acme Corporation estimates that the seasonal index for February is 109. How can this information be used to modify the forecast in a? What assumptions underlie this modification? Once this modification is made, what is the forecast of the Acme Corporation's sales in February 1998?

4. During 1974–1985, the sales of the Xerox Corporation were as follows:

Year	Sales (billions of dollars)	Year	Sales (billions of dollars)
1974	3.5	1980	8.0
1975	4.1	1981	8.5
1976	4.4	1982	8.5
1977	5.1	1983	8.3
1978	5.9	1984	8.6
1979	6.9	1985	9.0

a. Calculate a least-squares linear trend line for the firm's sales.
b. Plot both the sales data and the trend line in the graph below.
c. Use this trend line to forecast the Xerox Corporation's sales in 1996.

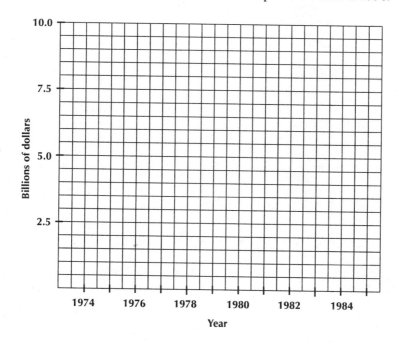

* 5. The Dickson Company's sales this year are $32 million, and its sales forecast for this year was $30 million. If the firm uses exponential smoothing to forecast sales and if the smoothing constant equals .15, what will be the firm's sales forecast for next year?

6. During 1974–85, the net income of the Rohm and Haas Corporation, the Philadelphia-based chemical producer, was as follows:

Year	Net income (millions of dollars)	Year	Net income (millions of dollars)
1974	74	1980	94
1975	25	1981	93
1976	−12	1982	86
1977	38	1983	138
1978	55	1984	172
1979	103	1985	141

a. Calculate a least-squares linear trend line for the firm's net income.
b. Plot both the net income data and the trend line in the graph below.
c. Use this trend line to forecast the Rohm and Haas Corporation's net income in 1996.
d. Do you think this forecast will be very accurate? Why or why not?

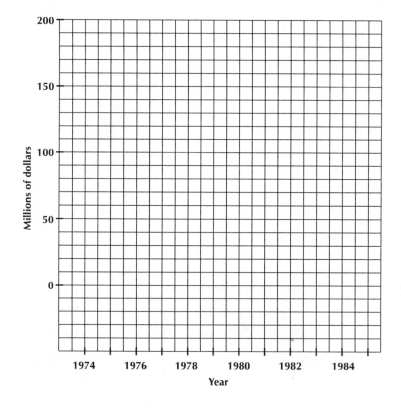

* This question pertains to the chapter appendix in the text.

7. The Moss Company's controller calculates a seasonal index for the firm's sales, the results being shown in the second column below. The firm's monthly 1996 sales are shown in the third column.

Month	Seasonal index	1996 sales (millions of dollars)
January	97	3.2
February	96	3.4
March	97	3.6
April	98	4.0
May	99	4.7
June	100	5.0
July	101	5.6
August	103	6.2
September	103	7.0
October	103	7.7
November	102	8.5
December	101	9.0

a. If one divides each month's sales figure by its seasonal index (divided by 100), it is said to be "deseasonalized," that is, the seasonal element is removed from the data. Calculate deseasonalized sales figures for 1996.
b. Why would the managers of the Moss Company want deseasonalized sales figures?

8. The equation describing the sales trend of the Miami Company is

$$S = 13.7 + 1.1t,$$

where S is the trend value of sales (in millions of dollars per month) of the firm, and t is time measured in months from January 1996. The firm's seasonal index of sales is

January	103	May	101	September	121
February	80	June	104	October	101
March	75	July	120	November	75
April	106	August	136	December	78

Construct a monthly sales forecast for the firm for 1998.

Answers

Completion
1. long-term 2. quadratic, exponential 3. Exponential 4. seasonal
5. trough 6. extrapolation 7. Leading indicators 8. exponential
smoothing 9. little 10. trend

True or False
1. True 2. True 3. False 4. True 5. False 6. True

Multiple Choice
1. d 2. b 3. d 4. c 5. e 6. d

Problems

1. From seasonal variation alone we would expect December's sales to be $110 \div 95 = 1.158$ times November's sales. Thus, allowing for seasonal variation, sales increased less than expected from November to December.

2. a. Yes.
   b. Sales tend to be high in the summer and low in the winter.
   c. Between April and May we would expect an increase of $\left(\dfrac{123.0}{106.3} - 1\right)100$,

   or 15.7 percent. Thus, this increase of 14.3 percent in 1996 is somewhat less than would be expected. Allowing for seasonal variation, sales did not increase between April and May in 1996.

3. a. If January 1990 is $t = 0$, then February 1998 is $t = 97$. Thus, the forecasted value of sales is

   $$5 + 0.1(97) = 5 + 9.7 = 14.7.$$

   That is, the forecast is \$14.7 million.
   b. Using this information, we can try to include seasonal factors as well as trend in the forecast. If we are willing to assume that the seasonal variation in the future will be like that in the past, the forecast is

   $$(1.09)(14.7) = 16.02.$$

   That is, the forecast is \$16.02 million.

4. a. The least-squares trend line is

   $$Y_t = -1060.536 + 0.53916t,$$

   where Y_t is the trend value of Xerox's sales in year t.

   b.

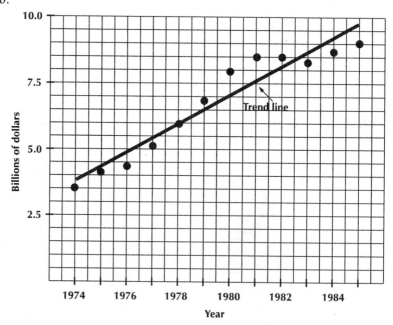

   c. \$15.6 billion.

5. .15(32) + (1 − .15)30 = 4.8 + 25.5 = 30.3 millions of dollars.

6. a. The least-squares trend line is

$$Y_t = -23,829 + 12.0804t,$$

where Y_t is the trend value of Rohm and Haas' net income in year t.

b.

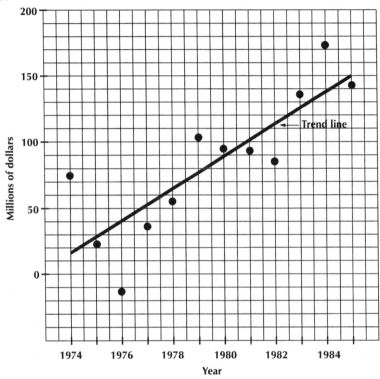

c. $283 million.
d. This is a very crude forecasting technique.

7. a.
January	3.30
February	3.54
March	3.71
April	4.08
May	4.75
June	5.00
July	5.54
August	6.02
September	6.80
October	7.48
November	8.33
December	8.91

b. Such figures indicate how sales are changing when the seasonal factor is removed.

8. For January 1998, $t = 24$. Thus, the trend values of sales are shown below. Multiplying them by the seasonal index, we get the forecasts in the last column.

| | | Millions of dollars | |
Month of 1998	Seasonal index	Trend value	Forecasted Sales
January	103	40.1	41.3
February	80	41.2	33.0
March	75	42.3	31.7
April	106	43.4	46.0
May	101	44.5	44.9
June	104	45.6	47.4
July	120	46.7	56.0
August	136	47.8	65.0
September	121	48.9	59.2
October	101	50.0	50.5
November	75	51.1	38.3
December	78	52.2	40.7

CASE ONE

How H-P Used Tactics of the Japanese to Beat Them at Their Game

Stephen Kreider Yoder

It was such sweet revenge.

Last year, Hewlett-Packard Co. faced a challenge from NEC Corp. The Japanese giant had plans to attack H-P's hegemony in the burgeoning computer-printer market in time-honored Japanese fashion: by undercutting prices with new, better-designed models. Over a decade ago, the tactic helped other Japanese companies grab the lead from H-P in a business it had pioneered, hand-held calculators.

This time it didn't work. Months before NEC could introduce its inexpensive monochrome inkjet printer, H-P launched an improved color version and slashed prices on its bestselling black-and-white model by 40% over six months. NEC withdrew its entry, now overpriced and uncompetitive, after about four months on the market.

"We were too late," says John McIntyre, then a marketing director at NEC's U.S. Unit. "We just didn't have the economies of scale" to compete with H-P.

A few year ago, U.S. companies were ruing Japan's unbeatable speed to market and economies of scale in many industries, and printers were a prime example: Japan made four out of five personal-computer printers that Americans bought in 1985. But now many American and Japanese com- panies are trading places, a shift confirmed by an annual global survey that reported Tuesday that the U.S. has replaced Japan as the world's most competitive economy for the first time since 1985.

H-P is one of the most dramatic of an increasing number of U.S. take-back stories, in technologies including disk drives, cellular phones, pagers and computer chips. H-P didn't even start making PC printers until 1984, but it is expected to have about $8 billion in printer revenue this year.

Among other things, the H-P story dispels common myths about the relative strengths of the U.S. and Japan, showing how big U.S. companies, under proper leadership, can exploit American creativity while using their huge resources to deploy "Japanese" tactics. H-P used its financial might to invest heavily in a laboratory breakthrough, then kept market share by enforcing rules that are gospel in Japan: Go for mass markets, cut costs, sustain a rapid fire of product variations and price cuts, and target the enemy.

Richard Hackborn, the H-P executive who led the charge, also succeeded because he could do what his Japanese counterparts couldn't: Buck the system. His printer-business teams were in outposts like Boise,

67

Idaho—far from H-P's increasingly bureaucratic Palo Alto, Calif., headquarters—where they were permitted, though sometimes reluctantly, to go their own way.

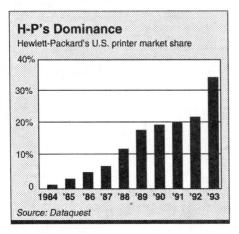

H-P's Dominance
Hewlett-Packard's U.S. printer market share

Source: Dataquest

H-P's other top executives for the most part preached high-profit, high-cost products for niche markets—which is how H-P lost the calculator business. Mr. Hackborn's troops set profit margins below the corporate norm and went for the mass market themselves. They moved fast and defied corporate rules when it meant winning customers.

"If you're going to leverage American culture but compete globally, you need a balance of entrepreneurship and central leverage," says Mr. Hackborn, who retired last year to become an H-P director. "The rugged individualism of cowboy culture alone doesn't work; but to be centrally directed doesn't either, because you lose the tremendous contribution of local innovation and accountability."

Japanese industrialists have often sermonized about U.S. complacency and myopia, but Japanese success, it turns out, can breed the same. H-P kept its huge lead because Japanese manufacturers, flush with success, spent too long squeezing profits out of old technologies and ignored signs that the American market—the bellwether— was rapidly changing.

"H-P understood computers better, it understood American customers better, it got good products to market faster," says Takashi Saito, head of Canon Inc.'s inkjet-printer business. Japanese makers' culture hindered the kind of quick decision-making needed in the fast-paced U.S. computer market, he says, and as a result, "The market is H-P's garden."

Hewlett Packard's journey to the top of the printer market began with a laboratory accident in 1979 and culminated in a rout of the Japanese beginning in 1992.

When H-P started thinking of entering the printer market, it realized it couldn't unseat the dominant Japanese makers, such as Seiko Epson Corp. and Oki Electric Industry Co., without a technological advance. Japan had a lock on the mass market with low-cost, well-engineered "dot matrix" printers, which form relatively rough letters.

The seeds for the H-P breakthrough had been nurtured by engineers in a converted janitor's closet at a Vancouver, Wash., plant since 1980. The year before, an H-P scientist noticed drops of liquid splattered over his lab bench. He had been testing a thin metal film by zapping it with electricity; when the metal grew hot, liquid trapped underneath began to boil and spurted out. The discovery evolved into the "thermal" inkjet.

Mr. Hackborn saw that inkjet technology had compelling advantages over laser printers for the mass market: It was cheaper, it was more easily adaptable for color printing and no one else had perfected it. The idea of using a jet to spit ink on paper had been around for years, but no one had found a good way to pump the ink through tiny holes.

H-P's first inkjet printer in 1984 was hardly a knockout. It needed special paper, the ink tended to smear and it could print only 96 dots per inch, compared with today's 600 dots. "H-P's first inkjet was terrible quality," says Norio Niwa, president of Epson's U.S. unit. "Our engineers thought that if they announced such a product, they'd lose face."

H-P saw it differently. It had also introduced a successful line of expensive laser printers for corporate customers, but the company believed that ordinary computer users would soon demand higher-quality printouts of text, graphics and photographs. There was a mass market in the making—the kind that H-P had previously blown. To prevent a repeat, H-P had to invest heavily in its low-cost inkjet technology, Mr. Hackborn says, and "learn from the Japanese" by building it into a family of products.

Meanwhile, the Japanese were making mistakes. Canon, which had edged ahead of H-P in patenting early inkjet designs but had agreed to share the patents, chose a complex implementation that would set it years behind. And Epson, the king of dot-matrix printers, ignored warnings of changing consumer tastes.

Executives from Epson's U.S. unit began traveling to Japan around 1985 to tell headquarters that low-budget PC users would soon demand high-quality printers and that Epson should invest more in technologies such as inkjets, says Peter Bergman, a former Epson marketing executive. "Their approach was, 'Who are these Americans to come over and tell me how to build our products?'" he says.

Epson had an inkjet technology of its own, but it was an expensive variation. Besides, says Mr. Niwa, the Epson executive, "Every engineer was looking at dot matrix because we had a big market, big profits, big business, and the technology itself had a long history."

The same kind of mistake could have happened at H-P. Headquarters became increasingly bureaucratic, with product plans requiring many levels of approval. But business units are set up as fiefs, each having great autonomy. "We had the resources of a big company, but we were off on our own," says Richard Belluzzo, who has taken over from Mr. Hackborn. "There wasn't central planning . . ., so we could make decisions really fast."

A PATENT OFFENSE

Based on decisions made in the hinterlands, H-P engineers adopted two Japanese tactics: They filed a blizzard of patents to protect their design and frustrate rivals, and embarked on a process of continual improvement to solve the inkjet's problems. They developed print heads that could spit 300 dots an inch and made inks that would stay liquid in the cartridge but dry instantly on plain paper. One engineer tested all types of paper: bonded, construction, toilet—and, for good measure, added sandpaper, tortillas and socks.

In 1988, H-P introduced the Deskjet, the plain-paper printer that would evolve into the model now taking market share away from the Japanese. No rivals loomed, but the line still wasn't meeting sales goals in 1989. It was competing with H-P's own more costly laser printers. Sales were too low to pay the high costs of research and factories. The inkjet division needed new markets to avert a financial crisis.

That autumn, a group of engineers and managers assembled for a two-day retreat at a lodge on Oregon's Mount Hood. They pored over market-share charts. That, says Richard Snyder, who now heads H-P's PC inkjet business, is "when the lights went on." H-P hadn't targeted the right enemy. Instead of positioning the inkjet as a low-cost alternative to H-P's fancy laser printers, the managers decided, they should go after the Japanese-dominated dot-matrix market.

Dot matrix, the biggest section of the market, had serious flaws—poor print quality and color. Epson, the No. 1 player, had a soft underbelly: No competitive inkjet and the distraction of an expensive and failing effort to sell a PC. "We said, 'Maybe this is a good time to attack,'" Mr. Snyder says.

H-P did so with the obsessive efficiency of a Japanese company. A week later, H-P teams were wearing "Beat Epson" football jerseys. The company began tracking Epson's market share, studying its marketing practices and public financial data, surveying loyal Epson customers and compiling profiles of Epson's top managers. Engineers tore apart Epson printers for ideas on design and manufacturing, a tactic the Japanese often use.

Among the findings: Epson's marketers got stores to put their printers in the most prominent spots; Epson used price cuts as tactical weapons to fend off challengers; consumers like Epson machines for their reliability; Epson's printers were built to be manufactured easily. H-P responded, demanding that stores put its inkjet printers alongside Epson's. It tripled its warranty to three years and redesigned printers with manufacturing in mind.

Engineers learned Epson got huge mileage out of a product by creating a broad line consisting of slight variations of the same basic printer. By contrast, "we were taken with the notion at H-P that you had to come up with a whole new platform every time," Mr. Snyder says. Change came hard. In 1990, as H-P was developing a color printer, engineers were set on creating a completely new, full-featured mechanical marvel. Marketers suggested that a simpler, slightly clumsier approach, would be good enough for most consumers.

TWEAKING A "KLUDGE"

There was a near mutiny among the engineers until a product manager named Judy Thorpe forced them to do telephone polls of customers. It turned out people were eager for the product the engineers considered a "kludge." H-P learned that "you can tweak your not-so-latest thing and get the latest thing," Ms. Thorpe says. By sticking to the existing platform, H-P was able to get the jump on competitors in the now-booming color-printer market.

By 1992, it became clear to Japanese makers that dot-matrix printers were under

assault, with sales falling for the first time as inkjet sales soared.

When the Computer City division of Tandy Corp., the Fort Worth, Texas, company, was preparing to open its first stores in the summer of 1991, it told printer makers that it expected inkjets to be a hot category, says Alan Bush, president of the chain. The Japanese responded that they didn't have anything ready. "We were very astounded," says Mr. Bush. "In the summer of '91, for an inkjet-product line you had your choice: H-P, H-P or H-P.

When Japanese printer makers that had been investing in inkjet research tried to move into the market, they ran into a brick wall: H-P had a lock on many important patents. Citizen Watch Co. found H-P had "covered the bases to make it very difficult for anyone else to get there," says Michael Del Vecchio, senior vice president of Citizen's U.S. unit. Citizen engineers trying to develop print heads learned H-P had some 50 patents covering how ink travels through the head. "It's like being in a maze: You go down this path and suddenly you're into an area that may infringe on their main patents and you have to back up and start over."

This barrier to entry meant competitors lost valuable time. "Every year that went by that we and other people were unsuccessful in reinventing the wheel, [H-P] got a greater and greater lead," says Mr. McIntyre, the former NEC executive.

Then there were H-P's economies of scale, which allowed it to undercut almost anyone else's prices; by the time Canon came out with the first credible competition, H-P had sold millions of printers and had thousands of outlets for its replacement cartridges. And H-P used its experience to make continual improvements in manufacturing. In constant dollars, for example, today's Deskjet costs half as much to make as the 1988 model.

This has allowed H-P to carry out a vital strategy: When a rival attacks, hit back quickly and hard. When Canon was about to introduce a color inkjet printer last year, H-P cut the price of its own version before its rival had even reached the market. The black-and-white printer, priced at $995 in 1988, now lists for $365.

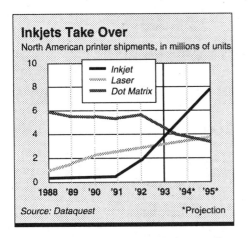

Inkjets Take Over
North American printer shipments, in millions of units

Source: Dataquest *Projection

"They've been very good about eating their own young," Mr. McIntyre says.

And consuming the competition as well. H-P now holds 55% of the world market for inkjets. The success in printers, including lasers, has propelled enormous overall growth at H-P, making it one of the two fastest-growing major U.S. multinationals (the other is Motorola Inc.). H-P's other divisions have been transformed by the printer people's mass-market approach and now seek to make the lowest-cost personal and hand-held computers on the market.

H-P's lead in printers could bring even more profits because inkjet mechanisms are finding their way into facsimile machines and color copiers. Sales could explode if, as expected, inkjet becomes the technology of choice inside TV-top printers

for interactive-TV services. Printers will "be like toilets," says Mr. Hackborn. "They'll play a central role in the home."

Questions

1. Before introducing its inkjet printers, did Hewlett-Packard have to estimate the demand curve for them? Why or why not?

2. When studying Epson before going after the Japanese-dominated dot-matrix market, did Hewlett-Packard try to determine which factors would have an important influence on the demand curve for its product? If so, what factors seemed to be particularly important?

3. Hewlett-Packard cut the price of its black-and-white printer from $995 to $365. If the quantity of such printers that it sold per year increased tenfold, does this mean that the (arc) price elasticity of demand for this product was about 1.8? Why or why not?

4. Can the data in the graph on page 68 be used to determine the trend in Hewlett-Packard's printer market share? What are the limitations of these data for such purposes?

5. If you were hired by Hewlett-Packard to forecast how many inkjet printers it would sell next year, how would you go about doing it? What data would you need? What techniques would you use? How accurate do you think your forecast would be?

CASE TWO

K. M. Westelle and Associates, Inc.
Rhonda L. Aull

KATHLEEN WESTELLE; CHIEF EXECUTIVE OFFICER
CHUCK KULLMAN; GENERAL MANAGER, DIVISION R
RUTH CUSHMAN; INVENTORY MANAGER, DIVISION R
CHARLIE VACHRIS; PRODUCTION SUPERVISOR, DIVISION R
STEVE BOSSI; DIRECTOR OF MARKETING

CHUCK: We just lost the Tellarunner account. And, to add insult to injury, Kathleen Westelle has just informed me that our division's second quarter costs are up 10% over the first quarter.

RUTH: Why did we lose the account? Tellarunner has been one of our biggest customers for five years.

CHUCK: Well, we've been backlogged on their last six orders by at least two weeks. As a result, their retail business is now backordered; so they've decided not to renew their contract with us. You can't blame them.

RUTH: Let me see what inventories look like on their remaining contract. (*Ruth pulls up the information on her terminal screen.*) My goodness! We have only one partial shipment in the warehouse and that was promised to them three weeks ago! We've been trying to build inventory over the past six months so that this wouldn't happen. But, it seems like one month we're overstocked and the next we're backlogged. That alone adds to our costs. Let me call Charlie and see what he's got scheduled for Division R next week. (*Ruth dials Charles Vachris, the production supervisor for Division R at Westelle.*) Charles, this is Ruth at the warehouse. What do you have scheduled next week on Tellarunner's order? We're extremely backlogged on that order and need something out the door ASAP.

CHARLIE: Let me see. I've got 2,200 pairs scheduled for that Tellarunner order. Unfortunately, I can't give you any more because changing the production mix is just too expensive at this stage of the game. I've already gotten two lectures from my boss about keeping production costs down.

RUTH: Well, we just lost that account and we may lose more if we don't do something about these backlogged orders. Steve Bossi personally managed the Tellarunner account and he's not happy over this news. He's blaming the loss on P&I. (*The Production and Inventory Departments are commonly referred to as "P&I".*)

CHARLIE: Wait a minute. Steve Bossi gave me monthly forecasts for that shoe model. I planned production according to his estimates but I guess those forecasts were off a bit. He must have underestimated; but, there's nothing I can do about it now. It's just too costly to change over that production equipment at this stage of the game just to make Tellarunner's order. It'd cost my division more money than we'd make on that order.

RUTH: (*turning to Chuck.*) What did Kathleen Westelle say she wanted to do? Does she want to cut production costs or would she rather service these customers?

CHUCK: Kathleen wants this division to do both.

COMPANY BACKGROUND

K. M. Westelle and Associates, Inc. is a manufacturer of athletic footwear. The company was founded in 1963 by Kathleen M. Westelle, a former design engineer for a major American footwear company. In the late 60's, the company held a substantial portion of the American market share for an all-purpose athletic shoe. During the 70's fitness boom, the company saw a niche for expansion into more specialized shoe lines. By 1990, the company was producing running, aerobic, tennis, and cycling shoes. Westelle sells only to distributors of athletic products. Individual sales orders are accepted only from Westelle employees and their families. The majority of company stock is held by the Westelle family and all remaining shares are held by Westelle employees.

The company consists of six departments—Accounting, Manufacturing Engineering, Marketing, Personnel, Purchasing, and Research and Development—that each service two manufacturing divisions, Division A and Division R. Division A produced the aerobic, tennis, and cycling shoe lines. Division R produces only the running shoe line which consists of three models, the Sprint, the Marian, and the Springtelle. Each model is described below.

The Sprint, introduced in 1979, is the oldest shoe in the line. Even with yearly upgrades, the Sprint has reached the end of its life cycle and has been replaced with Westelle's newer Springtelle model. Westelle has phased out production of the Sprint and current sales are being filled solely from final inventories of this model.

The Springtelle is a racing shoe specially engineered to give the runner added spring and cushion when racing on hard surfaces. A key selling point is its patented design and sales have steadily increased since its introduction in 1986.

The Marian is a training shoe which has been part of Westelle's running line since 1983. Yearly upgrades to the Marian trainer have helped keep its sales level steady.

The Manufacturing Process

All models in the running shoe line are processed through two areas: stamping and interfacing. Raw materials for each shoe model are first measured and cut in the stamping area. These materials are then routed by conveyor belt to the interfacing area for final assembly.

The stamping area consists of 20 stamping machines and raw material cutting for the Marian and Springtelle models is divided among these 20 machines. During May, 1991, 12 stamping machines were assigned to cut raw materials for the Marian model and the remaining 8 machines to cut raw materials for the Springtelle model. This allocation of stamping capacity between the two shoe models is subject to change monthly. Each stamping machine is targeted to operate continuously over one 9-hour shift, 5 days per week. A stamping machine cuts raw material for each pair at the rate of six pairs per hour, regardless of the shoe model. Historical production records indicate that the monthly production cutting rate for each shoe model is relatively constant at 1170 pairs per stamping machine.

The interfacing area consists of two separate assembly lines. One assembly line originates from the set of stamping machines that cuts raw materials for the Springtelle model, the other originating from those stamping machines that cut raw materials for the Marian model. Each assembly line operation can assemble raw materials for at most 90 pairs per hour. Thus, due to capacity constraints in the interfacing area, each shoe model can be scheduled for no more than 75% (that is, 15 stamping machines) of overall total cutting capacity in stamping. Figure 1 shows the layout of the manufacturing process for May, 1991.

The Cost Accounting System

At the end of each month, the Accounting Department prepares a report giving pro-duction levels and standard cost information for that month. Exhibit 1 is the report issued to Division R at the end of May, 1991. Due to blanket purchases made by Westelle, raw material costs are expected to remain constant over the next six months and union contracts insure that all hourly labor cost rates will remain constant over the next six months.

Each of the 20 stamping machines is capable of stamping for either the Springtelle or the Marian model. However, a changeover cost is incurred when a stamping machine interchanges production between the two shoe models. Costly specially trained maintenance personnel must adjust and realign machine settings when a production changeover on a machine occurs. Following realignment, finetuning of the stamping machine also causes raw material waste. Manufacturing Engineering has estimated that a changeover between the two shoe models on a single stamping

EXHIBIT 1   **Production and Standard Cost Information, May 1991**

	MARIAN	SPRINGTELLE	TOTAL
Production (pairs)	14,020	9,370	23,390
Ending Inventory (pairs)	800	0	800
Manufacturing Cost			
Raw Materials ($/pair)	$22.50	$26.30	
Direct Regular Labor*	.20 hrs/pair	.25 hrs/pair	
Direct Overhead			
Inventory Charges†	$ 446.50	$ 0.00	
Machine Changeovers‡			
Number of Changeovers			2
Special Labor Cost per Changeover			$ 3,800
Downtown and Scrap Cost per Changeover			$ 2,700
Total Changeover Cost			$ 13,000
Allocated Overhead			$127,700

Note: * Regular labor rate is $27 per hour.
†Monthly inventory carrying cost per pair is estimated to be 2% of raw material and direct labor costs. This cost includes insurance, taxes, warehouse handling, and the cost of capital.
‡Stamping machine changeovers require special maintenance labor and this labor is charged to Division R at a rate of $45 per hour.

FIGURE 1
Layout of Manufacturing Process, May 1991

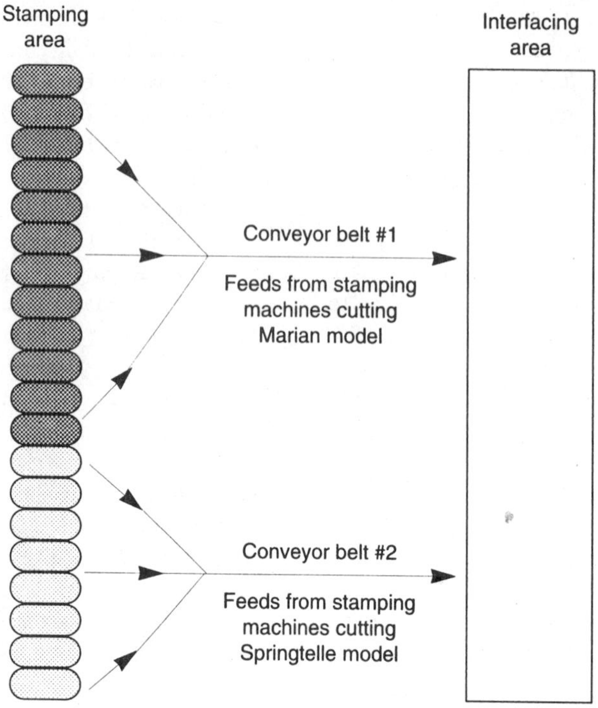

machine costs Division R $6500 in labor and raw material scrap costs. Changeover costs are charged to Division R as direct overhead expense.

Inventory carrying cost is also considered direct overhead expense because it is computed directly from ending monthly warehouse inventory levels for the Springtelle and Marian models. Division R is also charged a fixed monthly amount of allocated overhead that does not vary with production in Division R. This allocated overhead consists of operating expenses from the six departmental units. Westelle uses a volume-based cost accounting system, that is, one that computes unit costs by allocating to Division R a portion of departmental overhead expenses according to direct regular labor dollars. Exhibit 2 gives final unit costs and gross margins for each running shoe model for May, 1991.

Current Production Planning Procedures

Prior to 1990, all orders for the Springtelle and Marian models were phoned in directly to the production planning staff of Division R. Since orders for the Springtelle and Marian models were phoned in directly to these three planners, their knowledge of the immediate market was quite good. Using this market information to form subjective sales forecasts, appropriate production levels for the Marian and Springtelle shoe models were established for the upcoming three-month period. Each planner has been with the company at least 15 years, two of whom started as production line workers.

Since 1988, sales for the Marian model have been steady, enabling production planners to give very accurate subjective short-term (one-month ahead) forecasts

EXHIBIT 2   Unit Costs and Gross Margin for the Marian and
            Springtelle Models, May 1991

	MARIAN	SPRINGTELLE
Raw Material	$ 22.50	$ 26.30
Direct Regular Labor	$ 5.40	$ 6.75
Overhead (Reg Labor $ Basis)	$ 5.49	$ 6.86
Departmental $ 127,700.00		
Inventory 446.40		
Changeover 13,000.00		
Total $141,146.40		
Standard Unit Costs	$ 33.39	$ 39.91
Actual Selling Price	$ 49.95	$ 56.95
Gross Margin	33%	30%

for this model of shoe. Their prediction of short-term sales for the Marian shoe was about 98% accurate, winning the staff the "Crystal Ball Award" in 1989. Since the Springtelle shoe is still in the early stages of its life cycle, sales are not quite as steady as sales for the Marian model. Planners knew that sales were gradually increasing but their subjective opinions often produced forecasts that were severely low one month, severely high the following month or vice-versa.

Last year, the task of forecasting sales for both shoe models was turned over to the marketing unit. Now, all orders are phoned into the marketing unit and a three-month sales forecast is compiled. This forecast is then passed to the production planning staff so that production can be planned accordingly. Despite the marketing staff's lack of training in quantitative forecasting methods, their forecasts for the Marian shoe are extremely accurate. On the other hand, forecasting accuracy for the Springtelle model has shown little improvement since this job was reassigned to the marketing area. Exhibit 3 lists actual sales for the Marian and Springtelle shoes over the previous 29-month period.

In 1990, forecasting errors prompted the marketing department to establish a new inventory policy. To guard against stockouts, minimum inventory levels of 1,900 pairs and 400 pairs for the Springtelle and Marian shoe lines, respectively, became mandatory. Planners are now expected to schedule production for each shoe model so that the projected monthly ending inventory level of that model does not fall below its required minimum inventory level.

The Present Situation

At the beginning of each month, Charlie Vachris, the production supervisor for Division R, sets production levels of the Marian and Springtelle shoe models for the upcoming three-month period. This specific plan is actually enacted only during the first month. Once updated monthly sales forecasts are received from the marketing unit, Charlie then uses these newer forecasts to update his production plan over the next three-month period.

At the beginning of each month, the Marketing Department prepares monthly sales forecasts, for both shoe models, for the upcoming three-month period. Historically, these forecasts for the Marian model have been adequate. However, forecasting accuracy for the Springtelle shoe has been poor and Charlie Vachris feels that this forecasting error has contributed to some of the increase in production costs for Division R.

It is currently the beginning of June, 1991. Last month's production assignment in the stamping area was 12 machines cutting for the Marian model and 8 machines cutting for the Springtelle model. (See Figure 1.) Higher customer service levels and lower production costs appear to be contrary objectives for Division R. Kathleen Westelle has recognized the seriousness of Division R's problems and has ordered Chuck Kullman to turn the division around during the next three-month operating period.

EXHIBIT 3 **Actual Sales for Springtelle and Marian Models, January 1989 to May 1991**

YEAR	MONTH	MARIAN*	SPRINGTELLE*
1989	January	11.0	7.2
	February	11.7	6.2
	March	11.5	5.8
	April	11.8	8.1
	May	11.6	7.8
	June	11.2	6.9
	July	11.3	5.3
	August	12.1	5.8
	September	11.0	5.9
	October	11.2	8.0
	November	10.7	5.3
	December	10.9	6.5
1990	January	10.8	8.7
	February	11.2	7.6
	March	11.7	6.5
	April	11.9	10.4
	May	12.2	8.6
	June	11.8	7.4
	July	11.3	6.5
	August	11.4	6.4
	September	11.1	5.9
	October	10.8	8.2
	November	10.2	7.6
	December	10.4	7.2
1991	January	10.7	9.3
	February	11.2	7.8
	March	11.8	6.8
	April	11.5	10.7
	May	12.6	9.2

*Sales are given in thousands of pairs.

Questions

1. This case begins with Ruth asking Chuck what they should do: cut costs or provide service for the customers. How can a top manager figure out how far he or she should go in providing service for customers? What criteria can be used?

2. In what ways have Steve Bossi's forecasting errors cost the firm money?

3. Using the available data, describe how you would forecast the monthly sales of the Marian shoe model.

4. Describe how you would forecast the monthly sales of the Springtelle shoe model.

5. What sorts of conflicts seem to exist between the production and marketing segments of this firm? Do you think that production and marketing departments often stress different objectives? If so, why?

Part Three
PRODUCTION AND COST

CHAPTER 7

Production Theory

Chapter Profile

The production function is the relationship between the quantities of various inputs used per period of time and the maximum quantity of the good that can be produced per period of time. Given the production function for a particular firm, one can calculate the average product of an input (total output divided by the amount of the input) and the marginal product of an input (the addition to total output resulting from the addition of the last unit of input, when the amounts of other inputs used are held constant).

To determine how much of a particular input to utilize, a firm should compare the marginal revenue product of the input (the amount that an additional unit of the input adds to total revenue) with the marginal expenditure on the input (the amount that an addi-tional unit of the input adds to total cost). To maximize profit, the firm should utilize the amount of the input that results in the marginal revenue product being equal to the marginal expenditure.

An isoquant is a curve showing all possible (efficient) combinations of inputs that are capable of producing a particular quantity of output. The marginal rate of technical substitution shows the rate at which one input can be substituted for another input if output remains constant. No profit-maximizing firm will operate at a point where the isoquant is positively sloped.

To minimize the cost of producing a particular output, a firm should allocate the expenditures among various inputs in such a way that the ratio of the marginal product to the price is the same for all inputs used. Graphically, this amounts to choosing the input combination where the relevant isoquant is tangent to an isocost curve.

Many firms produce goods in lots. The optimal lot size equals $\sqrt{2SQ/b}$, where S is the cost per setup, Q is the total annual requirement of the relevant good, and b is the annual cost of holding each identical good of this sort in inventory for a year. It is important that firms produce lots of approximately optimal size; otherwise, their costs will be higher than is necessary or desirable.

If the firm increases all inputs by the same proportion and output increases by more (less) than this proportion, there are increasing (decreasing) returns to scale. Increasing returns to scale may occur because of indivisibility of inputs, various geometrical relations, or specialization. Decreasing returns to scale can also occur; the most frequently cited reason is the difficulty of managing a huge enterprise. Whether or not there are constant, increasing, or decreasing returns to scale is an empirical question that must be settled case by case.

Using techniques of the sort described in Chapter 5, business analysts, engineers, and others have estimated production functions in many firms and industries. Statistical analyses of time series and cross-section data, as well as engineering data, have been carried out. Many studies have fit the so-called Cobb-Douglas production function to the data. Also, competitive benchmarking is frequently used. The results have proved of considerable value to managers, here and abroad.

Questions

Completion

1. At the Manchester Corporation, the average product of labor equals $3L$, where L is the number of units of labor employed per day. The total output produced per day if 4 units of labor are employed per day is _____. The total output produced per day if 5 units of labor are employed per day is _____. The marginal product of the fifth unit of labor employed per day is _____.

2. In the _____ , all inputs are variable.

3. The _____ production function can be written $Q = AL^{\alpha_1}K^{\alpha_2}$.

4. A fixed input is _____.

5. A variable input is _____.

6. In both the short run and the long run, a firm's productive processes generally permit substantial _____ in the proportions in which inputs are used.

7. The average product of an input is total product divided by _____.

8. The marginal product of an input is the addition to total output resulting from _____.

9. Underlying the law of diminishing marginal returns is the assumption that technology remains _____.

10. Two isoquants can never _____.

True or False

_____ 1. If the average product of labor equals $10/L$, where L is the number of units of labor employed per day, total output is the same regardless of how much labor is used per day.

_____ 2. The law of diminishing marginal returns is inconsistent with increasing returns to scale.

_____ 3. The marginal rate of technical substitution equals -1 times the slope of the isoquant.

_____ 4. Isoquants are always straight lines.

_____ 5. All production functions exhibit constant returns to scale.

_____ 6. Increasing returns to scale can occur because of the difficulty of coordinating a large enterprise.

_____ 7. Whether there are increasing, decreasing, or constant returns to scale in a particular case is an empirical question.

_____ 8. Statistical studies of production functions are hampered by the fact that available data do not always represent technically efficient combinations of inputs and outputs.

_____ 9. The production function is not closely related to a firm's or industry's technology.

_____ 10. The law of diminishing marginal returns applies to cases where there is a proportional increase in all inputs.

Multiple Choice

1. At the Martin Company, the average product of labor equals $5 \div \sqrt{L}$, where L is the amount of labor employed per day. Thus,

   a. labor always is subject to diminishing marginal returns.
   b. labor is subject to diminishing marginal returns only when L is greater than 5.
   c. labor always is not subject to diminishing marginal returns.
   d. labor always is not subject to diminishing marginal returns when L is greater than 5.
   e. none of the above.

2. Suppose that the production function is as follows:

Quantity of output per year	Quantity of input per year
2	1
5	2
9	3
12	4
14 ⌣	5
15	6
15	7
14	8

   The average product of the input when 7 units of the input are used is

   a. 7.
   b. 15.
   c. 15/7.
   d. 7/15.
   e. none of the above.

3. If the production function is as given in question 2, the marginal product of the input when between 1 and 2 units of the input is used is

   a. 2.
   b. 5.
   c. 3.
   d. 4.
   e. none of the above.

4. If the production function is as given in question 2, the marginal product of the input begins to decline

   a. after 3 units of input are used.
   b. after 2 units of input are used.
   c. after 4 units of input are used.
   d. after 7 units of input are used.
   e. none of the above.

5. If the production function is as given in question 2, the marginal product of the input is negative when more than

   a. 7 units of input are used.
   b. 6 units of input are used.
   c. 5 units of input are used.
   d. 4 units of input are used.
   e. none of the above.

6. The marginal product equals the average product when the latter is

   a. 1/2 of its maximum value.
   b. 1/4 of its maximum value.
   c. equal to its maximum value.
   d. 1 1/2 times its maximum value.
   e. none of the above.

Problems

1. a Suppose the production function for a cigarette factory is as given below, there being only one input:

Amount of input (units per year)	Amount of output (units per year)
1	7
2	14.5
3	22
4	29
5	35
6	39
7	39

Plot the average product curve for the input in the graph below.

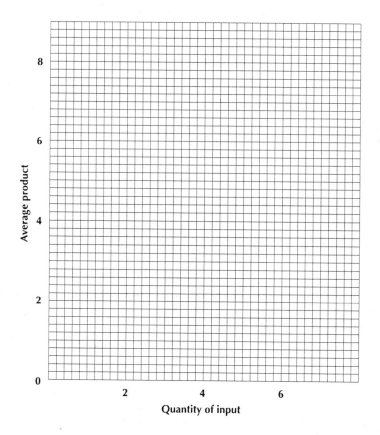

b. On the basis of the production function given in the first part of this question, plot the marginal product curve of the input.

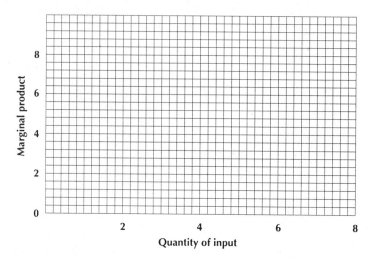

2. a. In the Cobb-Douglas production function, is the exponent of labor generally larger or smaller than that of capital?

b. Suppose that in a chemical plant $Q = AL^\alpha K^\beta$, where Q is the output rate, L is the rate of labor input, and K is the rate of capital input. Statistical analysis indicates that $\alpha = 0.8$ and $\beta = 0.3$. The owner of the plant claims that there are increasing returns to scale in the plant. Is he right?

c. What is the value of the output elasticity in the firm in part b?

3. Suppose you are assured by the owner of an aluminum plant that his plant is subject to constant returns to scale, labor and capital being the only inputs. He claims that output per worker in his plant is a function of capital per worker only. Is he right?

4. The Concord Company produces 20,000 parts of a particular type per year. The cost of each setup is $5,000, and the annual cost of holding each identical part of this sort in inventory for a year is $2. What is the optimal lot size?

5. In industries like consumer electronics, steel, and autos, the Japanese have increased their share of the American market. An engineering comparison of a compact-car plant in Japan and the United States is as follows:

	United States	Japan
Parts stamped per hour	325	550
Manpower per press line	7–13	1
Time needed to change dies	4–6 hours	5 minutes
Average production run	10 days	2 days
Time needed per small car	59.9 hours	30.8 hours
Number of quality inspectors	1 per 7 workers	1 per 30 workers

a One of the concepts at the core of Japanese production management is "just-in-time" production, which calls for goods being produced and delivered just in time to be sold, subassemblies to be produced and delivered just in time to be assembled into finished goods, and fabricated parts to be produced and delivered just in time to go into subassemblies. What are the advantages of this system?

b. What are the disadvantages of this system?

c. Another major Japanese production concept is "total quality control," or "quality at the source," which means that errors should be found and corrected *by the people performing the work.* In the West, inspection has often been performed by statistical sampling *after* a lot of goods is produced. What are the advantages of the Japanese system?

6. The production function for the Roundtree Laser Company is

$$Q = 10L^{.5}K^{.3}M^{.3},$$

where Q is the number of lasers produced per week, L is the amount of labor used per week, K is the amount of capital used per week, and M is the quantity of raw materials used per week.

a Does this production function exhibit diminishing marginal returns?

b. Does this production function exhibit decreasing returns to scale?

c. Does the average product of labor depend on the amount of the other inputs used?

7. At the Oklahoma Piano Company, the average product of labor equals 5, regardless of how much labor is used.

a What is the marginal product of the first unit of labor?

b. What is the marginal product of the eightieth unit of labor?

c. By how much will output increase if labor is increased by 100 units?

d. By how much will output fall if labor is reduced by 50 units?

e. Does this case conform to the law of diminishing marginal returns? Why or why not?

f. Does this case seem realistic? Why or why not?

8. The Torch Corporation, a hypothetical producer of paper napkins, claims that in 1996 it has the following production function:

$$Q = 3 + 4L + 2P,$$

where Q is the number of paper napkins it produces per year, L is the number of hours of labor per year, and P is the number of pounds of paper used per year.

a Does this production function seem to include all of the relevant inputs? Explain.

b. Does this production function seem reasonable if it is applied to all possible values of L and P? Explain.

c. Does this production function exhibit diminishing marginal returns?

9. Fill in the blanks in the following table:

Number of units of variable input	Total output (number of units)	Marginal product* of variable input	Average product of variable input
3	——	Unknown	30
4	——	20	——
5	130	——	——
6	——	5	——
7	——	——	$19^1/_2$

*These figures pertain to the interval between the indicated amount of the variable input and one unit less than the indicated amount of the variable input.

10. As the quantity of a variable input increases, explain why the point where *marginal* product begins to decline is encountered before the point where *average* product begins to decline. Explain too why the point where *average* product begins to decline is encountered before the point where *total* product begins to decline.

11. The Deering Company's production function is $Q = 20LK$, where Q is the output rate, L is the number of units of labor it uses per period of time, and K is the number of units of capital it uses per period of time. The price of labor is $4 a unit, and the price of capital is $10 per unit. What combination of inputs should the firm use to produce 200 units of output per period of time?

12. The Barton Company is a manufacturer of spectrometers. Barton's vice president for operations has determined that the firm's output (Q) is related in the following way to the number of engineers used (E) and the number of technicians used (T):

$$Q = -5.682 \qquad - .316E - .417T + 6.3512 \sqrt{E}$$
$$+ 8.5155 \sqrt{T} + .3410 \sqrt{ET}.$$

Suppose the wage of an engineer is $36,000, the wage of a technician is $24,000, and the total amount that the firm spends on both engineers and technicians is limited to $6 million. Find two equations that must be satisfied simultaneously to obtain the optimal values of E and T.

13. The owner of the Martin Marina believes that the relationship between the number of boats serviced and labor input is

$$Q = -3 + 8.5L - 2L^2,$$

where Q is the number of boats serviced per hour, and L is the number of people employed. Her firm receives $20 for each boat serviced, and the wage rate for each person employed is $10.

a. How many people should she employ to maximize profit?
b. What will be the firm's hourly profit? (Assume that the only cost is labor cost.)

Answers

Completion
1. 48, 75, 27   2. long run   3. Cobb-Douglas   4. fixed in quantity
5. variable in quantity   6. variation   7. the quantity of the input
8. an extra unit of the input   9. constant   10. intersect

True or False
1. True   2. False   3. True   4. False   5. False   6. False   7. True
8. True   9. False   10. False

Multiple Choice
1. a   2. c   3. c   4. a   5. a   6. c

Problems
1. a   The average product curve is as follows:

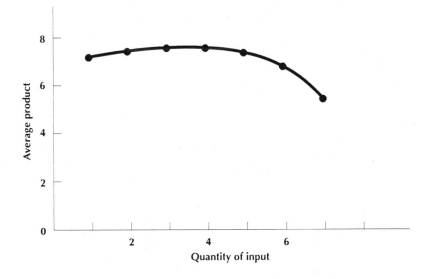

b. The marginal product curve is as follows:

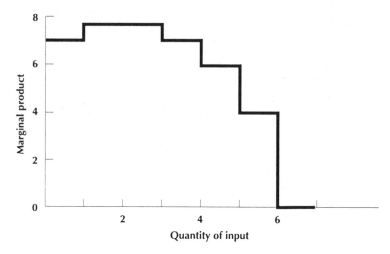

2. a It is generally larger than the exponent of capital.
   b. Yes.
   c. 1.1.

3. Yes.

4. The optimal lot size equals $\sqrt{2(5,000)\,(20,000) \div 2}\ = 10,000$.

5. a Because of its hand-to-mouth nature, just-in-time production means that a
      firm holds fewer inventories of parts, subassemblies, and finished goods.
      Because it is expensive to hold inventories, this is an advantage. Also,
      defects tend to be discovered more quickly, and their causes may be nipped
      in the bud.
   b. If goods, subassemblies, and parts are to be produced and delivered just in
      time for use or sale, they must be produced in small lots, which means that
      the equipment used to produce them must be set up more often. Each setup
      is expensive; it often involves moving heavy dies into place, making
      adjustments, and inspecting the results until the settings are right. To
      overcome this disadvantage, the Japanese have worked very hard to reduce
      setup costs. For example, Toyota has reduced the time to set up 800-ton
      presses used in forming auto hoods and fenders from an hour in 1971 to
      about 10 minutes or less.
   c. Higher quality of product, less waste of materials, a heightened awareness
      of the causes of defects on the part of the people doing the work, and fewer
      inspectors.

6. a Yes.
   b. No.
   c. Yes.

7. a 5.
   b. 5.
   c. 500.
   d. 250.
   e. No.
   f. No.

8. a No. It seems likely that some capital and land are used.
   b. No. It says that an extra 1/4 hour of labor or an extra 1/2 pound of paper will result in an extra paper napkin, regardless of the number of paper napkins produced. Beyond some output level, one would expect the marginal product of labor and of paper to fall. Also, this seems to be a lot of labor and paper to produce one napkin!
   c. No.

9. The complete table is:

Number of units of variable input	Total output (number of units)	Marginal product of variable input	Average product of variable input
3	90	Unknown	30
4	110	20	$27\frac{1}{2}$
5	130	20	26
6	135	5	$22\frac{1}{2}$
7	$136\frac{1}{2}$	$1\frac{1}{2}$	$19\frac{1}{2}$

10. Because of the law of diminishing marginal returns, the marginal product begins to decline at some point. If the marginal product exceeds the average product at that point, the marginal product can fall to some extent without reducing the average product. Only when it falls below zero will the total product begin to decrease.

11. The firm wants to minimize

$$C = 4L + 10K.$$

Since $K = 200 \div (20L) = 10 \div L$, the firm wants to minimize

$$C = 4L + 10 \left(\frac{10}{L}\right).$$

Setting $dC/dL = 0$, we find that

$$\frac{dC}{dL} = 4 - \frac{100}{L^2} = 0,$$

so $L = 5$. Thus, $K = 10 \div 5 = 2$. In other words, the firm should use 5 units of labor and 2 units of capital.

12. If the Barton Company is to maximize output, it must choose a combination of engineers and technicians such that

$$\frac{MP_E}{P_E} = \frac{MP_T}{P_T},$$

where MP_E is the marginal product of an engineer, MP_T is the marginal product of a technician, P_E is the wage of an engineer, and P_T is the wage of a technician. From the production function given in the question,

$$MP_E = \frac{\partial Q}{\partial E} = -.316 + 3.1756\sqrt{\frac{1}{E}} + .1705\sqrt{\frac{T}{E}}$$

$$MP_T = \frac{\partial Q}{\partial T} = -.417 + 4.2578\sqrt{\frac{1}{T}} + .1705\sqrt{\frac{E}{T}}.$$

Substituting for MP_E and MP_T, and noting that $P_E = 36$ and $P_T = 24$ (since wages are measured in thousands of dollars), it follows that

$$\frac{1}{36}\left\{-.316 + 3.1756\sqrt{\frac{1}{E}} + .1705\sqrt{\frac{T}{E}}\right\}$$

$$= \frac{1}{24}\left\{-.417 + 4.2578\sqrt{\frac{1}{T}} + .1705\sqrt{\frac{E}{T}}\right\}.$$

Also, since the firm wants to spend only $6 million on engineers and technicians,

$$36E + 24T = 6,000.$$

These last two equations must be solved simultaneously. (It turns out that the Barton Company should hire about 91 engineers and about 114 technicians.)

13. a   The marginal revenue product of a worker equals

$$20\left(\frac{dQ}{dL}\right) = 20\,(8.5 - 4L) = 170 - 80L.$$

Setting the marginal revenue product equal to the marginal expenditure on labor (which equals the wage), we find that

$$170 - 80L = 10,$$

which means that $L = 2$. She should employ 2 people.

b. Hourly profit equals

$$20[-3 + 8.5(2) - 2(2)^2] - 2(10)$$
$$= 20(17 - 11) - 20 = 100.$$

Thus, hourly profit equals $100.

CHAPTER 8

Technological Change and Industrial Innovation

Chapter Profile

Technological change is the advance of technology, such advance often resulting in a change in the production function for an existing product or in a new product. The rate of technological change is often measured by the change in the total productivity index. Such indexes are often used by firms as rough measures of changes in efficiency.

Research and development can be regarded as a process of uncertainty reduction, or learning. Chance plays a large role in research and development, and many projects use parallel efforts to help cope with uncertainty. Techniques are presented in this chapter to indicate when parallel efforts should be used.

An R and D project's likelihood of economic success is the product of three separate factors: (1) the probability of technical success, (2) the probability of commercialization (given technical success), and (3) the probability of economic success (given commer-cialization). All three seem to be directly related to how quickly an R and D project is evaluated for its economic, as opposed to only technical, potential.

To promote successful R and D, there must be a strong linkage between R and D and marketing personnel, the firm's R and D portfolio must be properly balanced between short-term and long-term projects, and project selection techniques must be effective. However, this does not mean that the more complicated quantitative selection techniques need be used.

For a particular innovation, there is likely to be a time-cost trade-off function. If the firm cuts the total time taken to develop and introduce the innovation, it incurs higher costs. Time-cost trade-off functions vary from firm to firm, because some firms are more adept and experienced than others in developing and introducing a particular innovation. The optimal duration of the project is the time interval where the discounted gross profits exceed the discounted cost by the maximum amount.

In many industries, there is a learning curve, which shows the extent to which the average cost of producing an item falls in response to increases in its cumulative total output. This learning curve plays an important role in pricing. For example, Texas Instruments successfully priced its product at less than its then-current average cost to move quickly down the learning curve. Regression techniques can be applied to estimate the learning curve for a particular product.

As the number of firms adopting an innovation increases, the probability of its adoption by a nonuser increases. Also, the probability that a nonuser will adopt the innovation is higher for more profitable innovations than for less profitable innovations, and for innovations requiring small investments than for those requiring large invest-ments. A model based on these propositions can sometimes be of use in forecasting the rate of diffusion of an innovation.

Questions

Completion

1. Technology is _____ regarding the industrial arts.
2. Technological change results in a _____ in the production function.
3. The total productivity index is _____.
4. An invention, when applied for the first time, is called an _____.
5. The rate of diffusion of an innovation depends heavily on the innovation's

    _____.

6. The proportion of firms using a new process often increases over time in rough accord with the _____ curve.
7. R and D can be regarded as a process of _____ reduction.
8. As the number of firms adopting a new process increases, the probability of its adoption by a nonuser (increases, decreases) _____.
9. The closer the link between _____ and R and D, the greater the probability that R and D will be commercialized, given technical completion.

True or False

_____   1. A firm almost never is wise to wait more than a few weeks in introducing an innovation.

_____   2. Learning takes place among the users of an innovation but not among the producers of an innovation.

_____   3. There is no real difference between invention and innovation.

_____   4. The percentage of total innovation cost devoted to marketing start-up is higher in the United States than in Japan.

_____   5. The learning curve is often represented as $\log C = \log a + b \log Q$.

_____   6. The closer the link between marketing and R and D, the greater the probability of commercialization (given technical completion).

_____   7. To measure the rate of technological change, total factor productivity is generally preferred over labor productivity.

_____ 8. Japanese firms in many high-technology industries have time-cost trade-off functions that are to the left of their American rivals for innovations based on external technology.

_____ 9. IBM does not use parallel efforts in its R and D.

_____ 10. The percentage of total innovation cost devoted in Japan to tooling and manufacturing equipment and facilities is almost double that in the United States.

Multiple Choice

1. The rate of growth of output per hour of labor is

   a. an adequate measure of the rate of technological change.
   b. influenced by the rate of technological change.
   c. independent of the rate of technological change.
   d. constant in the United States.
   e. none of the above.

2. An R and D project's probability of economic success depends on

   a. the probability of technical success.
   b. the probability of commercialization (given technical success).
   c. the probability of economic success (given commercialization).
   d. all of the above.
   e. none of the above.

3. If $R(t)$ is the present value of gross profit when the duration of an R and D project is t years, and if the time-cost trade-off function is $C(t)$,

   a. profit equals $R(t) - C(t)$.
   b. the first order condition for profit maximization is $\dfrac{dC}{dt} = \dfrac{dR}{dt}$.
   c. the firm should choose t to minimize $C(t)$.
   d. all of the above.
   e. both a and b.

4. The equation for the logistic curve is

   a. $e^{-(A + Bt)}$.
   b. $1 + e^{-(A + Bt)}$.
   c. $\dfrac{1}{1 + e^{-(A + Bt)}}$.
   d. all of the above.
   e. none of the above.

5. One simple way to estimate the parameters (A and B) of the logistic curve is to

   a. regress $\ln P(t)$ on t.
   b. regress $\ln[1 - P(t)]$ on t.
   c. regress $\ln \{P(t)/[1 - P(t)]\}$ on t.
   d. all of the above.
   e. none of the above.

97

Problems

1. Ever since the Arab oil embargo of late 1973, both the private and public sectors have been engaged in a great many projects to develop new ways to power our economy. Shale, found in large amounts in Colorado, Utah, and Wyoming, is a potentially important source of synthetic oil. However, one problem with shale is that it involves a waste-disposal program. The spent shale could fill an enormous volume, and the danger of environmental damage must be considered.

   Coal gasification is another potentially important source of energy. The United States is endowed with huge deposits of coal (about 20 percent of the world's supply), but there is no commercially successful way of burning much of it cleanly. One way to get around the environmental problems involved in using coal as a fuel is to convert coal to a clean gas. At present, much of this work is still in the stage of R and D. A substantial portion of this R and D has been funded by the government. Since there is so much uncertainty concerning the relative merits of various processes, the government has helped to finance a number of parallel approaches to the problem. It will be some time before anyone can tell which of these processes, if any, is economically viable.

   a. If any of these technologies were to be successfully commercialized, would this result in an increase in productivity? If so, how quickly would such an increase occur?

   b. Why has the government financed a number of parallel approaches to the problem? Why hasn't it focused on a single approach?

2. For a particular machine tool, a doubling of cumulative output results in a 25 percent reduction in average cost. The cost of producing the 100th of these machine tools is $10,000.

   a. What is the cost of producing the 200th of these machine tools?

   b. What is the cost of producing the 400th of these machine tools?

3. An automobile manufacturer is trying to develop an improved engine that will emit fewer pollutants. There are two possible approaches to this technical problem. If either one is adopted, there is a 50–50 chance that it will cost $2 million to develop the engine and a 50–50 chance that it will cost $1 million to do so. The expected cost of development is the sum of the total costs of development if each possible outcome occurs times the probability of the occurrence of this outcome.

   a. If the firm chooses one of the outcomes and carries it to completion, what is the expected cost of developing the engine?

   b. If the two approaches are run in parallel and if the true cost of development using each approach can be determined after $250,000 has been spent on each approach, what is the expected cost of developing the engine? (Note that the total cost figure for each approach, if adopted, includes the $250,000.)

4. Technological change is called labor saving if it results in a decrease in the marginal rate of technical substitution of labor for capital. Under these circumstances, does technological change result in a greater increase in the marginal product of capital than in the marginal product of labor (at a given capital-labor ratio)? Does it result in the firm's using more capital relative to labor?

5. a Is the growth of output per hour of labor a complete measure of the rate of technological change? If not, why not? Is it commonly used for this purpose?
   b. What advantages does the total productivity index have over output per hour of labor?

6. a According to John Kendrick, output per unit of labor input increased by 5.1 percent per year in the tobacco industry during 1899–1953 and by 3.5 percent per year in the chemical industry during 1899–1953. The chemical industry has spent much more on R and D than has the tobacco industry. Does this mean that R and D has relatively little impact on an industry's rate of technological change?
   b. The annual rate of increase of the total productivity index during 1899–1953 was 3.5 percent in the transportation equipment industry and 1.6 percent in the beverage industry. What sorts of factors may be able to explain this difference?

7. Figures provided by the Bureau of Labor Statistics show that output per hour of labor in blast furnaces using the most up-to-date techniques was about twice as large as the industry average. How can such large differences exist at a given point in time? Why don't all firms adopt the most up-to-date techniques at every point in time? Do differences of this sort persist today?

8. The Chester Company produces a numerically controlled machine tool. A member of the firm's engineering staff regresses the logarithm of the input cost (in dollars) of the Qth machine tool produced on the logarithm of Q, the result being

$$\log C = 3 - 0.3 \log Q.$$

   a What is the estimated input cost of the 10th machine tool produced?
   b. What is the estimated input cost of the 100th machine tool produced?
   c. What is the estimated input cost of the 400th machine tool produced?

9. The Elwyn Corporation wants to estimate the proportion of paper companies that will be using a particular new process in the year 2000. The firm's executive vice president regresses $\ln\{m(t)/[n - m(t)]\}$ on t, where $m(t)$ is the number of paper firms using this process in year t, and n is the total number of paper firms that can use this process. Measuring t in years from 1970, this regression is

$$\ln\left[\frac{m(t)}{n - m(t)}\right] = -3.0 + .15t.$$

   Forecast the proportion of paper firms that will be using this new process in the year 2000.

10. The Wilmington Company is developing and introducing a new biotechnology product. The firm's president decides to develop and introduce this product as quickly as possible. Under what conditions is this the optimal strategy? Under what conditions is it a poor strategy?

11. The Cornell Corporation uses three inputs: labor, energy, and materials. In 1996, it uses 10,000 hours of labor, 20,000 kilowatt-hours of energy, and 8,000 pounds of materials to produce 100,000 pounds of output. In 1997, it uses 20,000 hours of labor, 90,000 kilowatt-hours of energy, and 12,000 pounds of materials to produce 300,000 pounds of output. In 1996, the price of labor is $10 per hour; the price of a kilowatt-hour of energy is 2 cents, and the price of a pound of materials is $5.

    a. What was total factor productivity in 1996?
    b. What was total factor productivity in 1997?

12. The manager of a commercial laboratory estimates that the cost (in millions of dollars) of developing and introducing a new product equals

$$C = 50 - 10t + t^2, \text{ for } 1 \le t \le 5,$$

    where t is the number of years taken to develop and introduce the new drug. The discounted profit (gross of innovation cost) from a new drug of this type (in millions of dollars) is estimated to equal

$$R = 100 - 6t, \text{ for } 1 \le t \le 5.$$

    a. The managers of the laboratory are committed to develop and introduce this new drug within 5 years, and it is impossible to develop and introduce it in less than 1 year. What project duration would minimize cost?
    b. What is the optimal project duration? Why?

13. The Japanese emphasis on low-cost manufacturing (and high quality of product) has paid off well. Faced with intense competition from the Japanese and others, many American firms have begun to redesign their products in order to make them cheaper to produce. Consider the Sunbeam Appliance Company, which launched a program in 1982 aimed at getting 30 percent of the world market for steam irons. Sunbeam's existing product used 97 parts with 18 fasteners in 10 configurations. After intensive analysis, Sunbeam's managers decided that the key to cost reduction was to reduce the number of parts. Eventually, a design was developed that used 51 parts and 3 fasteners in 2 configurations. The new design, implemented in 1986, was substantially cheaper to produce than either of Sunbeam's previous designs.[4] Did this new design result in a shift in Sunbeam's production function?

Answers

Completion

1. society's pool of knowledge   2. change   3. $Q \div (a_1I_1 + a_2I_2 + \ldots + a_nI_n)$, where Q is output, I_i is the amount of the ith input used, and a_i is the price of the ith input in the base period.   4. innovation   5. profitability   6. logistic   7. uncertainty   8. increases   9. marketing

True or False

1. False   2. False   3. False   4. True   5. True   6. True   7. True
8. True   9. False   10. True

---

[4] A. Lehnard, "Revitalizing the Manufacture and Design of Mature Global Products," in B. Guile and H. Brooks, eds., *Technology and Global Industry* (Washington, D.C.: National Academy Press, 1987).

Multiple Choice

1. b   2. d   3. e   4. c   5. c

Problems

1. a   To the extent that these technologies use less input per unit of output than the technologies they replace, productivity will increase. But, in general, productivity will not increase merely because new technologies are introduced (because they are new). The first commercial introduction of a new technology may have little effect. How quickly productivity increases in response to a new technology depends on the rate of diffusion, which depends on the profitability of using the technology, among other things.

   b.   Because of the uncertainties concerning which approach is best.

2. a $7,500.

   b. $5,625.

3. a   If a single approach is used, the expected costs of development are 0.5 × $2 million + 0.5 × $1 million, or $1.5 million, since there is a 0.5 probability that total costs with any single approach will be $2 million and a 0.5 probability that they will be $1 million.

   b.   The expected total costs of development are 0.25 × $2 million + 0.75 × $1 million + $250,000, or $1.5 million, if each approach is carried to the point at which $250,000 has been spent on it, and if the cheaper approach is chosen at that point (and the other approach is dropped). Why? Because there is a 0.25 probability that total costs with the better of the two approaches will be $2 million and a 0.75 probability that they will be $1 million. In addition, there is the certainty that a cost of $250,000 will be incurred for the approach that is dropped. The reason why there is a 0.25 chance that total costs with the better of the two approaches is $2 million is that this will occur only when the total cost of both approaches turns out to be $2 million—and the probability that this will occur is 0.5 × 0.5, or 0.25.

4. Yes. Yes.

5. a   No. It is influenced by many factors other than the rate of technological change—for example, changes in capital per worker. Yes.

   b.   The total productivity index takes explicit account of capital input as well as labor input.

6. a   No. Many factors other than technological change also influence output per hour of labor.

   b.   Differences in R and D expenditures and economies of scale, among others.

7. A profit-maximizing firm generally will not scrap existing equipment merely because somewhat better equipment is available. The new equipment must be sufficiently better to offset the fact that the old equipment is already paid for, whereas this is not the case for the new. Yes.

8. a. $501.
   b. $251.
   c. $166.

9. $\ln \left[\dfrac{m(t)}{n - m(t)} \right] = -3.0 + .15(30) = 1.5.$

   Thus,

   $$\frac{m(t)}{n - m(t)} = 4.48,$$

   and

   $$m(t)/n = 4.48 \left[1 - \frac{m(t)}{n} \right]$$

   $$m(t)/n = \frac{4.48}{5.48} = .82.$$

   The forecasted proportion is .82.

10. It is the optimal strategy if the discounted revenues from the new product fall greatly if the product's introduction is delayed even slightly. Often, however, the discounted revenues do not fall so greatly. Because the discounted costs of developing and introducing the new product often drop if it is delayed, it may be worthwhile to develop and introduce it more slowly.

11. a. $\dfrac{100,000}{10,000(10) + 20,000(.02) + 8,000(5)} = \dfrac{100,000}{140,400} = 0.712.$

    b. $\dfrac{300,000}{20,000(10) + 90,000(.02) + 12,000(5)} = \dfrac{300,000}{261,800} = 1.146.$

12. a. To minimize C, we set $\dfrac{dC}{dt}$ equal to zero, the result being

    $$\frac{dC}{dt} = -10 + 2t = 0,$$

    which means that $t = 5$. Thus, to minimize cost, the drug should be developed and introduced in 5 years.

    b. The discounted profit equals

    $$\pi = R - C = 100 - 6t - (50 - 10t + t^2)$$

    $$= 50 + 4t - t^2, \text{ for } 1 \leq t \leq 5.$$

    Setting $\dfrac{d\pi}{dt} = 0$, we find that

    $$\frac{d\pi}{dt} = 4 - 2t = 0,$$

    which means that $t = 2$. Thus, to maximize profit, the drug should be developed and introduced in 2 years.

13. Yes. Note too that the product may have changed somewhat.

CHAPTER 9

The Analysis of Costs

Chapter Profile

Managerial economists define the cost of producing a particular product as the value of the other products that the resources used in its production could have produced instead. This is the product's opportunity cost, and it may differ from historical cost, which is generally the basis of accounting statements.

In the short run, it is important to distinguish between a firm's fixed and variable costs. The firm's total and average costs, total and average fixed costs, and total and average variable costs can all be plotted against output. So can the firm's marginal cost. The resulting cost functions, or cost curves (as they are often called), show how changes in output will affect the firm's costs, a major concern of any firm.

The long-run average cost function shows the minimum cost per unit of producing each output level when any desired scale of plant can be built. The long-run average cost function is tangent to each of the short-run average cost functions at the output where the plant corresponding to the short-run average cost function is optimal. The long-run average cost curve is important for practical decision making because it shows the extent to which larger plants have cost advantages over smaller ones.

Many studies based on the statistical analysis of cross-section and time-series data, as well as engineering studies, have been carried out to estimate the cost functions of particular firms. The regression techniques described in Chapter 5 have played an important role here.

In choosing among plants, a major consideration is flexibility if the output of the plant is highly uncertain. Some plants, while they have higher costs than others at the most likely output, have lower costs than the others over a wide range of output. If one cannot predict output reasonably well, flexible plants of this sort may be best.

Break-even analysis compares total revenue and total cost, graphically or algebraically. A break-even chart combines the total cost function and the total revenue curve, both of which are generally assumed to be linear, and shows the profit or loss resulting from each sales level. The break-even point is the sales level that must be achieved if the firm is to avoid losses. Firms often find it useful to carry out various types of profit contribution analysis. The profit contribution is the difference between total revenue and total variable cost; on a per-unit basis, it is equal to price minus average variable cost.

Questions

Completion

1. If the average fixed cost of producing 10 units of output at the Hollywood Manufacturing Company is $10, the average fixed cost of producing 20 units is _____. If the marginal cost of each of the first 20 units of output is $5, the average variable cost of producing 20 units is _____, and the average total cost of producing 20 units is _____.

2. Total cost equals _____ plus variable cost.

3. Average cost must equal marginal cost at the point where average cost is a _____.

4. The long-run total cost equals output times _____.

5. _____ include opportunity costs of resources owned and used by the firm's owner.

6. An important criticism of cross-section studies of cost functions is that they sometimes are subject to the _____.

7. Some determinants of the shape of the long-run average cost curve are _____.

8. The average variable cost curve turns up beyond some output level because of the _____.

9. The marginal cost curve turns up beyond some output level because of the _____.

10. Average variable cost equals the price of the variable input divided by _____, if the price of the variable input is constant.

11. Marginal cost equals the price of the variable input divided by _____, if the price of the variable input is constant.

12. Statistical estimates of cost functions based on cross-section data sometimes run into problems because firms' _____ methods are different.

True or False

_____ 1. If average variable cost always equals $20 when output is less than 100 units, marginal cost is less than $20 when output is in this range.

_____ 2. Long-run marginal cost can never differ from short-run marginal cost.

_____ 3. Costs that have already been incurred are important factors in making production decisions.

_____ 4. The opportunity cost doctrine says that the production of one good may reduce the cost of another good.

_____ 5. When the firm has constructed the scale of plant that is optimal for producing a given level of output, long-run marginal cost will equal short-run marginal cost at that output.

_____ 6. The shape of the long-run average cost function is due primarily to the law of diminishing marginal returns.

_____ 7. Average cost must exceed marginal cost at the point where average cost is a minimum.

_____ 8. The break-even point lies well above the output level that must be reached if the firm is to avoid losses.

_____ 9. Empirical studies often indicate that the short-run average cost curve is S-shaped.

_____ 10. The survivor technique is a way of estimating a firm's short-run cost function.

Multiple Choice

1. The Moulton Corporation's average total cost per month equals $5 \times Q$, where Q is the number of units of output produced per month. The marginal cost of the third unit of output produced per month is

   a. $15.
   b. $20.
   c. $25.
   d. $30.
   e. none of the above.

2. The curve in the graph below has the shape of

    a a marginal cost curve.
    b. an average variable cost curve.
    c. an average fixed cost curve.
    d. all of the above.
    e. none of the above.

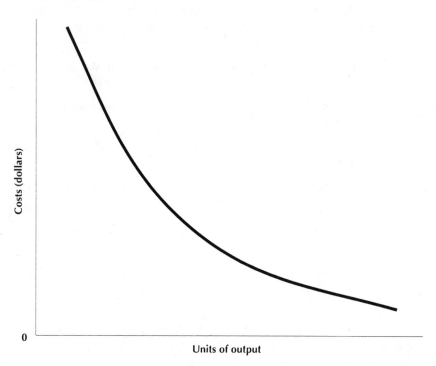

3. The firm's cost functions are determined by

    a the price of its product.
    b. its assets.
    c. its production function.
    d. the age of the firm.
    e. none of the above.

Problems

1. Suppose that a machine shop's daily costs are as shown below.

Units of output	Total fixed cost (dollars)	Total variable cost (dollars)
0	$500	0
1	500	50
2	500	90
3	500	140
4	500	200
5	500	270
6	500	350
7	500	450
8	500	600

a Draw the firm's average fixed cost function below.

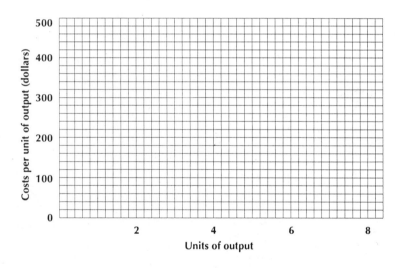

b. Draw the firm's average variable cost function below.

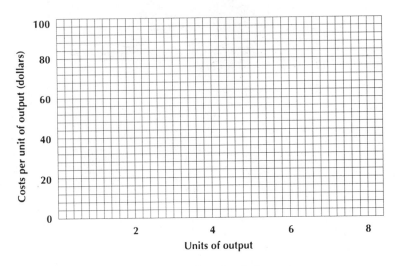

c. Draw the firm's average total cost function below.

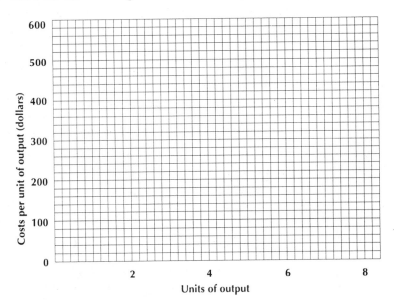

d. Draw the firm's marginal cost function below.

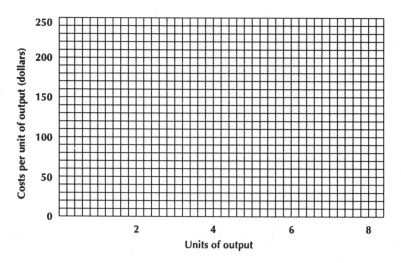

2. a. Suppose you are a consultant to Harper & Row, the book publisher. Suppose the firm is about to publish a book that will sell for $10 a copy. The fixed costs of publishing the books are $5,000; the variable cost is $5 a copy. What is the break-even point for this book?

   b. If the price were $8 rather than $10, what would be the break-even point?

3. a. Suppose two firms have exactly the same marginal cost curve, but their average fixed cost curve is not the same. Will their average variable cost curve be the same? Why or why not?

   b. A firm's marginal product of capital is twice its marginal product of labor; the price of labor is $6, and the price of capital is $3. Is the firm minimizing cost? If not, how can it reduce its costs? Explain.

4. Brady Farms is a profit-maximizing, perfectly competitive producer of tomatoes. It produces tomatoes using one acre of land (price of the land equals $2,000) and varying numbers of workers (wage per worker equals $500 per week). The production function is as follows:

Number of workers (per week)	Output of tomatoes per week (in truckloads)
0	0
1	1
3	2
7	3
12	4
18	5
25	6

Show that this farm is subject to increasing marginal cost as output increases.

5. The Miracle Manufacturing Company's short-run average cost function in 1996 is

$$AC = 3 + 4Q,$$

where AC is the firm's average cost (in dollars per pound of the product), and Q is its output rate.

   a. Obtain an equation for the firm's short-run total cost function.
   b. Does the firm have any fixed costs? Explain.
   c. If the price of the Miracle Manufacturing Company's product (per pound) is $2, is the firm making profits or losses? Explain.

6. Show that a firm will maximize output—for a given outlay—by distributing its expenditures among various inputs in such a way that the marginal product of a dollar's worth of any input is equal to the marginal product of a dollar's worth of any other input that is used. At any point on a firm's cost function, is the firm maximizing output for a given outlay?

7. a. Suppose that capital and labor are the only inputs used by the Golden Printing Company and that capital costs $1 a unit and labor costs $2 a unit. Draw the isocost curves corresponding to an outlay of $200 and $300.

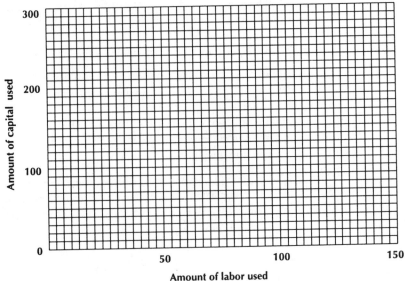

b. To produce each unit of output, the Golden Printing Company must use 1 unit of labor and 1 unit of capital. What is the firm's cost of producing 200 units of output? Of producing 300 units of output?

8. The Barbizon Corporation is considering two types of plants to make an electric motor. For each type of plant, average variable cost is constant so long as output is less than capacity, which is the maximum output of the plant. The cost structure for each type of plant is as follows:

	Plant X	Plant Y
Average variable costs		
Labor	$24.40	$12.10
Materials	14.10	14.05
Other	11.20	10.80
Total	$49.70	$36.95
Total fixed cost	$150,000	$400,000
Annual capacity	80,000	160,000

a. Derive the average cost of producing 40,000, 80,000, and 160,000 motors per year with plant X. (For outputs exceeding the capacity of a single plant, assume that more than one plant of this type is built.)

b. Derive the average cost of producing 40,000, 80,000, and 160,000 motors per year with plant Y.

c. If these are the only plants to produce these motors, plot the points on the long-run average cost curve for the production of these motors for outputs of 40,000, 80,000, and 160,000 per year.

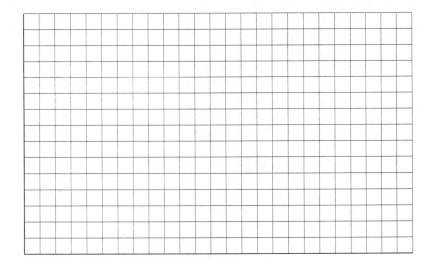

9. The Suffern Company's total cost function is

$$C = 100 + 3Q - 2Q^2 + 3Q^3,$$

where C equals total cost, and Q equals output per day.

a. What is the equation for the firm's average cost curve?

b. What is the equation for the firm's marginal cost curve?

c. At what output is marginal cost a minimum?

10. The Swarthmore Company is considering three types of plants to make a particular product. Plant I is much more highly automated than plant II, which in turn is more highly automated than plant III. For each type of plant, average variable cost is constant so long as output is less than capacity, which is the maximum output of the plant. The cost structure for each type of plant is as follows:

	Plant I	Plant II	Plant III
Average variable costs			
Labor	$1.60	$4.60	$5.80
Materials	1.10	1.50	1.90
Other	.60	.90	1.50
Total	$3.30	$7.00	$9.20
Total fixed costs	$600,000	$200,000	$100,000
Annual capacity (units)	200,000	100,000	50,000

   a Derive the average cost of producing 200,000 units per year with plant I.
   b. Derive the average cost of producing 200,000 units per year with plant II. (For outputs exceeding the capacity of a single plant, assume that more than one plant of this type is built.)
   c. Derive the average cost of producing 200,000 units per year with plant III. (For outputs exceeding the capacity of a single plant, assume that more than one plant of this type is built.)

11. The Allentown Corporation, a retail seller of sofas, wants to determine how many sofas it must sell in order to earn a profit of $15,000 per month. The price of each sofa is $400, and the average variable cost is $150.
   a What is the required sales volume if the Allentown Corporation's monthly fixed costs are $4,000 per month?
   b. If the firm sold each sofa at a price of $500, rather than $400, what would be the required sales volume?
   c. If the price is $500 and if average variable cost is $100, rather than $150, what would be the required sales volume?

12. According to a statistical study, the following relationship exists between a firm's total cost (TC) and its output (Q):

$$TC = 40 + 3Q + 2Q^2.$$

At what output is average total cost a minimum?

13. Martin-Brower, a leading food distributor, pared its customer list to only eight fast-food chains. Its strategy was to satisfy the specialized needs of these customers at very low cost. To do so, it stocked only their narrow product lines, located its warehouses near their locations, and geared its order-taking procedures to their purchasing cycles. While Martin-Brower was not the lowest-cost distributor in serving the market as a whole, it was the lowest-cost in serving its particular part of the market, the result being that it was fast-growing and relatively profitable.[5] Is it always a good strategy for a firm to serve a highly specialized market?

Answers

Completion
1. $5, $5, $10   2. fixed cost   3. minimum   4. long-run average cost
5. Implicit costs   6. regression fallacy   7. economies and diseconomies of scale
8. law of diminishing marginal returns   9. law of diminishing marginal returns
10. average variable product   11. marginal product   12. accounting

True or False
1. False   2. False   3. False   4. False   5. True   6. False   7. False
8. False   9. False   10. False

Multiple Choice
1. c   2. c   3. c

Problems
1. a

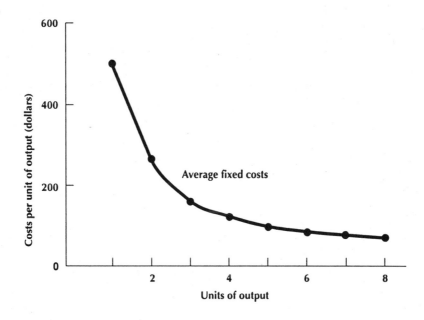

[5] M. Porter, *Competitive Strategy* (New York: Free Press, 1980).

b.

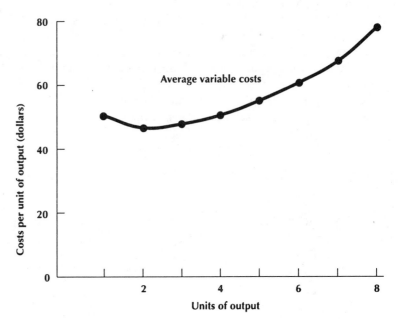

c.

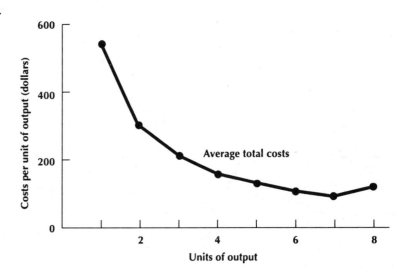

d.

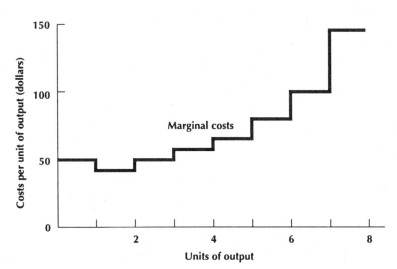

2. a. 1,000 copies sold.
   b. 1,667 copies sold.

3. a. Yes.
   b. No. Since the ratio of the marginal product of capital to the price of capital exceeds the ratio of the marginal product of labor to the price of labor, the firm can lower its costs by substituting capital for labor.

4. The *extra* labor needed to produce the first, second, third, fourth, fifth, and sixth truckloads of tomatoes are 1, 2, 4, 5, 6, and 7 workers. Thus, the marginal costs of the first, second, third, fourth, fifth, and sixth truckloads are $500, $1,000, $2,000, $2,500, $3,000, and $3,500.

5. a. Since total cost equals average cost times output, the firm's total cost function is

$$C = AC \times Q = 3Q + 4Q^2.$$

   b. No, since total cost equals zero when $Q = 0$.
   c. If the price is $2, total revenue ($R$) equals $2Q$. Thus, the firm's profit equals

$$\pi = R - C = 2Q - (3Q + 4Q^2) = -Q - 4Q^2.$$

If Q is greater than zero, π must be negative, and the firm is incurring losses. If the firm is producing nothing, it is incurring neither profits nor losses. Thus, the firm is better off to produce nothing.

6. Draw the firm's isoquants, as shown below. Also draw the isocost curve corresponding to a given outlay. Clearly, point *P* is the input combination that maximizes output for this outlay. Since the firm's isoquant is tangent to the isocost curve at point *P*, the slope of the isocost curve (which equals –1 times the price of input 1 + price of input 2) must equal the slope of the isoquant (which equals –1 times the marginal product of input 1 + marginal product of input 2). Thus, at point *P*, the ratio of the marginal product to the price of each input must be the same. Yes.

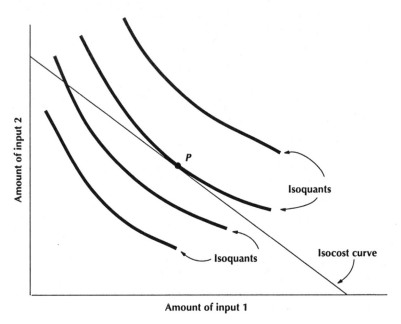

7. a The isocost curves are as follows:

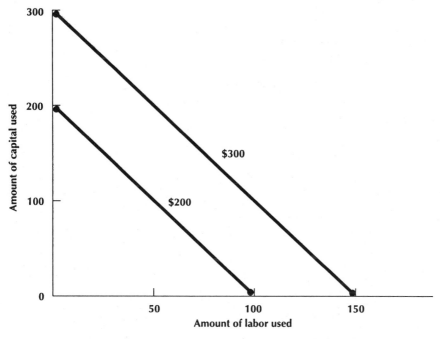

b. $600, $900.

8. a The average cost of producing 40,000 motors per year is $49.70 + $\dfrac{\$150,000}{40,000}$ = $49.70 + $3.75 = $53.45. For 80,000 and 160,000 motors, it is $49.70 + 1.88 = $51.58.

b. For 40,000 motors, it is $36.95 + $\dfrac{\$400,000}{40,000}$ = $46.95. For 80,000 motors, it is $36.95 + $\dfrac{\$400,000}{80,000}$ = $41.95. For 160,000 motors, it is $36.95 + $\dfrac{\$400,000}{160,000}$ = $39.45.

c.

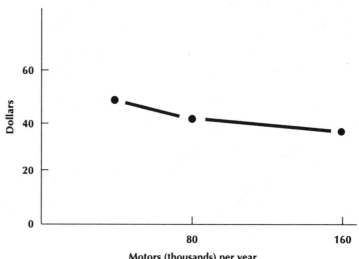

Motors (thousands) per year

9. a $AC = \dfrac{100}{Q} + 3 - 2Q + 3Q^2.$

b. $MC = 3 - 4Q + 9Q^2.$

c. $\dfrac{dMC}{dQ} = -4 + 18Q.$

Setting $\dfrac{dMC}{dQ}$ equal to zero, $Q = 4/18 = 0.22.$

10. a $\$3.30 + \dfrac{\$600{,}000}{200{,}000} = \$6.30.$

b. $\$7.00 + \dfrac{\$200{,}000}{100{,}000} = \$9.00.$

c. $\$9.20 + \dfrac{\$100{,}000}{50{,}000} = \$11.20.$

11. a Profit equals $250Q - 4{,}000$, where Q is the number sold. If $250Q - 4{,}000 = 15{,}000$, $Q = 19{,}000 + 250 = 76.$

b. $Q = 19{,}000 + 350 = 54.3.$

c. $Q = 19{,}000 + 400 = 47.5.$

12. Average total cost equals

$$ATC = \dfrac{40}{Q} + 3 + 2Q,$$

and

$$\dfrac{dATC}{dQ} = \dfrac{-40}{Q^2} + 2.$$

Setting $\dfrac{dATC}{dQ} = 0$, $Q = \sqrt{20} = 4.47.$

13. No. A firm frequently can make more money by serving a broader market.

CHAPTER 10

Linear Programming

Chapter Profile

Linear programming is a technique that allows decision makers to solve maximization and minimization problems where there are certain constraints that limit what can be done. It is useful to look at production decisions from the programming point of view because, unlike conventional theory, linear programming does not take the production function as being given to the analyst or manager before he or she attacks the problem. Also, the programming analysis is easier to apply in many respects, and powerful computational techniques are available to obtain solutions.

A firm often has to choose which one (or which combination) of a number of alternative processes to use to produce a particular product, given that it has only a limited amount of certain inputs. We solved this problem by graphical techniques. Isoprofit curves were constructed and superimposed on a diagram showing the feasible input combinations, and the point was chosen that, among those that were feasible, was on the highest isoprofit curve. In addition, we considered a variant of this problem in which the firm is no longer constrained by limitations on inputs.

Frequently, a firm produces more than one product, and has various fixed facilities that set limits on the amount of each product that can be produced. The firm's managers must determine the optimal combination of outputs of the products. This problem was also solved by graphical means, with isoprofit lines superimposed on a diagram showing feasible output combinations. In addition, in the context of this example, we discussed the fact that the optimal solution of a linear-programming problem will lie at one of the extreme points or corners of the feasible area.

Every linear-programming problem has a corresponding problem called its **dual**; the original problem is called the **primal problem**. If the primal is a maximization problem, the dual is a minimization problem; if the primal is a minimization problem, the dual is a maximization problem. In the example concerning the optimal combination of outputs of two products, whereas the primal looked for optimal output rates for the two products, the dual seeks to impute values to the fixed facilities. These imputed values, or shadow prices, are very useful, since they show what would happen to the firm's profits if the company somehow were able to increase each type of capacity.

A slack variable represents the amount of an input that is unused. When slack variables are introduced, the constraints can be converted from inequalities into equations.

Once such a conversion is made, one can use algebraic techniques to solve a linear-programming problem. The procedure is to evaluate the objective function, which is what we are trying to maximize or minimize, at each corner of the feasible area. The corner where the objective function is highest or lowest is the optimal solution.

 * Most linear-programming problems faced by firms are too complex to be solved by graphical methods. Instead, computer programs are used. For example, LINDO (Linear Interactive Discrete Optimizer) is one easy-to-use software package.

Questions

Completion

1. When linear programming is applied, there is some _____ function to be maximized or minimized.

2. In linear-programming problems, the objective function is a _____ function of the variables to be determined.

3. In linear-programming problems, the values of the variables must satisfy certain _____ , which are in the form of _____ .

4. Every linear-programming problem has a corresponding problem called its _____ .

5. If the primal problem is a minimization problem, its dual is a _____ problem.

6. If a resource is not fully utilized, its shadow price will be _____ .

7. If a resource is fully utilized and its opportunity cost is positive, its shadow price will be _____ .

8. A _____ variable is used to represent the amount of an input that is unused.

9. If the slack variable for an input turns out to be positive in the solution to a firm's problem, some of this input is _____ .

10. If the primal problem is to find the outputs of two products that maximize profit, subject to constraints on labor and equipment time, the dual problem is to _____ the total value of _____ and _____ available.

True or False

_____ 1. Linear programming involves constraints that are inequalities.

_____ 2. Linear programming is a purely mathematical technique.

_____ 3. Linear programming seems to conform more closely than conventional

---

 * This paragraph refers to the chapter appendix in the text.

analysis to the way managers tend to view production.

_____ 4. Linear programming works only when there are fewer than 10 constraints.

_____ 5. Isoquants are horizontal in the case of linear programming.

_____ 6. The optimal solution of a linear programming problem will occur at an extreme point.

_____ 7. The simplex method is a technique designed to determine how many processes the firm should utilize.

_____ 8. To every linear-programming problem there corresponds a dual problem.

_____ 9. The solutions to the dual problem are the shadow prices.

_____ 10. If the slack variable for an input turns out to be positive, some of this input is redundant.

Multiple Choice

1. In linear programming, isoquants are

   a. positively sloped.
   b. smooth.
   c. a series of connected line segments.
   d. all of the above.
   e. none of the above.

2. In linear programming, the objective function is

   a. a summary of the constraints.
   b. what you want to maximize or minimize.
   c. always nonnegative.
   d. all of the above.
   e. none of the above.

3. If the slack variable for an input turns out to be zero,

   a. this input is fully utilized when the firm is maximizing profit.
   b. this means that some of this input is redundant.
   c. none of this input should be used.
   d. all of the above.
   e. both a and b.

4. The shadow price of a resource is

    a. the opportunity cost of using this resource.
    b. zero if an extra unit of the resource would not increase profit.
    c. positive if the resource is fully utilized and more of it would increase profit.
    d. all of the above.
    e. only a and b.

Problems

1. The Hogan Company can use three processes, A, B, and C, to produce motors. To make one motor, process A requires 1 hour of labor and 4 hours of machine time, process B requires 2 hours of labor and 2 hours of machine time, and process C requires 5 hours of labor and 1 hour of machine time.

    a. In the graph below, draw the rays corresponding to the three processes.
    b. In the graph below, draw the isoquant corresponding to an output of 200 motors.

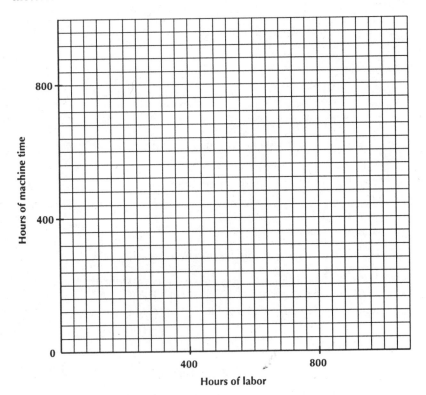

2. The Hogan Company must pay $10 an hour for labor and $15 an hour for machine time.

    a If the firm can hire as much labor and machine time as it wants, draw two isocost curves for this firm in the graph below.

    b. Which of the three processes described in question 1 should Hogan's managers choose?

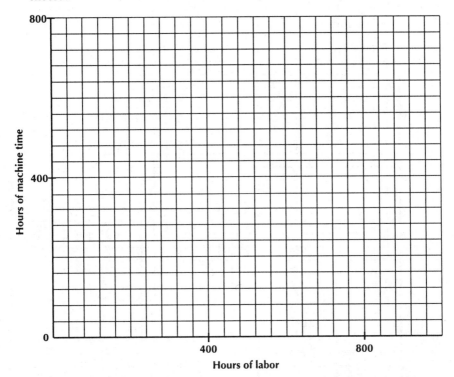

3. Suppose that the Hogan Company can use no more than 1,000 hours of labor time and 2,000 hours of machine time, and that, regardless of which process the firm uses, it receives a price of $100 per motor.

    a How much profit does the firm receive for each motor made by process A?

    b. How much profit does the firm receive for each motor made by process B?

    c. How much profit does the firm receive for each motor made by process C?

4. Under the circumstances set forth in question 3, the Hogan Company wants to know how it should allocate its available labor time and machine time among the three processes.

    a. What is the objective function?
    b. What are the constraints?
    c. In the graph below, plot the feasible input combinations.
    d. In the graph below, plot several isoprofit curves.
    e. Solve the firm's problem.

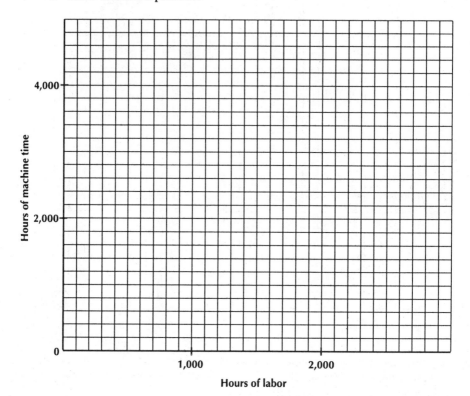

5. The Cook Company produces large and small chairs. The profit contribution per chair is $100 for a large chair and $40 for a small chair. To produce each large chair, the firm requires 20 hours of labor and 10 hours of machine time. To produce each small chair, the firm requires 10 hours of labor and 3 hours of machine time. The firm has available only 1,000 hours of labor and 400 hours of machine time per day.

    a   If the Cook Company wants to maximize the total profit contribution from the two types of chairs, what is the objective function?
    b. What are the constraints?
    c. In the graph below, plot the feasible combinations of output of large and small chairs.
    d. In the graph below, plot three isoprofit lines, and solve the firm's problem.

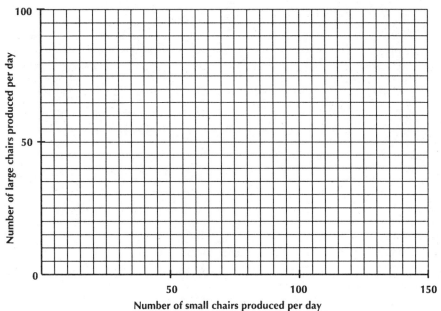

6. a   In question 5, what is the dual problem?
    b. In the dual problem, what is being maximized or minimized?
    c. In the dual problem, what are the constraints?
    d. In the dual problem, what is the solution?
    e. What are the shadow prices of labor time and machine time, and why are they of importance to the managers of the Cook Company?

7. a In question 5, show how slack variables can be used to convert the constraints from inequalities into equalities.
   b. If one of these slack variables turns out to be zero in the solution of the problem, what does this mean?

8. The Livermore Company has two factories and three warehouses. The factories are in New Jersey and Wisconsin. The warehouses are in Georgia, Tennessee, and Oregon. The cost of shipping a ton of the firm's product from each factory to each warehouse is as follows:

| | --------- Warehouse --------- | | |
Factory	Georgia	Tennessee	Oregon
New Jersey	$ 8	6	14
Wisconsin	10	9	11

The capacity of the New Jersey factory is 1,000 tons per week; for the Wisconsin factory, it is 2,000 tons per week. The weekly requirements of the three warehouses are Georgia, 800 tons; Tennessee, 1,200 tons; and Oregon, 1,000 tons.

   a If the Livermore Company wants to minimize shipping cost, what is the objective function?
   b. What are the constraints?
   * c. What is the solution?
   * d. What is the minimum value of the firm's weekly shipping cost?

Answers

Completion
1. objective 2. linear 3. constraints, inequalities 4. dual
5. maximization 6. zero 7. positive 8. slack 9. unutilized
10. minimize, labor, equipment

True or False
1. True 2. True 3. True 4. False 5. False 6. True 7. False
8. True 9. True 10. True

Multiple Choice
1. c 2. b 3. a 4. d

---

* This question is for students having access to a computer package like LINDO. See the chapter appendix in the text.

Problems

1. a and b.

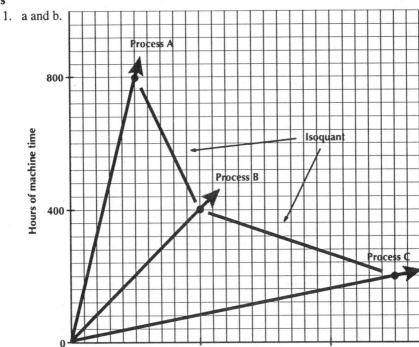

2. a.

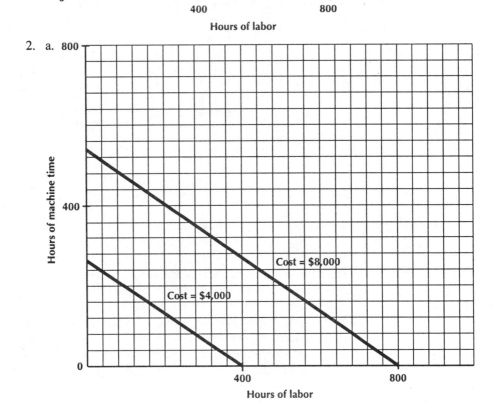

    b.   Process B.

3. a $100 – $70 = $30.
    b. $100 – $50 = $50.
    c. $100 – $65 = $35.

4. a   Maximize $30A + 50B + 35C$.
    b. $A + 2B + 5C \leq 1,000$.
        $4A + 2B + C \leq 2,000$.
        $A \geq 0, B \geq 0, C \geq 0$.
    c.   The feasible input combinations are in the rectangle $0XYZ$.

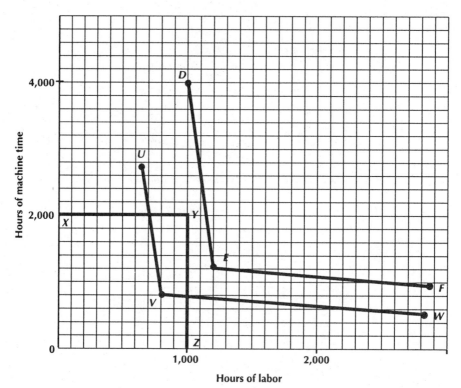

    d.   Let's construct the isoprofit curve for a profit level of $20,000. To obtain this much profit from process A, $20,000 + $30 = 666 2/3 motors must be produced, which requires 666 2/3 hours of labor and 2,666 2/3 hours of machine time. To obtain this much profit from process B, $20,000 + $50 = 400 motors must be produced, which requires 800 hours of labor and 800 hours of machine time. To obtain this much profit from process C, $20,000 + $35 = 571 motors must be produced, which requires 2,855 hours of labor and 571 hours of machine time. Thus, the isoprofit curve is UVW in the graph in the answer to part c. Using the same technique, we can derive the isoprofit curve for a profit level of $30,000, which is DEF in this graph.

e. Based on the diagram in the answer to part c, it is evident that the point in the feasible area $0XYZ$ that is on the highest isoprofit curve is point Y. Since points U and D pertain to process A and points V and E pertain to process B, only processes A and B are used. Thus,

$$A + 2B = 1,000$$

$$4A + 2B = 2,000,$$

where A is the number of motors produced with process A, and B is the number of motors produced with process B. Solving these two equations simultaneously, $A = 333\ 1/3$ and $B = 333\ 1/3$. Thus, the optimal solution is for the firm to produce 333 1/3 motors with process A and 333 1/3 motors with process B.

5. a. The Cook Company should maximize $100L + 40S$, where L is the number of large chairs produced, and S is the number of small chairs produced per day.

b. $20L + 10S \leq 1,000$
$10L + 3S \leq 400$
$L \geq 0, S \geq 0.$

c. If the constraint on labor time is satisfied,

$$20L + 10S \leq 1,000,$$

which implies that

$$L \leq \frac{1,000}{20} - \frac{10S}{20} = 50 - 0.5S.$$

If the constraint on machine time is satisfied,

$$10L + 3S \leq 400,$$

which implies that

$$L \leq \frac{400}{10} - \frac{3S}{10} = 40 - 0.3S.$$

Thus, the feasible combinations of output are points within 0*ABC* in the graph below:

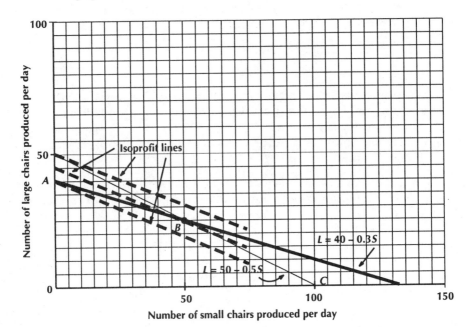

d. The total profit contribution is $100L + 40S$. Thus, if the total profit contribution per day equals π,

$$L = \frac{\pi}{100} - \frac{40}{100}S.$$

To obtain the isoprofit lines in the graph above, we set $\pi = 5{,}000$, $4{,}500$, and $4{,}000$.

Clearly, the point in the feasible area (0*ABC*) on the highest isoprofit line is point *B*. This is the point of intersection between the following two lines:

$$L = 40 - 0.3S$$
$$L = 50 - 0.5S.$$

Solving these two equations simultaneously, we get $L = 25$ and $S = 50$, which are the coordinates of point *B*. Thus, the Cook Company should produce 25 large chairs and 50 small chairs per day.

6. a. Minimize $1{,}000G + 400H$ subject to

$$20G + 10H \geq 100$$
$$10G + 3H \geq 40$$
$$G \geq 0, H \geq 0.$$

b. $1{,}000G + 400H$.
c. $20G + 10H \geq 100$
$10G + 3H \geq 40$
$G \geq 0, H \geq 0.$

d. If the first constraint is satisfied,

$$G \geq \frac{100}{20} - \frac{10H}{20} = 5 - 0.5H.$$

If the second constraint is satisfied,

$$G \geq \frac{40}{10} - \frac{3H}{10} = 4 - 0.3H.$$

Thus, if both constraints are satisfied, only points on or above XYZ in the graph below can be considered. Letting $1,000G + 400H = M$,

$$G = \frac{M}{1,000} - \frac{400}{1,000}H = \frac{M}{1,000} - 0.4H.$$

Each dashed line in the graph below shows the values of G and H resulting in a given value of M (5,000 or 4,500). To minimize M, we must find the point on or above XYZ that is on the lowest dashed line. Clearly, this point is Y, where $G = 2.5$ and $H = 5$.

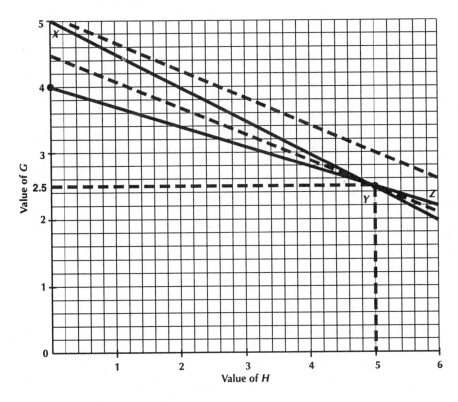

e. The solutions to the dual problem—that is, the values of G and H found in part d—are the shadow prices of labor time and of machine time. Thus, the shadow price of labor time is $2.50 per hour, and the shadow price of machine time is $5 per hour. These shadow prices are important because they indicate what an extra hour of labor time or machine time would be worth to the Cook Company.

7. a. Let U be the number of hours of available labor time that is unutilized. Let V be the number of available machine time that is unutilized. Then the constraints on labor time and machine time are

$$20L + 10S + U = 1,000$$

$$10L + 3S + V = 400.$$

Because of the utilization of the slack variables (U and V), these constraints are now equalities, not inequalities.

b. It means that all of the relevant resource is used. Thus, if U equals zero, all of the available labor time is used. If V equals zero, all of the available machine time is used.

8. a. Livermore wants to minimize

$$8I + 6J + 14K + 10N + 9P + 11R,$$

where I is the number of tons per week shipped from the New Jersey factory to the Georgia warehouse, J is the number of tons per week shipped from the New Jersey factory to the Tennessee warehouse, K is the number of tons per week shipped from the New Jersey factory to the Oregon warehouse, N is the number of tons shipped per week from the Wisconsin factory to the Georgia warehouse, P is the number of tons shipped per week from the Wisconsin factory to the Tennessee warehouse, and R is the number of tons shipped per week from the Wisconsin factory to the Oregon warehouse.

b. $I + J + K \leq 1,000$
$N + P + R \leq 2,000$
$I + N \geq 800$
$J + P \geq 1,200$
$K + R \geq 1,000$
$I \geq 0, J \geq 0, K \geq 0, N \geq 0, P \geq 0, R \geq 0.$

c. The solution is that the New Jersey factory should ship 1,000 tons per week to the Tennessee warehouse, and the Wisconsin factory should ship 800 tons per week to the Georgia warehouse, 200 tons per week to the Tennessee warehouse, and 1,000 tons per week to the Oregon warehouse. The computer printout is shown below:

```
    min 8I + 6J + 14K + 10N + 9P + 11R
? s.t.
? I + J + K < 1000
? N + P + R < 2000
? I + N > 800
? J + P > 1200
? K + R > 1000
? I > 0
? J > 0
? K > 0
? N > 0
? P > 0
? R > 0
? end
: look all

MIN      8 I + 6 J + 14 K + 10 N + 9 P + 11 R
SUBJECT TO
          2)    I + J + K <=    1000
          3)    N + P + R <=    2000
          4)    I + N >=    800
          5)    J + P >=    1200
          6)    K + R >=    1000
          7)    I >=    0
          8)    J >=    0
          9)    K >=    0
         10)    N >=    0
         11)    P >=    0
         12)    R >=    0
END
```

```
: go
LP OPTIMUM FOUND    AT STEP        4
                OBJECTIVE FUNCTION VALUE
1)              26800.0000

VARIABLE          VALUE            REDUCED COST
       I          .000000            1.000000
       J        1000.000000           .000000
       K          .000000            6.000000
       N         800.000000           .000000
       P         200.000000           .000000
       R        1000.000000           .000000

    ROW       SLACK OR SURPUS       DUAL PRICES
    2)            .000000            3.000000
    3)            .000000             .000000
    4)            .000000          -10.000000
    5)            .000000           -9.000000
    6)            .000000          -11.000000
    7)            .000000             .000000
    8)         1000.000000            .000000
    9)            .000000             .000000
   10)          800.000000            .000000
   11)          200.000000            .000000
- -More- -
   12)         1000.000000            .000000

NO.  ITERATIONS=       4
```

d. As the above printout shows, the minimum cost is $26,800 per week.

CASE THREE

Production Functions and Cost Functions in Oil Pipelines
Leslie Cookenboo

This case is concerned with a discussion of long-, short-, and intermediate-run costs of operating crude oil pipe lines. For the benefit of the reader not conversant with economic jargon, it might be well to begin with a description of the three cost categories. First, it is necessary to distinguish between the various types of costs that may be considered under any of these three categories. "Total" cost (be it long-, short-, or intermediate-run) is the total expenditure necessary for producing a given output. "Average" cost is the cost per unit of producing a given output; it is equal to total cost divided by output. For example, if the total expenditure for an output of 100 units is $1,000, then total cost is $1,000 and average cost (per-unit cost) is $10 per unit ($1,000 divided by 100 units). "Marginal" cost is the change in total cost associated with changes in output. If 100 units cost $1,000 and 101 units cost $1,008, then "marginal" cost is $8 (the change in total cost divided by the change in output). "Fixed" and "variable" costs are simply parts of total (or average) cost. Fixed costs are those incurred even when no output is produced, for example, interest on the money borrowed to buy machinery, pay taxes, and so forth. Variable costs (out-of-pocket costs) are expenditures that would

not be necessary were no output produced, for example, expenditures for labor and raw materials. Total cost is equal to the sum of total fixed cost and total variable cost. Average cost is equal to the sum of average fixed cost and average variable cost.

A "short-run" cost curve shows the cost of producing various outputs with a given amount of fixed capital equipment. In other words, it is the cost curve for a given size of plant, the output of which can be changed simply by using more or less labor and raw materials. Changes in short-run costs with changes in output represent changes in expenditures for items of variable cost *only;* no extra machinery or other capital equipment is needed to increase output.

A long-run cost curve (also called a "planning" curve) is an "envelope" of all possible short-run curves. It shows the least possible expenditure for producing any output. That is, it takes into account all individual plant cost curves in order to determine which plant can produce each output for the least amount possible (relative to all other plants). This is illustrated in Figure 1.

This diagram shows per-unit cost plotted against output (the short-run cost curves) for each of six possible plants (A–F) that might be used to produce some

This case comes from Leslie Cookenboo's book, *Crude Oil Pipe Lines and Competition in the Oil Industry*, published by the Harvard University Press. Reprinted with permission.

135

product. The long-run average cost curve is the envelope of these short-run curves. . . . It shows the least possible expenditure for any given output in the range of outputs under consideration. Output Q_0 might be produced with either plant A, B, C, D, E, or F. However, D's short-run cost curve lies beneath all the others at Q_0; therefore its cost is the least possible for producing Q_0, and it may be said to be the "optimum" plant for producing that output. In the range of outputs where its cost curve lies beneath all others, its short-run cost is equal to long-run cost. A long-run cost curve such as that in Figure 1 is called a "planning" curve because it shows the least amount that could be spent to produce various outputs if a firm had the option of choosing from several sizes of plants. Such a long-run cost curve would be of value when building a new plant or when contemplating entering an industry. Once a plant is built, it is the short-run curve for this plant which shows what the firm would spend in order to produce various outputs.

Note the paradox in Figure 1 that D is *not* the optimum plant for the output at which it itself is most efficient (Q_1). Its most efficient output is the output which it produces at the least possible cost per unit that *it* is capable of achieving. In Figure 1, plant E could produce D's optimum output (Q_1) more cheaply than could D; hence E is the optimum plant at D's optimum output. It is a question of optimum *plant* relative to all *other* plants, versus optimum *output* for a *given* plant (without consideration of others) once that plant is built. Because of this paradox, any plant in Figure 1, say D, would be built originally to produce an output less that its own optimum output. Hence, it could subsequently increase its output, should it so desire, and thereby achieve a lower per-unit cost. Indeed, it could increase its output to Q_2 before average costs became higher than they were at the design output. It might be asked why a firm would ever consider producing Q_2 with D when E and F can produce it for less. If the need for Q_2 had been foreseen before any plant was built, then plant E would probably have been built. However, if the original output desired was Q_0, the correct choice would have been D. A subsequent expansion to Q_2 could then be made with plant D. This would be done instead of building a new plant if the cash costs of operating plant D at Q_2 were less than the total costs of operating plant F at Q_2.

One other "paradox" should be pointed out in Figure 1. Note that the short-run average costs decrease and then rise, even though the long-run cost curve falls throughout the range of outputs. Consequently, a U-shaped short-run average cost curve may occur for each plant while long-run average costs decline continuously.

In the range of outputs where long-run average costs decrease (in this case throughout the range), there are said to be "economies of scale." That is, by producing larger amounts conglomerately in larger plants, it is possible to achieve lower per-unit costs, better known as "mass-production economies." If the long-run average cost curve declines throughout the range of outputs, then no plant can achieve the least possible (long-run) cost of producing the product, unless there is some size of plant, say F, which is the largest possible for one reason or another. However, something approaching the least possible long-run cost can be had with the large plants, for example, E and F in Figure 1, since the average cost curve declines more and more slowly as output rises. From the point of view of both society and the firm, plants in an industry having costs such as those shown in Figure 1 should be as large as possible in order to achieve as low average costs as possible—apart from any political or sociological disadvantages of large business.

Cost per unit

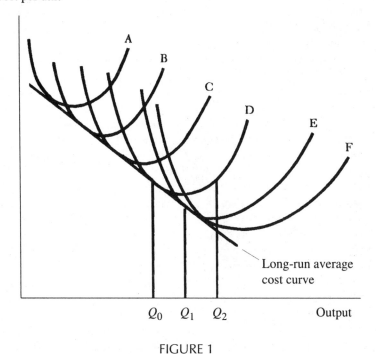

FIGURE 1

Long- and Short-run Average Cost Curves

In the case of pipe lines it is also necessary to utilize the concept of "intermediate-run" costs. If the curves labeled A–F in Figure 1 were the basis of a planning curve for pipe lines, they would be called not "short-run," but "intermediate-run" pipeline cost curves, each representing a given line size carrying various "throughputs." (Pipe-line output is called "throughput"—the volume of liquid carried per unit of time.) In some industries the output of individual plants can be expanded above the original output simply by adding more labor or raw materials; these may be described with short-run cost curves. However, in the case of pipe lines, throughput can be increased above the designed capacity only by the addition of more capital equipment (pumping stations), along with extra labor and fuel. Short-run cost curves which allow for a fixed amount of capital

equipment are "reversible." That is, when output is decreased (by laying off workers and buying smaller amounts of raw materials), the short-run curve shows the appropriate cost for the lower output. On the other hand, intermediate-run cost curves which include costs of varying amounts of capital equipment are not reversible. If pipe line D (again referring to Figure 1, this time as a series of intermediate-run curves) were built for throughput Q_0, then the costs of carrying throughput less than Q_0 in line D would *not* be shown by the curve labeled D; these costs would be higher for all throughputs less than Q_0. Why? The curve D would be based, for planning purposes, on the proper (minimum possible) number of pumping stations for each throughput. It takes more stations of a given size to push larger throughputs through a given size pipe. Consequently, the number of stations

137

built on line D for throughput Q_0 would be larger than needed for lesser throughputs. If throughput is cut below Q_0, the number of stations cannot be cut (as could the number of workers in some other industry), since stations represent fixed capital investments—investments which incur costs even if the stations are not needed. In short, too many pumping stations would be present for any lower throughput; consequently there would be higher average costs than if the line had been designed for the lower throughput with the minimum number of stations required for that throughput. Hence, the necessity of the hybrid term "intermediate-run" in the pipe-line case. In this case the long-run curve is the envelope of the intermediate-run curves, not of the short-run curves.

With this digression into the principles of economics in mind, it is possible to proceed with the discussion of pipe-line costs. The costs computed for this study were determined primarily by the method of engineering estimation, not by the use of actual historical costs. Where engineering estimation is feasible for cost studies it should be used, since actual costs may be subject to any number of erratic variations arising from construction or operating conditions unique to particular cases. In the case of the majority of the cost items, the process of computation involved a physical determination of the amount of equipment or services required, followed by the pricing of this amount from current price quotations furnished by suppliers and/or pipe-line companies. In some cases where particular items did not readily lend themselves to a priori engineering estimation, it was necessary to use historical costs. One example of this is the construction materials cost of pumphouses, for which actual costs obtained from a pipe-line company were used as the basis of computation. This particular item also illustrates the dangers

of using historical costs. The stations were built in a period of unusually bad weather; hence the labor costs were much higher than would be the case normally. The materials costs were usable, but the labor costs had to be estimated from other sources. The notable exceptions where actual costs were used as the principal basis for computation include costs of surveying the right-of-way, mainline valves, office operation, site improvement at stations, and the pipe-line communications system. Since the details of this cost study are reported elsewhere,[1] it will not be necessary to engage here in an extended discussion of such problems as optimum operating pressure, safety factor, wall thickness of pipe, centrifugal versus reciprocating pumps, diesel engines versus electric motors, and so forth. However, it is necessary to discuss in summary form certain points about pipe-line technology and the results of the cost study, since this information is all-important for the subsequent discussion.

PRODUCTION FUNCTION

In order to determine costs by engineering estimation, it is necessary to compute an "engineering production function" relating the factors of production (the goods and services used to produce a product) and output. Such a function shows the possible combinations of the factors of production which can be used to produce various levels of output.

A basic choice between two "factors of production" exists in the determination of the optimum line diameter for carrying any particular throughput. A given size of line may be used for several different throughputs by applying different amounts of power (hydraulic horsepower) to the oil carried—the more horsepower, the more throughput (but less than proportionately

---

[1] See L. Cookenboo, Jr., "Costs of Operating Crude Oil Pipe Lines," *Rice Institute Pamphlet.*

more). Conversely, any given throughput can be achieved by the use of several possible sizes of lines with the proper amount of horsepower applied. There are, in short, variable physical proportions of these two basic factors of production, line diameter and horsepower, which may be used to develop any given throughput. As a result, the management of a pipe-line company is forced to choose between several sizes of line when planning to develop a given throughput. Furthermore, the long-run cost of carrying crude oil might vary with throughput, as did the long-run costs in Figure 1. Larger throughputs might cost less or more per barrel. Managements, then, not only have the option of several sizes of line for each throughput, they also may have the option of choosing throughputs having different costs per barrel. Other

things being equal, a pipe-line company planning to build a line should select the cheapest combination of line diameter and horsepower for the throughput which can be carried at the least cost per barrel.

A production function relating line diameter, horsepower, and throughput can be derived for crude oil pipe lines. Indeed, many such functions could be derived, depending on the density and viscosity of the oil carried, the wall thickness of pipe used, and so forth. However, for the purposes of this monograph one function will suffice. The only differences among the cost curves derived from different functions are in absolute dollars per barrel-mile for each throughput, not in the relative positions of the intermediate-run cost curves for each line. The latter is the important point for public policy considerations.

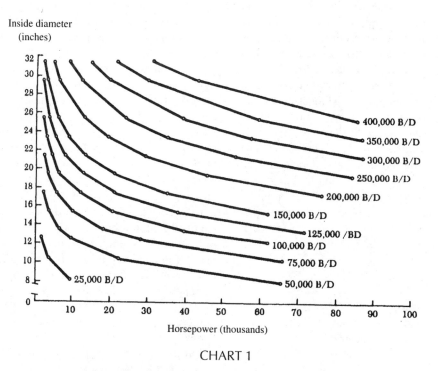

Inside diameter (inches)

Horsepower (thousands)

400,000 B/D
350,000 B/D
300,000 B/D
250,000 B/D
200,000 B/D
150,000 B/D
125,000 /BD
100,000 B/D
75,000 B/D
50,000 B/D
25,000 B/D

CHART 1

Production Function for Crude Oil Trunk Pipe Lines:
Line Diameter versus Horsepower versus Throughput—1,000-mile Lines*

*Assumptions: 60 SUS, 34° A.P.I. Crude; no influence of gravity on flow; 5 percent terrain variation (equalized up and down hill); 1/4-in. pipe throughout.

A crude oil trunk pipe-line production function is shown in Chart 1. This chart assumes a more or less typical Mid-Continent (60 SUS viscosity, 34° A.P.I. gravity) crude, 1/4-inch pipe throughout the lines, lines 1,000 miles in length with a 5 percent terrain variation (giving 1,050 miles of pipe), and no net gravity flow in the line (there may be hills as long as there are offsetting valleys). The production function covers throughputs of 25, 50, 75, 100, 125, 200, 250, 300, 350, and 400 thousand barrels per day; this encompasses the range of throughputs for crude oil trunk lines which have yet been built. The curves in the chart show the amounts of horsepower required for the several line sizes which might be used for a given throughput; each curve applies to one of the throughputs listed. The line sizes used are 8 5/8, 10 3/4, 12 3/4, 14, 16, 18, 20, 22, 24, 26, 30, and 32 inches (outside diameter) all having 1/4-inch walls. This covers all line sizes used for recent crude trunk lines. (Standard line pipe is only available in these sizes in the 8–32-inch range.) It will be noted that this is in reality a three-dimensional function, with line diameter and horsepower on a plane and with the throughput axis rising perpendicularly to this plane. The production function was computed by the use of a hydraulic formula for computing required horsepowers for various volumes of liquid flow in pipes of the sizes just noted, with appropriate constants for oil of the type used. This formula, simplified, is

$$T^{2.735} = (H) (D^{4.735}) \div (0.01046),$$

where,

T = Throughput,

H = Horsepower, and

D = Inside diameter of pipe.

Chart 2 shows vertical cross sections of the production function drawn perpendicular to the line-diameter axis. These are intermediate-run physical productivity curves which show the amount of horsepower that must be used with any given line size for various throughputs. They are analogous to traditional physical productivity curves of economic theory. Such a physical productivity curve in the textbooks might show the amount of wheat that can be produced from an acre of land by the use of varying numbers of workers, where line diameter is equivalent to the fixed factor (land) and horsepower is more or less equivalent to the variable factor (labor). These curves are not, however, precisely equivalent to the traditional physical productivity curves, since the horsepower factor includes some capital equipment. When it is necessary to expand output over the designed capacity of the line, it is necessary to add more capital equipment as well as more labor. When throughput is decreased below the designed capacity, unnecessary capital equipment exists— equipment on which fixed costs are incurred. Hence, as was noted above, the designation "intermediate-run" instead of short-run.

It will be observed that these productivity curves exhibit decreasing returns (marginal and average) throughout the range of throughputs. That is, there is a less than proportionate increase in throughput for a given increase in horsepower in a particular size of line. This is a physical phenomenon deriving from the characteristics of liquid flow in pipes. Other things being equal, this would mean that intermediate-run average costs attributable to horsepower should rise throughout the range of throughputs. (If the price of horsepower were constant and an addition to horsepower gave a less than proportionate increase in throughput, then the horsepower cost per barrel of throughput would rise.)

On the other hand, average costs attributable to line diameter will perforce fall throughout the range of throughputs for any given line size, since these costs are fixed in total. There are, then, offsetting forces at work, one tending to increasing average costs, the other to decreasing

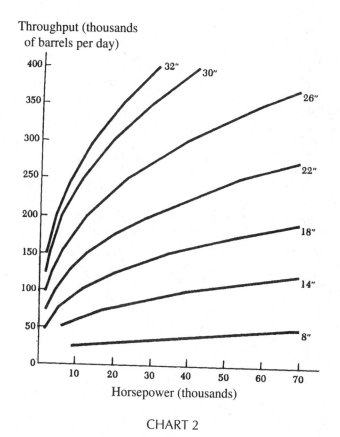

Throughput (thousands
of barrels per day)

CHART 2

**Vertical Cross Section of Production Function:
Horsepower versus Throughput—Line Diameter Held Constant**

average costs. Whether aggregate average costs would rise, fall, or both, depends on the relative magnitudes of the horsepower and line diameter costs. In this case it will be seen that U-shaped intermediate-run average cost curves result. That is, average costs fall at first, but then level off and rise as more and more horsepower is added to a given line. (The initial fall is accentuated by the fact that the price of horsepower falls somewhat as total horsepower used on a given line increases, thereby offsetting to some extent the decreasing physical returns.)

Chart 3 shows vertical cross sections of the production function drawn perpendicular to the horsepower axis, as opposed to those in Chart 2 which are drawn perpendicular to the line-diameter axis. These cross sections indicate what happens when horsepower is held constant and additional throughput is obtained by the use of more line-diameter (a long-run movement over the production function surface that is possible only when planning the line, not after the line is built). It will be observed that these curves exhibit *increasing* physical returns (average and marginal) to scale. This means that the same amount of horsepower applied in a large-diameter line as in a small-diameter line will give a more than proportionate increase in throughput. In other words, there is more throughput per horsepower in a large line than in a small one. Since this relationship is the basic reason for the shape of the long-run cost curve, and is therefore the basis for the public policy conclusions which may be

141

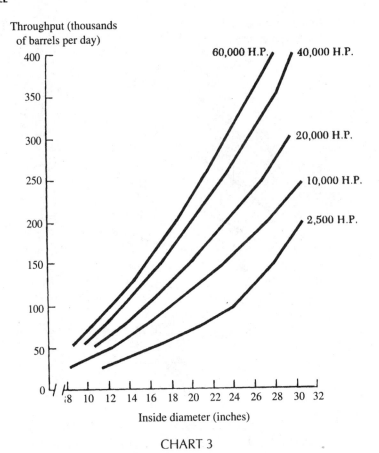

Throughput (thousands of barrels per day)

60,000 H.P.   40,000 H.P.

20,000 H.P.

10,000 H.P.

2,500 H.P.

Inside diameter (inches)

CHART 3

Vertical Cross Section of Production Function:
Line Diameter versus Throughput for Selected Horsepowers

drawn from the long-run curve, it will be well to examine the physical reason for these increasing returns.

The increasing returns are attributable to the fact that there is less friction incurred per barrel of oil carried in a large-diameter pipe than in a small-diameter pipe. Friction is created by only that part of the oil which touches the inside surface of the pipe. Hence it is the amount of surface area per barrel of oil carried that determines the amount of friction per barrel of oil carried. Solid geometry tells us that there is less surface area per unit of volume in a large-diameter cylinder (in this case the line pipe) of a given length than in a small-diameter cylinder of the same length. An open-ended cylinder of inside radius r and length L has a volume of $\pi r^2 L$ and an inside surface area of $2\pi rL$. A larger open-ended cylinder, say of inside radius $r + x$, and the same length, has a volume of $\pi(r + x)^2 L$ and a surface area of $2\pi(r + x)L$. The volume increases more than the surface area. This may be shown as follows (where V_1 and A_1 are the volume and surface area of the smaller open-ended cylinder and V_2 and A_2 are the volume and area of the larger open-ended cylinder):

$$V_1 = \pi r^2 L$$
$$V_2 = \pi(r + x)^2 L = \pi(r^2 + 2xr + x^2)L = \pi r^2 L + 2\pi xrL + \pi x^2 L$$
$$\Delta V = V_2 - V_1 = 2\pi xrL + x^2\pi L$$
$$A_1 = 2\pi rL$$
$$A_2 = 2\pi(r + x)L = 2\pi rL + 2\pi xL$$

142

$\Delta A = A_2 - A_1 = 2\pi xL.$
Since $2\pi xrL + x^2\pi L > 2\pi xL$,
$\Delta V > \Delta A$.

The volume increased by ($2\pi xrL + x^2\pi L$), while the surface area increased only by $2\pi xL$. It may be concluded that there is more volume per unit of surface area in a large than in a small pipe. This means that more oil can be transported per unit of surface area touched in a large than a small pipe. Since the amount of friction generated depends on the amount of surface area touched, it follows that more oil can be carried per given amount of friction developed in a large than in a small pipe. Therefore, the horsepower required to overcome a given amount of friction will propel more oil per day through a large pipe than through a small pipe. In short, because of the volume-area relationship it is possible to develop more throughput per horsepower applied in large pipes than in small ones. (It is interesting to note that the volume-area relationship is responsible for many other important technical economies of scale in industry, for example, economies of large tanks, heat containment, and so forth.) [2]

Chart 4 indicates the physical returns to scale characteristic of pipe-line operation. It will be remembered that there are decreasing physical returns as more horse-power is added to a given line, but that there are increasing physical returns from using larger lines with a given amount of horsepower. Which of these counteracting tendencies predominates in long-run movements where throughput is increased or decreased by varying the amounts of both factors used? In other words, are there increasing or decreasing returns to scale (to larger size) from carrying larger amounts of oil in the same facilities? This is shown physically by the shape of vertical cross sections of the production function

drawn through the origin. Chart 4 shows such a cross section drawn at a 45° angle through the origin of the function. This section indicates the returns to scale when throughput is increased by increasing the use of horsepower and line diameter in equal proportions. (Note that this is only an approximation, since the production function is only realistic at certain points, not over its whole surface; consequently, the 45° line would only by chance intersect each throughput at a point where an available line size exists.) The curve exhibits increasing (average and marginal) returns to scale throughout the range of throughputs. In other words, if the amounts of horse-power and line diameter used are increased in equal proportions, then there would be a more than proportionate increase in throughput. This indicates that on an a priori basis it would be expected that long-run decreasing average costs would characterize pipe-line operation. Only if the price of one or both of the factors should increase sufficiently with the amount of the factor used to offset the increasing returns, would the long-run cost curve turn up. Actually, the price of horsepower decreases somewhat with the amount used, and the price of line diameter does not fluctuate sufficiently with the amount used to offset the physical relationship.

Lest the reader object to drawing these general conclusions only on the basis of an example where expansion is by increased utilization of the factors in equal proportions, it should be pointed out that this is a "homogeneous" production function. Homogeneous production functions exhibit the same type of returns to scale on all parts of the surface. The function used reduces to:

$$T^{2.735} = (H)(D^{4.735})(C), \text{ or}$$
$$T = (H^{\frac{1}{2.735}})(D^{\frac{4.735}{2.735}})(C)$$
$$= (H^{.37})(D^{1.73})(C).$$

---

[2]See H. B. Chenery, *Engineering Bases of Economic Analysis* (unpublished doctoral thesis deposited in Widener Library, 1950), pp. 140–141, and E. A. Robinson, *Structure of Competitive Industry* (London, 1935), p. 29.

[C is a constant.] This is a function of the form,

$$T = H^m D^n C.$$

Such a function is homogeneous if $(m + n)$ is a constant, as it is in this case, where $(m + n) = 2.1$. This also indicates that there are marked increasing returns to scale, since the function is of order 2 (constant returns to scale are implied from a function having an order of one).

The discussion of the technological relationships peculiar to pipe-line transportation of oil may now be summarized. A basic physical relationship may be deduced for the purpose of computing pipe-line costs. This relationship shows that there will be markedly increasing long-run physical returns to scale if larger and larger throughputs are carried. In the intermediate-run, physical returns decrease. It follows, assuming that factor prices are more or less constant with the amount of

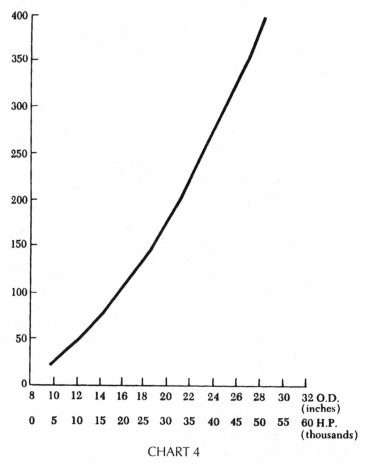

Throughput (thousands of barrels per day)

CHART 4

Physical Returns to Scale. Vertical Cross Section or Production Function Through Origin (45° angle)

the factor used, that there will be long-run decreasing costs (economies of scale) for pipe-line operation. Intermediate-run costs might rise, fall, or both—since the increasing average costs attributable to horsepower are counteracted by fixed costs attributed to line diameter. Under such conditions, U-shaped curves are feasible. These cost conclusions are based solely on the physical relationships discussed and are independent of the cost determination to be considered next. The conclusions would be invalidated only if the price of one or both of the factors rose sufficiently with increases in the amount of the factor used to offset the increasing physical returns to scale. This is not the case. (This may also be predicted to a considerable extent apart from actual cost determination, since the amounts of the most important single cost items included in each factor are proportional to the amounts of the factors used.)

COSTS

Pipe-line costs may be divided into three basic categories: (1) those variant with line diameter; (2) those variant with horse-power; (3) those variant only with through-put or length of line (a relatively small part of total cost). Since there is a choice for any given throughput among several possible combinations of line diameter and horsepower (as is shown in the production function in Chart 1), in order to be able to compute a long-run cost curve it is neces-sary to determine which of several possible combinations is least expensive for any throughput. This is done for each through-put by determining the total cost of each possible combination, on, say, an annual basis. That combination whose total cost is least for a given throughput is the opti-mum combination for that throughput. Note that it is only the costs of line diameter and horsepower which must be so mani-

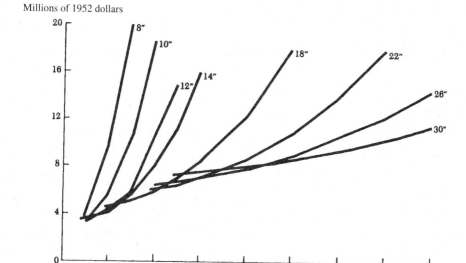

Millions of 1952 dollars

CHART 5

Annual Total Costs of Operating Crude Oil Trunk Pipe Lines

Source: L. Cookenboo, Jr., "Costs of Operating Crude Oil Pipe Lines," *Rice Institute Pamphlet.*

pulated, since the other costs are irrelevant to the choice of the optimum combination of these two. The other costs are, of course, incurred and cannot be ignored; but they do not influence the choice of the proper size line for a given throughput.

Annual total intermediate-run costs are shown in Chart 5; these are derived by plotting annual cost against throughput for each line diameter covered in the study. The shaded envelope of the intermediate-run cost curves is the long-run total cost curve. Chart 6 shows intermediate-run costs per barrel per 1,000 miles (that is, average costs). This is a chart analogous to Figure 1 above. Its envelope is the long-run

average cost curve. In the range of throughputs where the average cost curve of a given line size lies below all the other average cost curves, that line is the optimum line for the throughputs covered. For example, the 30-inch line lies beneath all others between about 225,000 and 325,000 barrels per day; hence, it is the optimum line for throughputs between those limits.

The intermediate-run cost curves also show what it would cost to carry larger quantities of oil than the design throughput if stations were added subsequent to the building of the line. (Pipe-lines cannot be operated at throughputs greater than the designed capacity without the additions of

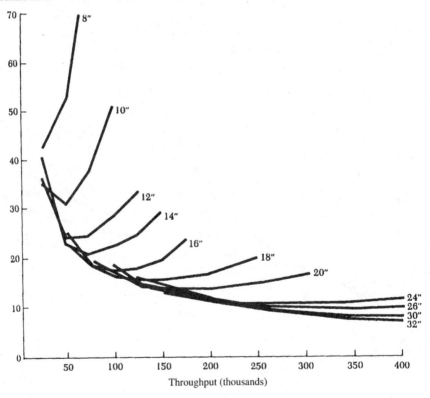

CHART 6

Costs per Barrel of Operating Crude Oil Trunk Pipe Lines

Source: L. Cookenboo, Jr., "Costs of Operating Crude Oil Pipe LInes," pp. 106–107 (Table 19).

more stations, since the design capacity would require the highest operating pressures permitted by the safety factor.) Remember that the intermediate-run curve does *not* show the costs of throughputs less than the design throughputs.

While, as was pointed out above, the details of the cost study lying behind the totals in Charts 5 and 6 are discussed at length elsewhere,[3] a word or two should be said about the assumptions involved in the engineering-type cost determination. The principal items involved in the cost of line diameter are all represented by initial outlays made during the construction of the line. The most important line costs are the service costs of laying the line, and the material costs of steel, pipe coating, line block valves, corrosion protection, and so forth. The assumptions of the characteristics of the lines, listed above, were 1,000 miles of 1/4-inch pipe having 50 miles of terrain variation (with no net gravity flow). This means that the line costs include the material and service costs of laying 1,050 miles of pipe (coated in accord with the best coating practice and protected by magnesium anodes).

The principal items involved in the costs of horsepower are the annual expenditures for electric power and labor (and of less importance, maintenance) to operate the pumping stations. This category also includes the initial cost of the stations; this represents the most difficult, time-consuming part of a pipe-line cost computation (even though station costs are not too important in relation to total costs). The stations used on the pipe-lines described in Charts 5 and 6 are semiautomatic, equipped with centrifugal pumps and electric motors. Stations pumping over 100,000 barrels per day are equipped with three full-size pumps and motors (one motor per pump) which together deliver the capacity throughput, and one half-size pump and motor. This provides flexibility

of operation which would otherwise be unattainable with constant speed electric motors. (With, as they say, 3 1/2 pumps, seven stages of operation are possible: no pumps, 1/2 pump, 1 1/2, 2, 2 1/2, and 3 for capacity.) Stations pumping less than 100,000 barrels per day utilize two full-size pumps and one half-size pump. Each station utilizes in-an-out piping to permit the bypassing of any one pump without shutting down the whole station. The labor force required for such semiautomatic stations is two men per shift (regardless of the level of operation), unless the stations are very large; none used in this study was large enough to require extra operators. (In a semiautomatic pumping station the principal tasks of the operators are to watch the controls, shut off motor-operated valves when necessary, and maintain the equipment.)

The principal costs involved in the "other" category are the initial costs of (1) tankage (the lines in this study have 12.5 days' supply of storage capacity along the line), (2) surveying the right-of-way, (3) damages to terrain crossed, and (4) a communications system (here assumed to be a 12-channel microwave system). It should be noted that while these costs vary either with throughput or with length of line, they are *proportional* to either throughput or length of line as the case may be. There are no significant per-barrel costs of a pipe-line which change with length. The only such costs are those of a central office force; these are inconsequential in relation to total. Hence, it is possible to state that costs per barrel-mile for a 1,000-mile trunk line are representative of costs per barrel-mile of any trunk line (those, say, 75 or 100 miles in length or longer).

It will be observed in Chart 6 that there are economies of scale (decreasing long-run average costs) throughout the range of throughputs covered. The analysis was

---

[3]Cookenboo, L., "Costs of Operating Crude Oil Pipe Lines," pp. 35–113.

only carried through 32-inch lines and 400,000 barrels per day. However, if larger lines could be had at a constant price per ton of steel (the only price per unit of material likely to change with larger amounts than those used), then the long-run average cost curve would fall even farther. On the other hand, pipe much larger than 34 or 36 inches might well require the creation of special pipe-making facilities and, consequently, might command a higher price per ton than the pipe sizes used in this study. In this case, the long-run average cost curve might turn up near, say, 500,000 barrels per day. In any event, the rate of decrease of the average cost curve has declined appreciably by the time a throughput of 400,000 barrels per day is reached. Consequently, the cost per barrel of carrying a throughput of 400,000 barrels per day is probably close to the minimum that can be achieved with present pipe-making facilities.

It may also be noted from Chart 6, especially in the case of the large-diameter lines, that throughput can be expanded appreciably over the design throughput before higher per-barrel costs than the original costs are incurred. (For a while, of course, there would actually be a decline in per-barrel costs.) For example, a 24-inch line built for 200,000 barrels per day could, if necessary, later be used for 300,000 barrels per day (after adding the required number of stations) without incurring increased costs per barrel.

Short-run cost curves could be computed for any of the possible combinations of line diameter and horsepower shown in Chart 1—since each line would have a different short-run cost curve for each throughput it might carry. Building seven stations on an 18-inch line would yield one short-run curve. Building ten stations on an 18-inch line would yield another short-run curve. Building seven stations on a 20-inch line would yield yet another short-run curve—ad infinitum. To avoid the labor involved in computing short-run costs for every combination of line diameter and horsepower covered in the study (75 in all), two were computed:

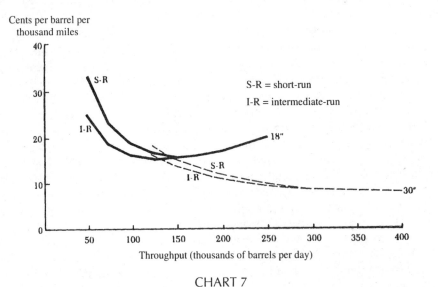

CHART 7

Short-run Average Costs of Transporting Crude Oil in Trunk Lines

Note: Eighteen-in. line designed for 150,000 barrels per day. Thirty-in. line designed for 300,000 barrels per day.

one for an 18-inch line carrying 100,000 barrels per day, another for a 30-inch line carrying 300,000 barrels per day. The relative positions of short- and intermediate-run curves would be the same for any other combinations of line diameter and horsepower. These short-run average cost curves are shown in Chart 7.

Observe that short-run average costs are always higher than intermediate-run average costs for throughputs less than the designed throughput (the short-run curve does not exist for higher throughputs, since pipe lines cannot be operated over the designed capacity without violating the safety factor). The significance of this is that a line built to carry 250,000 barrels per day will incur higher costs than necessary if it consistently carries 200,000 barrels per day. If it had been designed for 200,000 barrels per day, then the intermediate-run cost for 200,000 barrels per day would be the cost incurred. This figure is less than the short-run cost of 200,000 barrels per day on a line with a capacity of 250,000 barrels per day.

This may be made clear by discussing briefly the process of computation of short-run costs. The only significant cost of a pipe line that is not fixed once the line is built is the cost of electric power. If the line is run below capacity, as many workers are still needed; and, of course, the same number of stations and the same amount of pipe exists. The only significant saving is in power costs. In order to compute short-run costs one simply subtracts the cost of the appropriate amount of electric power which is saved when throughput is cut to various levels from the intermediate-run cost at the designed output. This figure must be higher than intermediate-run costs of lesser throughputs because these costs are computed upon the basis of the proper (smaller) number of stations for the smaller throughputs. It should be noted that a given cut in throughput means a more than proportionate saving in power requirements, since electric power requirements

vary with horsepower requirements. Remember that it takes a more than proportionate increase in horsepower to get a given increase in throughput; conversely, a decrease in throughput means a more than proportionate decrease in horsepower required—and hence a more than proportionate decrease in electric power required.

SUMMARY

Intermediate-, long-, and short-run costs for carrying crude oil were computed.

The long- and intermediate-run cost curves computed in a study of the engineering estimation type are of the same shape that would be predicted from the physical production functions for pipe-line transportation of crude (with no consideration of costs). The physical production function is homogeneous of order 2; under these conditions there will be marked economies of scale unless factor prices rise sharply with the amount of the factor used. This is not the case in the range of throughputs and line sizes covered.

The long-run average cost curve falls throughout the range of throughputs covered (see Chart 6), and it would continue to fall indefinitely if larger pipe could be obtained without paying a premium price. However, the rate of decline of long-run costs per barrel has slowed considerably by the time a throughput of 400,000 barrels per day is reached. Intermediate-run curves are U-shaped, but throughput can be increased appreciably over the designed level without increased per-barrel costs—especially in the case of large-diameter lines where the "U" is rather flat over wide ranges of throughputs.

Short-run costs are always greater than intermediate-run costs for a given line size. The only significant variable cost in pipe-line operation is the cost of power (or fuel).

It may be concluded from these cost curves that the economies of scale characteristic of the operation of pipe lines require that oil must be carried conglomerately in as large quantities as is possible in large-diameter line. This gives the least transportation costs obtainable—the optimum situation from the point of view of both the firm and society. Furthermore, pipe lines should not be run at throughputs appreciably below capacity; otherwise higher (short-run) costs per barrel will be incurred than need be. Finally, the capacity of a large line can be expanded appreciably without increasing average costs; indeed, *decreased* average costs can be obtained with moderate expansions.

Questions

1. For an 18-inch pipeline designed for 150,000 barrels per day, what is the short-run cost per barrel (per thousand miles) of transporting crude oil if the throughput is (a) 50,000 barrels per day, (b) 100,000 barrels per day, (c) 150,000 barrels per day?

2. Can a 16-inch pipeline with 10,000 horsepower transport 100,000 barrels of crude oil per day? If a firm has a 20-inch pipeline, how much horsepower must be used to transport 150,000 barrels per day?

3. Does it appear that there should be many pipelines competing to transport crude oil over a particular route? Why or why not?

4. According to Leslie Cookenboo, plant D in Figure 1 "is not the optimum plant for the output at which it itself is most efficient (Q_1)." How can this be? Explain.

5. Leslie Cookenboo stresses the difficulties and limitations of estimating cost functions on the basis of historical cost data, rather than engineering data of the sort he uses. What are these difficulties and limitations?

6. Explain in commonsense terms why there are economies of scale in pipelines.

7. Leslie Cookenboo has been senior economics adviser in the corporate planning department of the Exxon Corporation. In what ways might Exxon have made use of his findings?

CASE FOUR

A Managerial Application of Cost Functions by a Railroad
Edwin Mansfield and Harold H. Wein

There have been numerous studies where the relationship between cost and output has been estimated for manufacturing plants. These studies fall generally into two categories. In the first category, the chief purpose of the work has been to accumulate evidence concerning various cost curves that occupy an important place in economics. In the second category, the work has been done primarily with a view toward the direct usefulness of the relationship of cost and output to industrial managers. This paper falls into the second category.

We give an illustration here of how such a relationship may be used to formulate a simple control chart for costs, a topic which should be of interest to many applied statisticians and industrial managers. The problem of controlling performance and costs is important in almost every sector of industry and trade. Our data, and hence our specific results, pertain to the American railroad industry, but the statistical techniques that are used may be applicable to other industries as well.

FREIGHT YARDS AND COST CONTROL

Freight yards differ greatly in size, layout, and type, but they have certain physical characteristics and functions in common.

Physical Characteristics. All yards contain sets of tracks. In large yards they are generally of three types: receiving tracks where incoming freight cars are stored, classification tracks where cars are switched, and outbound tracks where cars that were situated on a classification track are stored until a locomotive hauls them away as a train.

Functions. Freight yards switch cars. That is, they sort incoming cars by putting them on the appropriate classification tracks, and in this way they break up incoming trains to form new trains. Most yards also deliver and pick up cars. Engines are assigned to deliver cars to industrial sidings and other yards and to pick them up there. Finally, many yards bill and inspect freight cars and perform such ancillary services as maintenance, repair, and storage.

This case is taken from an article in *Applied Statistics*. Reprinted with permission.

The importance of freight yards to a railroad is illustrated by the fact that about one-third of its total operating costs may arise in these yards. In view of this, it is clearly important that proper control be maintained over the performance of the yards. However, this problem of maintaining adequate control is made difficult by their number and their distribution over a large area. (For example, in the railroad we studied, about 200 freight yards are scattered along approximately 12,000 miles of track.) It is virtually impossible for any team of managers to have each day a reasonably complete knowledge of what happened at each yard. They must examine selected data concerning the performance of the yards during the day, and from these data they must somehow evaluate a yard's performance. In evaluating performance, one piece of information that is used is the costs incurred in the yard during the day.

At present, the data and techniques used by most railroads do not seem well suited for their purpose. Judging by the opinions of the railroad management with which we worked, their purpose is to detect those days when the costs at a yard are unusually high for the output produced and those series of days when the costs are repeatedly higher than would be expected. Detection of either of these would result in an inquiry concerning the causes of the apparent deterioration of yard performance. In addition, the management is interested in detecting days when costs are unusually low or when they are repeatedly lower than would be expected. In this case there would also be an inquiry, but the intention would be to encourage the responsible factors rather than to remedy them.

In this paper we discuss a control chart based on the relationship between cost and output that may be useful for these purposes. Before discussing the chart, it seems worthwhile to describe the measures of freight-yard output and costs that are used. The two most important services performed at a yard are switching and delivery; and it seems reasonable to use the number of "cuts" switched and the number of cars delivered during a particular period as a measure of output. A "cut" is a group of cars that rolls as a unit on to the same classification track; it is often used as a measure of switching output. The number of cars delivered includes both the cars delivered to sidings and other yards and those that are picked up. This output measure is not ideal, one difficulty being that it conceals considerable heterogeneity. For example, two groups of cars may be delivered but one may be hauled a greater distance than the other. Some of this heterogeneity could be eliminated by further refinements in the output measure, but the extra complexity with regard to data collection and computation might result in a loss of feasibility.

The costs used here include all money costs incurred in the yard except fixed charges, repair costs, maintenance and storage costs, and vacation costs. Only money costs are included; the costs that may be imputed to car delay are not taken into account. Fixed charges are excluded, but some of the included costs are essentially fixed in the very short run.

THE CONTROL CHART

The control chart contains the deviation of actual cost from the cost that would be expected on the basis of the average relationship between cost and output. These deviations are used to detect days when costs are suspiciously high or low. The model that underlies the chart is as follows: for a particular yard, the expected cost on the i'th day (C_i) is assumed to be a linear function of the number of cuts switched on the i'th day (S_i) and the number of cars delivered on the i'th day (D_i).

When the railroad management refer to unusually high or low costs, it seems clear that they mean costs that are unusual if the cost-output relationship and effects of numerous small disturbances remain at their previous, satisfactory levels. That is, they are interested in detecting those C_i that are unusually high or low if the average relationship between cost and output is unchanged. Similarly, when they refer to a sequence of days when costs are higher or lower than would be expected, it seems clear that they mean a run of the C_i that is unlikely if this relationship is unchanged.

If the model is adequate and if the average relationship between cost and output is known, it is a simple matter to set up a control chart that will aid the management. Each day, the deviation of actual cost from the cost that would be expected on the basis of this relationship can be plotted on a chart that has two sets of control limits. The outer control limits can be set so that, if this relationship remains the same, the probability that a point lies outside them is small. The inner control limits can be set so that, if this relationship remains the same, the probability that two consecutive points lie outside them (in one direction) is small. When a point lies outside the outer limits or a pair of points lies outside the inner limits, there is evidence that the relationship may have changed and that an inquiry should be made.

SETTING UP THE CHART

A control chart was set up at a freight yard located at Toledo, Ohio. This yard constitutes one of the largest and most important links in the railroad we studied. The chief types of freight that pass through the yard are livestock, perishables, coal, and automobiles. Table 1 shows the number of cars switched, the number of cuts switched, the number of cars delivered, the number of crews employed, the number of engine hours used, and the costs at the yard, for a sample one-week period.

The first step in setting up the chart was to gather historical data concerning cost and output. Data similar to those in Table 1 were collected for sixty-one days, and the average relationship between cost and output was estimated. The resulting relationship was

$$C_i = 4,914 + 0.42S_i + 2.44D_i \qquad (1)$$

The second step was to test some of the assumptions underlying the chart. Some of these tests are quite similar to those used in quality control to determine if the process is "in control." Taken together, the results of these tests did not cast any great sus-

TABLE 1

Output, Cost, and Employment, Freight Yard, Toledo, 7 Days*

ITEM	FRI.	SAT.	SUN.	MON.	TUES.	WED.	THURS.
Number of cuts switched	869	792	762	586	669	732	659
Number of cars switched	2534	2303	2521	1849	2090	2114	1979
Number of cars delivered[†]	1015	1003	820	548	877	706	1038
Number of crews used	45	45	40	38	46	46	46
Number of engine hours	372	369	329	309	385	381	386
Money costs ($)	7523	7464	6932	6550	7606	7757	7701

*Taken from records of cooperating railroad
[†]Includes number of cars picked up.

picion on the assumptions underlying the chart. Indeed, the results seemed to be quite compatible with these assumptions.

The third step was to draw the inner and outer control limits on the chart. The outer control limits were set at ±$804, and the inner control limits were set at ± $410. These limits (designated by ICL and OCL) are included in Figure 1. If there were no errors in the assumptions, the probability would be 0.05 that a point would lie outside the outer limits if the relationship remained fixed. Similarly, the probability would be about 0.03 that two consecutive points would lie outside the same inner control limit.

After setting the control limits, an attempt was made to determine if any assignable cause could be found for the days

that were "out of control." None could be found, and it was assumed that they were due to "chance." The number of such days was almost precisely what one would expect on a chance basis.

PERFORMANCE OF THE CHART

This section describes the performance of the chart during a six-week period that was several months subsequent to the time when the chart was set up. The results apply to the freight yard described above. On each day during the period data were collected concerning the money costs (C), the number of cuts switched (S), and the number of cars delivered (D) on the previous day. Then the deviation of actual cost from expected

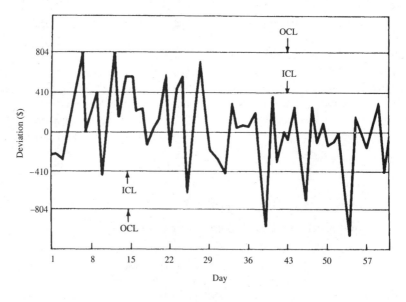

FIGURE 1

Deviation of Actual Cost from Expected Cost Based on Average Relationship Between Cost and Output: Freight Yard, 61 Days

Source: Records of cooperating railroad.

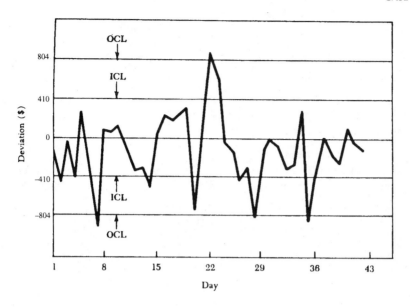

FIGURE 2

Control Chart for Costs: Freight Yard, 42 Days

Source: Records of cooperating railroad.

cost based on the average relationship in equation (1) was computed and plotted on the chart.[1] The deviations that were plotted are shown in Figure 2.

During the six-week period, four days seemed to be out of control, and in every case there seemed to be an assignable cause. One of these days was Labor Day. The exceptionally high costs on Labor Day can be attributed to the punitive wage-rates that were paid because it was a holiday. On the other days that were out of control (all of them Sundays) the exceptionally low costs can be attributed in part to the following circumstances: (1) Cars delivered to other yards constituted a large proportion of all cars delivered, and since such cars are relatively easy to deliver, costs were depressed. (2) More efficient methods were used to handle incoming cars. (3) Some work ordinarily performed by the yard was done by another yard; hence costs were reduced somewhat.

The basic data were collected by railroad employees and the points on the chart were computed by officials of the railroad. From their evaluation of the performance of the yard it appeared that the chart provided a reasonably faithful picture of the level of performance. Moreover, the chart stimulated some inquiries that indicated where improvements in yard performance might be made.

---

[1] Actually, the relationship was recomputed as more and more data became available.

Questions

1. Do managers often find it difficult to minimize costs? If so, why?

2. Can control charts of the sort described in this case help managers to minimize costs? If so, how?

3. Is equation 1 a short-run or long-run cost function? Why?

4. What is the marginal cost of switching a cut?

5. What is the marginal cost of delivering a car?

6. Does the average cost per cut switched exceed the marginal cost of switching a cut?

7. In what ways can these estimates of marginal and average cost be useful to railroad managers? Explain.

Part Four
MARKET STRUCTURE, STRATEGIC BEHAVIOR, AND PRICING

CHAPTER 11

Perfect Competition, Monopoly, and Monopolistic Competition

Chapter Profile

A perfectly competitive firm will set its output so that price equals marginal cost. If there exists an output rate where price exceeds average variable costs, it will pay the firm to produce, even though price does not cover average total costs. But if there does not exist an output rate where price exceeds average variable costs, the firm is better off to produce nothing at all. In the long run, the firm will produce at the minimum point on its long-run average total cost curve. Price tends to be at the level where the market demand curve intersects the market supply curve.

Under monopoly, a firm will maximize profit if it sets its output rate at the point where marginal revenue equals marginal cost. It does not follow that a firm that holds a monopoly over the production of a particular product must make a profit. If the monopolist cannot cover its variable costs, it, like a perfectly competitive firm, will shut down, even in the short run.

A firm sometimes requires the consumer to pay an initial fee for the right to buy its product as well as a usage fee for each unit of the product that he or she buys. This is called a two-part tariff. Another pricing technique sometimes used is bundling, in which a firm requires customers who buy one of its products to buy another of its products as well.

In contrast to perfect competition, where all firms sell an identical product, firms under monopolistic competition sell somewhat different products. Producers differentiate their product from that of other producers. Thus, the demand curve facing each firm slopes downward to the right—and is not horizontal, as it would be under perfect competition. Each firm will set marginal revenue equal to marginal cost. In the long run, each firm will produce to the left of the minimum point on its long-run average total cost curve.

Monopolistically competitive firms spend very large amounts on advertising. To maximize its profits, a firm should set its advertising so that the marginal revenue from an extra dollar of advertising equals the price elasticity of demand. A graph showing how both the price elasticity and the marginal revenue from an extra dollar of advertising vary with the amount spent by the firm on advertising can shed useful light on this topic.

Advertising of price changes may increase the price elasticity of demand for the product whose price is changed. This is because the advertising makes more consumers aware of the price changes. Measures of brand loyalty are useful in guiding decisions concerning promotional activities to increase sales of particular brands.

Questions

Completion

1. In the long run, a perfectly competitive firm's equilibrium position is at the place where its long-run average cost equals _____.
2. For a firm in a perfectly competitive market, if price is more than marginal cost, increases in output will _____ profit.
3. A monopolist can sell 12 units of output when it charges $8 a unit, 11 units of output when it charges $9 a unit, and 10 units of output when it charges $10 a unit. The marginal revenue from the eleventh unit of output equals _____. The marginal revenue from the twelfth unit of output equals _____.
4. A monopolist's demand curve is the same as the industry _____.
5. For a monopolist, marginal revenue is _____ than price.
6. Price will be _____ under monopoly than under perfect competition.
7. Output will be _____ under monopoly than under perfect competition.
8. A monopolistically competitive firm is in long-run equilibrium. Its marginal revenue equals $10. If its marginal revenue plus its economic profit equals one-half of its price, its price equals _____, and its marginal cost equals _____.
9. A measure of brand loyalty is the percentage of customers buying a particular brand today that will buy this brand _____.
10. In the case of coffee, coupon users tend to have a relatively (low, high) _____ brand loyalty.

True or False

____ 1. In the long run, equilibrium price under perfect competition may be above or below average total cost.

____ 2. Under perfect competition, one producer can produce a somewhat different good from other producers in the industry.

____ 3. Under perfect competition, each firm must be careful not to produce too much and spoil the market.

____ 4. At the equilibrium price, price will equal marginal cost (for all firms that choose to produce) under perfect competition.

____ 5. A profit-maximizing monopolist will always choose an output in the short run where average total cost is less than average revenue.

____ 6. A monopolist always produces an output such that the price elasticity of demand is 1.

_____ 7. A monopolistically competitive firm's short-run demand and cost curves are as follows:

Price (dollars)	Quantity demanded	Output	Total cost (dollars)
8	1	1	5
7	2	2	7
6	3	3	9
4	4	4	11
3	5	5	20

This firm, if it maximizes profit, will choose an output rate of 5.

_____ 8. One effect of advertising price changes is likely to be an increase in the price elasticity of demand for the product whose price is changed.

_____ 9. To maximize profit, a firm should set the marginal revenue from an extra dollar of advertising equal to the income elasticity of demand.

_____ * 10. To maximize profit, a firm with two plants, A and B, will allocate output between them so that the average cost at plant A equals the average cost at plant B.

Multiple Choice

1. The market demand curve for a particular kind of table is as follows:

Price (dollars)	Quantity demanded
30	200
20	300
10	400
5	600
3	800

The industry producing this kind of table has a horizontal long-run supply curve, and each firm has the following long-run total cost curve:

Output	Total cost (dollars)
1	10
2	12
3	15
4	30

(Each firm can produce only integer numbers of units of output.)
In the long run, the total number of firms in this industry will be about

a. 100.
b. 200.
c. 300.

* This question pertains to the chapter appendix in the text.

  d. 400.

  e. 500.

2. The long-run average cost curve of the Longacre Company, a perfectly competitive firm, is given below. Given that this curve does not shift, the long-run equilibrium output of this firm will be

  a. 4 units.

  b. 5 units.

  c. 6 units.

  d. 7 units.

  e. 8 units.

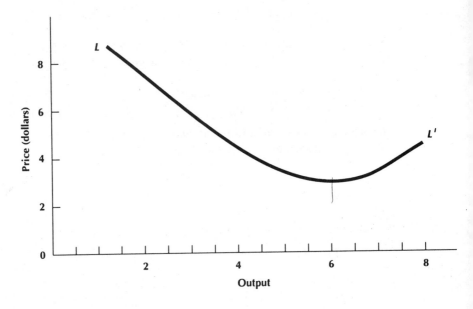

3. The total cost and total revenue of the Connors Company, a perfectly competitive firm, are shown below:

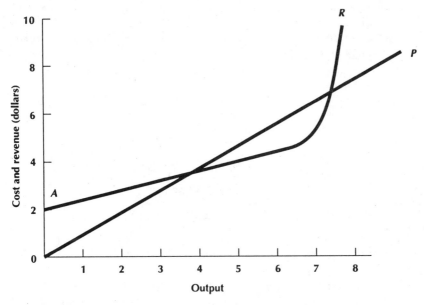

The line *OP* is

a. the total cost curve.
b. the total revenue curve.
c. the relationship between price and output.
d. all of the above.
e. none of the above.

4. A monopolist's total cost equals $100 + 3Q$, where Q is the number of units of output it produces per month. Its demand curve is $P = 200 - Q$, where P is the price of the product. The marginal revenue from the twentieth unit of output per month equals

a. $3,600.
b. $3,439.
c. $180.
d. $140.
e. none of the above.

5. A monopolistic firm will expand its output when

a. marginal revenue exceeds marginal cost.
b. marginal cost exceeds marginal revenue.
c. marginal cost equals marginal revenue.
d. marginal revenue is negative.
e. none of the above.

* 6. A profit-maximizing firm, if it owns a number of plants, will always

    a. produce some of its output at each plant.
    b. transfer output from plants with high marginal cost to those with low marginal cost.
    c. transfer output from plants with low marginal cost to those with high marginal cost.
    d. produce all of its output at a single plant and shut down the rest.
    e. none of the above.

Problems

1. In the cotton textile industry, each firm's marginal cost curve is

$$MC = 5 + 3Q,$$

where MC is its marginal cost (in dollars per ton), and Q is its output per day (in tons).

    a. If there are 1,000 firms in the cotton textile industry, derive the industry's short-run supply curve.
    b. If the price is $8, how much will the cotton textile industry produce per day?
    c. Can you derive each firm's total cost function? Why or why not?

2. Each firm in a perfectly competitive industry has the short-run total cost function shown below.

Output	Total cost (dollars)
0	10
1	12
2	16
3	22
4	30
5	40

There are 1,000 firms in this industry, and the market demand curve is as follows:

Price (dollars)	Quantity demanded
3	3,000
5	2,000
7	1,500
9	1,000

    a. What is the equilibrium price of the product? (Assume that the price must be $3, $5, $7, or $9.)
    b. What will be the output of each firm?
    c. If you were considering investing in this industry, would you forecast that in the long run firms would tend to enter or leave this industry?

---

* This question pertains to the chapter appendix in the text.

3. The Jackson Company, a perfectly competitive firm, has the following total cost function:

Total Output	Total cost (dollars)
0	20
1	30
2	42
3	55
4	69
5	84
6	100
7	117

How much will the Jackson Company produce, if the price is

a $13?
b. $14?
c. $15?
d. $16?
e. $17?

4. The Murphy Corporation's marginal cost curve is

$$MC = 4 + 3Q,$$

where MC is the cost (in dollars) of producing the Qth unit of its product, and Q is the number of units of its product produced per day. The price of a unit of its product is $3. A consultant hired by the Murphy Corporation argues that, based on this evidence, the firm would make more money by shutting down than by continuing to operate. Do you agree? Explain.

5. The Landau Company's average cost curve is

$$AC = \frac{400}{Q} + 3Q,$$

where AC is its average cost (in dollars), and Q is the number of units of its product that is produced per day. The price of a unit of its product is $3, regardless of how many units it sells.

a If the firm produces more than one unit per day, is it making profits or losses? Explain.
b. Is the firm better off to shut down or operate? Explain.

6. In the early 1950s, it was proposed that New York subway fares should be increased. William Vickrey of Columbia University was asked by the Mayor's Committee on Management Survey of the City of New York to make a study to help evaluate the proposal. Vickrey estimated the demand curve; part of his results are shown below. How would these data be useful in deciding whether or not to raise the subway fare from the then-prevailing level of 10 cents? What additional data would you need in order to come to a conclusion on this score? Do you think that data of this sort would be as useful now as in the early 1950s?

Fare (cents)	Passengers	Total revenue (dollars)
5	1,945	$ 97.2
10	1,683	168.3
15	1,421	213.2
20	1,159	231.8
25	897	224.2
30	635	190.5

Source: W. S. Vickrey. Passengers and revenues are in millions per year.

7. The Ardmore Company's marginal cost of production is zero if its output is less than (or equal to) 40 units per day.

a. If its output rate is 20 units per day, does its average total cost exceed its average fixed cost?
b. If the Ardmore Company is a perfectly competitive firm, will it produce less than 40 units per day? Why or why not?
c. If the Ardmore Company is a monopolist, under what conditions (if ever), will it produce less than 40 units per day? Explain.

8. The Towne Food Corporation has bought exclusive rights to sell chocolate bars in a local sports arena. The fee it paid for this concession was $1,000 per game. The cost (excluding this fee) of obtaining and marketing each candy bar is 10 cents. The demand schedule for candy bars in this arena is as follows:

Price per candy bar (cents)	Thousands of candy bars sold per game
20	10
25	9
30	8
35	7
40	6
45	5
50	4

It is assumed that prices must be multiples of a nickel.

a. What price should the Towne Food Corporation charge for a candy bar?
b. What is the maximum amount that the Towne Food Corporation should pay for this concession for a single game?

9. Beer manufacturers try to differentiate their products by advertising and by other means. In recent decades, there has been a reduction in the number of beer producers: in 1947, there were 404; in 1963, 150; and in 1974, 58. The rate of return, after taxes, on owner's equity in this industry was usually below 8 percent in the post–World War II period, but it increased to 9.1 percent in 1967, 10.1 percent in 1969, and 8.8 percent in 1971. For all manufacturing, the comparable rate of return in 1967, 1969, and 1971 was 11.7, 11.5, and 9.7 percent, respectively.

   a. Would you characterize the beer industry in the United States as monopolistically competitive? Why or why not?
   b. With regard to production differentiation, does it have the characteristics of a monopolistically competitive industry?
   c. Is its profit performance similar to what would be expected in a monopolistically competitive industry?
   d. Do you think that it is becoming closer to monopolistic competition than it used to be? Why or why not?

10. The Haas Company believes that the price elasticity of demand for its product equals 2. It also believes that an extra $1 million in advertising would increase its sales by $1.5 million.

   a. Is the Haas Company spending the optimal amount on advertising? Why or why not?
   b. If not, should it spend more or less on advertising? Explain.

11. For the Schmidt Company, the marginal revenue from an extra dollar of advertising is as shown below.

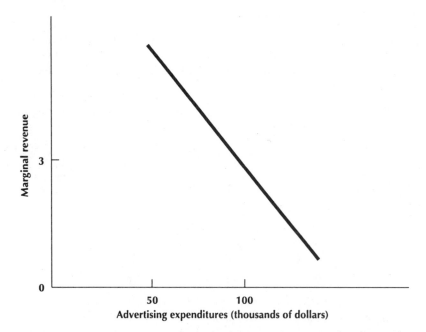

Advertising expenditures (thousands of dollars)

If the price elasticity of demand for the Schmidt Company's product is 3, regardless of how much is spent on advertising, how much should the firm spend on advertising?

12. The Rosemont Company is a member of a perfectly competitive industry. Like all members of the industry, its total cost function is

$$TC = 160,000 + 100Q + 4Q^2,$$

where TC is the firm's monthly total cost (in dollars), and Q is the firm's monthly output.

a. If the industry is in long-run equilibrium, what is the price of the Rosemont Company's product?

b. What is the firm's monthly output?

13. The London Corporation's total cost function (where TC is total cost in dollars, and Q is quantity) is

$$TC = 400 + 6Q + 3Q^2.$$

a. If the firm is perfectly competitive and if the price of its product is $36, what is its optimal output rate?

b. At this output rate, what are its profits?

14. The supply and demand curves for a product are as follows:

$$Q_S = 10,000P$$

$$Q_D = 25,000 - 15,000P,$$

where Q_S is the quantity (tons) supplied, Q_D is the quantity (tons) demanded, and P is the price per ton (in hundreds of dollars per ton).

a. What is the equilibrium price?

b. What is the equilibrium quantity?

15. The Nibelungen Company, an unregulated monopoly, finds that its marginal cost curve is $MC = 80 + 4Q$, where MC is marginal cost (in dollars), and Q is output. The demand curve for its product is $P = 200 - 2Q$, where P is the product price (in dollars), and Q is output.

a. If this firm wants to maximize profit, what output should it choose?

b. What price should it charge?

16. The Garfield Company's marketing manager believes that the price elasticity of demand for its product equals 1.8, and that the relationship between the amount spent by the firm on advertising and its sales is as follows:

Advertising expenditure	Sales
$200,000	$0.6 million
300,000	0.9 million
400,000	1.1 million
500,000	1.2 million

a. If the Garfield Company is spending $300,000 on advertising, what is the marginal revenue from an extra dollar of advertising?

b. Is $300,000 the optimal amount for the firm to spend on advertising?

c. If $300,000 is not the optimal amount, would you recommend that the firm spend more or less on advertising?

Answers

Completion
1. price   2. increase   3. –$1, –$3   4. demand curve   5. less
6. higher   7. lower   8. $20, $10   9. again when next they buy the product   10. low

True or False
1. False   2. False   3. False   4. True   5. False   6. False   7. False
8. True   9. False   10. False

Multiple Choice
1. b   2. c   3. b   4. e   5. a   6. b

Problems
1. a If *Q* is the quantity supplied by the industry (in tons per day) and *P* is the price (in dollars per ton),

$$Q = \frac{-5,000}{3} + \frac{1,000P}{3}.$$

   b. 1,000 tons.
   c. No.

2. a $5.
   b. 2 units.
   c. They will tend to leave this industry.

3. The Jackson Company's marginal cost curve is

Output	Marginal cost (dollars)
0 to 1	10
1 to 2	12
2 to 3	13
3 to 4	14
4 to 5	15
5 to 6	16
6 to 7	17

   a   If the price is $13, the Jackson Company will produce 2 or 3 units.
   b. 3 or 4 units.
   c. 4 or 5 units.
   d. 5 or 6 units.
   e. 6 or 7 units.

4. According to this evidence, the marginal cost of the first unit of output is 4 + (3)(1) = $7. Clearly, if the price of a unit of the product is $3, the firm loses money on each unit it sells. Indeed, it does not even cover its variable costs. Thus, the consultant is right; the firm should produce nothing.

5. a   The firm's total cost function is

$$C = AC \times Q = \left(\frac{400}{Q} + 3Q\right)Q = 400 + 3Q^2.$$

The firm's total revenue equals $R = 3Q$. Thus, its profit equals

$$\pi = R - C = 3Q - 400 - 3Q^2 = -400 - 3(Q^2 - Q) = -400 - 3Q(Q - 1).$$

If $Q > 1$, the firm incurs losses because $\pi = -400 - 3Q(Q - 1)$ is negative.

b.   Since $\pi = -400 - 3Q(Q - 1)$, the maximum value of π is not achieved at $Q = 0$. For example, if $Q = 1/2$, $\pi = -400 - 3(1/2)(-1/2) = -399 \ 1/4$. This is a higher value of π than -400, which is the value of π when $Q = 0$. Thus, assuming that the firm can produce fractional units of output per day, it is better off to operate than to shut down.

6. The demand for subway travel is shown by the table to be price inelastic at the then-prevailing fare of 10 cents. This means that increases in the fare would increase total revenues. Also, they would reduce the subway deficit because fewer passengers would mean lower costs (or at least no higher costs). But this is not the only consideration. You would probably want to investigate how such a fare increase would affect various parts of the population—the poor, the rich, rush-hour traffic, non-rush-hour traffic, and so on. Data of this sort would be just as relevant now as in the early 1950s.

7. a   No. They are equal.

b.   No, since marginal cost (which is zero) must be less than price (unless it too is zero).

c.   It will produce less than 40 units per day if marginal revenue equals zero (and thus is equal to marginal cost) at an output less than 40 units per day.

8. a   Since total cost (excluding the fee) is 10 cents times the number of candy bars sold, the Towne Food Corporation's total profit per game (before paying the fee) is shown below, under various assumptions concerning the price.

Thousands of candy bars	Price (cents)	Total revenue (dollars)	Total cost (dollars) (excluding fee)	Total profit (dollars)
10	20	2,000	1,000	1,000
9	25	2,250	900	1,350
8	30	2,400	800	1,600
7	35	2,450	700	1,750
6	40	2,400	600	1,800
5	45	2,250	500	1,750
4	50	2,000	400	1,600

Thus, the Towne Food Corporation will maximize profit if it sets a price of 40 cents.

b. $1,800, since this is the maximum amount it could make per game.

9. a The beer industry has some characteristics of monopolistic competition, but it departs from it in other respects. In a particular geographical market, there may be a limited number of beers that are distributed. In contrast, monopolistic competition occurs where there are a great many sellers. Also, the barriers to entry in the beer industry are not inconsiderable, whereas monopolistic competition assumes free entry.

b. Yes, the beer industry is characterized by product differentiation.

c. Its profits have not been above-average. In this respect, at least, its profit performance is similar to a monopolistically competitive industry.

d. No, because the number of breweries has declined, and it seems to be increasingly oligopolistic.

10. a No. It should set the marginal revenue from an extra dollar of its advertising equal to its price elasticity of demand.

b. Less.

11. $100,000.

12. a Average cost equals

$$AC = \frac{160,000}{Q} + 100 + 4Q.$$

Thus, the minimum value of average cost occurs when

$$\frac{dAC}{dQ} = \frac{-160,000}{Q^2} + 4 = 0$$

$$Q = 200.$$

Substituting 200 for Q in the equation for average cost, the minimum value of average cost equals

$$\frac{160,000}{200} + 100 + 4(200) = 1,700.$$

Thus, in the long run, price equals $1,700.

b. 200.

13. a Since marginal cost equals

$$MC = \frac{dTC}{dQ} = 6 + 6Q,$$

marginal cost equals price when

$$6 + 6Q = 36$$

$$Q = 5.$$

Thus, the optimal output rate is 5 units.

b. $5(36) - (400 + 6(5) + 3(25)) = 180 - 505 = -325.$

14. a Since Q_D must equal Q_S,

$$10,000P = 25,000 - 15,000P$$

$$P = 1.$$

b. 10,000 tons.

15. a   Setting marginal cost equal to marginal revenue,

$$80 + 4Q = 200 - 4Q$$

$$Q = 15.$$

   b. $P = 200 - 2(15) = 170.$

16. a   2.
    b.   No.
    c.   More.

CHAPTER 12

Oligopoly and Strategic Behavior

Chapter Profile

Oligopoly is characterized by a small number of firms and a great deal of inter-dependence, actual and perceived, among them. A good example of an oligopoly is the American oil industry, where a small number of firms account for the bulk of the industry's capacity.

Oligopolistic industries, like others, tend to pass through a number of phases—introduction, growth, maturity, and decline. As an industry goes through these phases, the nature of firm behavior often shifts. During the early stages, there often is considerable uncertainty regarding the industry's technology and concerning which markets will open up soonest. During the maturity phase, there frequently is a tendency for firms to attack the market shares of their rivals. In decline, there may be a tendency to get cash out of the firm as quickly as possible, but this may not be the best policy.

There is no single model of oligopoly. Instead, there are many models, depending on the circumstances. Conditions in oligopolistic industries tend to promote collusion, since the number of firms is small and firms recognize their interdependence. The advantages to be derived by the firms from collusion seem obvious: increased profits, decreased uncertainty, and a better opportunity to control the entry of new firms. However, collusive arrangements are often hard to maintain, since once a collusive agreement is made, any of the firms can increase its profits by "cheating" on the agreement.

In considering whether to make a move that threatens its rivals, an oligopolist should consider how likely it is that retaliation will occur, how soon it is likely to come, and how effective (and painful) it will be. It frequently is important that you convince your firm's rivals that your firm is committed to a strategic move it is making, that, if they make particular moves, your firm is committed to retaliate swiftly and effectively, and that your firm is committed not to make particular threatening moves against them.

The prisoners' dilemma is a type of game that is useful in analyzing oligopolistic situations, such as whether or not cartel members should cheat. If the game is played once, there are strong incentives to cheat, but if it is repeated, other strategies such as "tit for tat" may be better. Most-favored-customer clauses can be devices to discourage price cutting.

Another model of oligopolistic behavior is based on the supposition that one of the firms in the industry is a price leader, because it is a dominant firm. We have shown how under these circumstances this firm should set its price to maximize its profits. Also, game theory was used to analyze entry deterrence by oligopolists, as well as preemptive strategies.

Statistical studies based on data pertaining to hundreds of firms indicate (a) that the single most important factor influencing a business unit's profitability is the quality of its products and services, relative to those of rivals, and (b) that market share and profitability are strongly related.

Questions

Completion

1. All firms in an industry have marginal costs equal to $10 per unit of output. If they combine to form a cartel, the cartel's marginal cost (will, will not) _____ be $10 per unit of output. If the cartel maximizes profit, its marginal revenue will be (greater than, smaller than, equal to) _____ $10 per unit. Its price will be (greater than, smaller than, equal to) _____ $10 per unit.

2. Under oligopoly, each firm is aware that its actions are likely to elicit _____ in the policies of its competitors.

3. A good example of oligopoly in the United States is the _____ in-dustry.

4. According to the kinked oligopoly demand curve, firms think that if they raise their price, their rivals will _____.

5. According to the kinked oligopoly demand curve, firms think that if they lower their price, their rivals will _____.

6. A most-favored-customer clause means that if a firm reduces its price subsequently, earlier customers will get a _____ so they will pay __ more than those buying _____ the price reduction.

7. Most-favored-customer clauses can be devices to discourage _____.

8. Excess _____ can be used to forestall and resist entry.

9. According to PIMS data, the most important single factor influencing a business unit's profitability is the _____ of its products and services relative to those of rivals.

10. If the game of the prisoners' dilemma is repeated indefinitely, the best strategy for each player may not be to _____.

11. A commitment tends to be more persuasive if it seems _____ and _____.

12. The Cournot model assumes that each firm thinks that the other will hold its output constant at _____.

True or False

_____ 1. Collusion is often difficult to achieve and maintain because an oligopoly contains an unwieldy number of firms, or because the product is quite heterogeneous.

_____ 2. If a perfectly competitive industry is operating along the elastic portion of its demand curve, there is no point in trying to cartelize the industry.

_____ 3. Because a cartel maximizes profit, there is no incentive for a member to violate the rules of the cartel.

_____ 4. Cartels have been common and legally acceptable in Europe.

_____ 5. Cartels tend to be unstable because the demand curve facing a "cheater" is highly inelastic.

_____ 6. According to the dominant-firm model, the dominant firm allows the smaller firms to sell all they want at the price it sets.

_____ 7. Whether or not an industry remains oligopolistic in the face of relatively easy entry depends on the size of the market for the product relative to the optimal size of the firm.

_____ 8. A limit price is a price that is the maximum price the oligopolists can charge without courting the possibility of government antitrust action.

_____ 9. A Nash equilibrium exists for any and every game.

_____ 10. According to a tit-for-tat strategy, if one firm cheats on an agreement, the other firm should do the same.

_____ 11. Firms frequently send signals to one another indicating their intentions, motives, and objectives.

_____ 12. Firms never can alter the payoff matrix.

_____ 13. A firm may succeed in convincing a potential entrant not to enter its market by reducing its own profits if it does not resist entry.

Multiple Choice

1. A strategic move may be

   a. threatening to the firm's rivals.
   b. not threatening to the firm's rivals.
   c. met with substantial retaliation by the firm's rivals.
   d. met with little or no retaliation by the firm's rivals.
   e. all of the above.

2. A firm may be able to deter entry into its market by

   a. building excess production capacity.
   b. gaining a reputation for "irrational" resistance to entry.
   c. threatening to resist even though potential entrants believe that it is not in this firm's interest to resist.
   d. only a and b.
   e. all of the above.

3. If two rival firms both adopt a preemptive strategy with regard to capacity expansion,

   a. each tries to expand before the other does so.
   b. there may be two Nash equilibria.
   c. both firms are likely to profit greatly if the demand for the product grows more slowly than expected.
   d. both a and b.
   e. all of the above.

4. If D is the industry demand curve and marginal cost equals $2, the price that maximizes a cartel's profits is

   a. $12.
   b. $14.
   c. $16.
   d. $2.
   e. none of the above.

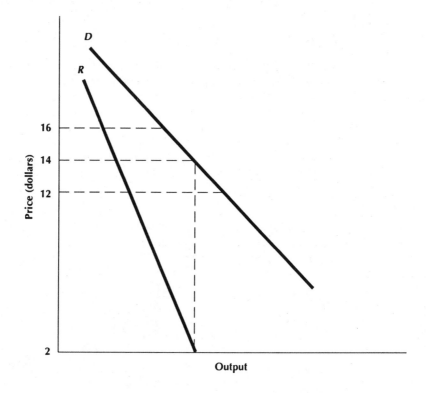

5. In the previous question, the R curve is

   a. the marginal revenue curve.
   b. the marginal cost curve.
   c. the reaction curve.
   d. all of the above.
   e. none of the above.

6. A dominant strategy is a strategy where

   a. the player loses.
   b. a second-best approach is used.
   c. pure strategies are mixed with impure strategies.
   d. all of the above.
   e. none of the above.

7. In the dominant-firm model, the dominant firm finds the demand curve for its output by

   a. using the unadjusted industry demand curve.
   b. adding up the small firms' demand curves.
   c. subtracting the small firms' supply from the industry demand curve.
   d. all of the above.
   e. none of the above.

Problems

1. During the 1960s and 1970s, the major U.S. automobile manufacturers were not very enthusiastic about producing small cars, owing in part to the fact that they made a larger profit on a larger car than a small one. But the explosion of gasoline prices and the press of foreign competition during the 1970s led the American producers to introduce new lines of smaller, fuel-efficient cars in the fall of 1980. The prices at which they and their Japanese competitors were offered were as follows:

Chevrolet Citation	$6,337	Subaru wagon	$5,612
GM "J" cars	6,300	Datsun 310	5,439
Ford Escort	6,009	Subaru hatchback	5,212
Dodge Omni	5,713	Mazda GLC	4,755

   a. According to some observers, "Detroit . . . priced these cars relatively high to replenish its depleted coffers as soon as possible." Is this necessarily the effect of charging relatively high prices?
   b. Some auto executives stated that the U.S. demand for smaller cars would be so great in the early 1980s that Detroit would be able to sell all such cars that it could produce. What implicit assumptions were they making?

2. Firms C and D are the only two producers and sellers of a particular type of electrical equipment. They each have two possible strategies for product development. The payoff matrix is as follows:

Possible strategies for firm C	Possible strategies for firm D	
	A	B
1	Firm C's profit: $5 million Firm D's profit: $6 million	Firm C's profit: $4 million Firm D's profit: $5 million
2	Firm C's profit: $6 million Firm D's profit: $5 million	Firm C's profit: $5 million Firm D's profit: $4 million

   a. What is firm C's optimal strategy?
   b. What is firm D's optimal strategy?
   c. Is this an example of the prisoner's dilemma?
   d. Is there a dominant strategy for firm C? Explain.
   e. Is there a dominant strategy for firm D? Explain.

3. If two firms are engaged in a game with the characteristics of the prisoner's dilemma, can the equilibrium depend on whether the game is played repeatedly or just once? Explain.

4. Two firms that are the only producers of a particular scientific instrument agree to maintain their prices at the monopoly level. In the event that either cheats on this agreement, both firms will adopt a strategy of tit for tat. Describe how each firm may attempt to determine whether the other firm is cheating.

5. There are ten identical producers of spring water. Each of these firms has zero costs of production, so long as it produces less than (or equal to) 10 gallons of water per hour. It is impossible for each firm to produce more than 10 gallons per hour. Suppose the market demand curve for this water is as follows:

Price (dollars per gallon)	Number of gallons demanded per hour	Price (dollars per gallon)	Number of gallons demanded per hour
11	0	5	60
10	10	4	70
9	20	3	80
8	30	2	90
7	40	1	100
6	50	1/2	105

   a. If the firms take the price of water as given (as in the case of perfect competition), what will be the price and output of each firm?
   b. If the firms form a completely effective cartel, what will be the price and output of each firm?
   c. How much money will each firm be willing to pay to achieve and enforce the collusive agreement described in part b?
   d. Suppose that one of the firms secretly breaks the terms of the agreement and shades price. What effect will this have on its profits?

6. John Milton and Alexander Pope are arrested for holding up a bank. The district attorney talks *separately* to each one, saying, "We've got lots of evidence indicating you robbed the bank, so you'd better confess. If you do, I'll give you a break. If you *alone* confess, I'll see to it you get only 6 months in jail. If you *both* confess, I'll see to it you get 10 years. But if you don't confess, and your partner *does*, I'll see to it you get 20 years." Both Milton and Pope are sure that if neither confesses, they will get 2 years.

    a. In this situation, what is the payoff matrix?

    b. What strategy will each choose, given that each tries to save his own skin?

7. The Aloha Company and the Crowe Corporation are producers of a product whose marginal cost equals $2. The marginal revenue curve for their combined output is

    $$MR = 10 - 2Q,$$

    where MR is marginal revenue (in dollars), and Q is the number of units of output sold by both together per hour. If the two producers decide to collude and share the monopoly profits, how much will be their combined output? Why?

8. A cartel is formed by three firms. Their total cost functions are as follows:

Units of output	Firm A	Firm B	Firm C
	Total cost (dollars)		
0	20	25	15
1	25	35	22
2	35	50	32
3	50	80	47
4	80	120	77
5	120	160	117

    If the cartel decides to produce 11 units of output, how should the output be distributed among the three firms, if they want to minimize cost?

9. In its annual report, Aluminium, Ltd., of Canada once noted, "World stocks of aluminum are not excessively large. They are in firm hands and do not weigh unduly upon the world market." What did it mean by "firm hands"? Do you think this phenomenon was at all related to the firmness of world aluminum prices during the relevant period? Under perfect competition, do you think aluminum prices would remain fairly constant in the face of sharp reductions in sales?

10. U.S. Steel (now USX) often was regarded as the price leader in steel, as was Alcoa in virgin aluminum, American Viscose in rayon, and Du Pont in nylon and polyester fibers. What characteristics tend to distinguish price leaders from other firms? If you had to predict which of a number of firms in an industry was the price leader, what variables would you use to make the forecast?

11. If the payoff matrix is as given below, what strategy will firm A choose? What strategy will firm B choose? (Assume firm A chooses its strategy first.)

Possible strategies for firm A	Possible strategies for firm B		
	1	*2*	*3*
	Profits for firm A, or losses for firm B (dollars)		
I	$10	$9.0	$11
II	8	8.5	10

12. According to the Federal Trade Commission, there was collusion among the leading bakers and food outlets in the state of Washington in the late 1950s and early 1960s. Prior to the conspiracy, bread prices in Seattle were about equal to the U.S. average. During the period of the conspiracy, bread prices in Seattle were 15 to 20 percent above the U.S. average. Is this consistent with the theory of collusive behavior? Why do you think bread prices in Seattle were not double or triple the U.S. average during the conspiracy?

Answers

Completion
1. will, equal to, greater than 2. changes 3. steel (among many others)
4. maintain their present price 5. lower their price too 6. rebate, no, after 7. price cutting 8. capacity 9. quality 10. confess 11. binding, irreversible 12. its existing level

True or False
1. True 2. False 3. False 4. True 5. False 6. True 7. True
8. False 9. False 10. True 11. True 12. False 13. True

Multiple Choice
1. e 2. d 3. d 4. b 5. a 6. e 7. c

Problems
1. a No. If a firm charges relatively high prices, it may sell relatively few units of its product, the result being that its profits may be lower than they would be if its price were somewhat lower.
   b. They were assuming that U.S. consumers would not buy imported smaller cars (instead of U.S. smaller cars) in such numbers that Detroit would be unable to sell all it could produce.

2. a Strategy 2.
   b. Strategy A.
   c. No.
   d. Yes. Strategy 2.
   e. Yes. Strategy A.

3. Yes. See the text.

4. In some cases, trade associations have been authorized to collect detailed information concerning each firm's transactions.

5. a The industry supply curve would be as shown below. This is the horizontal sum of the firm's marginal cost curves. Since this supply curve intersects the demand curve at a price of $1, this is the equilibrium price. Since the supply and demand curves intersect at an output of 100 gallons, this is the industry output. Each firm produces one-tenth of this output, or 10 gallons.

    The industry supply curve is

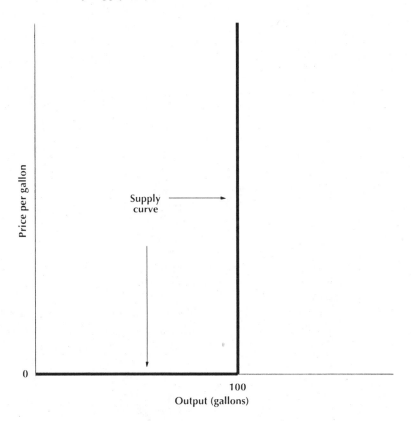

b. The cartel would expand output only so long as marginal revenue exceeds marginal cost. Since marginal cost is zero, this means that the cartel would expand output only so long as marginal revenue is positive. Marginal revenue is shown below.

Output	Total revenue (dollars)	Marginal revenue (dollars)
0	0	
		10
10	100	
		8
20	180	
		6
30	240	
		4
40	280	
		2
50	300	
		0
60	300	
		−2
70	280	
		−4
80	240	
		−6
90	180	
		−8
100	100	

Clearly, the cartel would restrict output to 50 gallons and charge $6 per gallon. (Alternatively, it could set output at 60 gallons, and charge $5 per gallon. The profit would be the same.)

c. If the alternative to the cartel is the arrangement described in part a, each firm would be willing to pay up to $20 per hour to achieve and enforce the cartel. With the cartel, each firm makes $30 per hour, since each produces 5 gallons per hour, and charges $6 per gallon. Under the arrangement in part a, each firm makes $10 per hour, since each produces 10 gallons per hour and charges $1 per gallon. Thus, each firm's profit per hour is $20 higher under the cartel.

d. If the cartel sets a price of $6 per gallon, this firm can increase its profits by selling an additional 5 gallons per hour at a price per gallon of $5. But if a substantial number of firms begin to act in this way, the cartel will break apart.

6. a The payoff matrix is as follows:

Possible strategies for Pope	Milton's payoff Possible strategies for Milton		Pope's payoff Possible strategies for Milton	
	Confess	Not confess	Confess	Not confess
	(Years of imprisonment for Milton)		(Years of imprisonment for Pope)	
Confess	10	20	10	1/2
Not confess	1/2	2	20	2

b. Milton's payoff matrix shows that, if Pope confesses, Milton is better off to confess than not to confess. If Pope does not confess, Milton is also better off to confess than not to confess. Thus, Milton's optimal strategy is to confess. Similarly, Pope's payoff matrix shows that Pope is better off to confess if Milton confesses and that Pope is also better off to confess if Milton does not confess. Thus, Pope's optimal strategy too is to confess.

7. The two producers will choose the monopoly output, where marginal revenue equals marginal cost. Since marginal cost equals $2, this means that

$$MR = 10 - 2Q = 2,$$

so

$$Q = \frac{8}{2} = 4.$$

Thus, their combined output will be 4 units per hour.

8. They should set the marginal cost at one firm equal to the marginal cost at each other firm. If firm A produces 4 units, firm B produces 3 units, and firm C produces 4 units, the marginal cost at each firm equals $30. Thus, this seems to be the optimal distribution of output.

9. It meant that the holders of these inventories were unlikely to sell them (and depress the price). Yes, by holding output off the market, producers could maintain prices. No.

10. The price leaders tend to be the largest firms. Also, historical factors play a role, and there is sometimes a tendency for low-cost (or medium-cost) firms to be leaders.

11. Firm A will choose strategy I.

    Firm B will choose strategy 2.

12. Yes. Because of possible entry, for one thing.

CHAPTER 13

Pricing Techniques

Chapter Profile

Empirical studies indicate that cost-plus pricing is used frequently by firms. In this approach, the firm estimates the cost per unit of output of the product (based on some assumed output level) and adds a markup to include costs that cannot be allocated to any specific product and to provide a return on the firm's investment. On the surface, it is questionable whether this approach can maximize profit, but if marginal cost (not average cost) is really what is being marked up, and if the markup is determined (in the appropriate way) by the price elasticity of demand of the product, cost-plus pricing can result in profit maximization.

Firms generally produce and sell more than one product. It is important for them to recognize the demand interrelationships among the products they sell. Also, a firm's products are often interrelated in production. If two products are produced jointly in fixed proportions, the profit-maximizing output is where the total marginal revenue curve—the vertical summation of the marginal revenue curves for the individual products—intersects the marginal cost curve for the bundle of products (assuming that the marginal revenue of each product is nonnegative).

If two products are produced jointly in variable proportions, one can construct isocost curves, each of which shows the combinations of outputs that can be produced at the same total cost. Also, isorevenue lines can be constructed, each of which shows the combinations of outputs that yield the same total revenue. For an output combination to be optimal, it must be at a point where an isorevenue line is tangent to an isocost curve. To determine which output combination is optimal, one compares the profit levels at the tangency points. The tangency point where profit is highest is the optimal output combination.

Price discrimination occurs when the same commodity is sold at more than one price, or when similar products are sold at prices that are in different ratios to marginal cost. A firm will be able and willing to practice price discrimination if various classes of buyers with different price elasticities of demand can be identified and segregated, and if the commodity cannot be transferred easily from one class to another. If the total market is divided into such classes, a firm that discriminates will maximize its profits by choosing prices and outputs so that the marginal revenue in each class is equal to marginal cost.

Many large firms are decentralized, and one division of the firm sells its product to another division of the firm. To maximize the firm's overall profit, it is important that the price at which this transfer takes place—the so-called transfer price—is set properly. If there is no market outside the firm for the transferred product, the transfer price should equal the marginal production cost at the optimal output. If there is a perfectly competitive market for the transferred product outside the firm, the transfer price should equal the price of this product in that market.

Questions

Completion

1. If a firm is maximizing profit, the percentage markup on a product is (directly, inversely) _____ related to the product's price elasticity of demand.

2. The price at which one division of a firm sells to another division is the _____ price.

3. If there is a perfectly competitive market for the transferred product, the transfer price should equal the _____ .

4. If two products are produced jointly in fixed proportions, the profit-maximizing output is where the _____ of the marginal revenue curves of the individual products intersects the _____ for the bundle of products.

5. The statement in the previous question assumes that the marginal revenue of each product is _____ .

6. If the Johnstown Company produces 1 unit of good X, it automatically produces 2 units of good Y. Goods X and Y are _____ products produced in _____ proportions.

7. From a production point of view, goods X and Y (in the previous question) are not separate products but should be viewed as a _____ .

8. A markup is meant to include costs that (can, cannot) _____ be allocated to any specific product and to provide a _____ on the firm's investment.

True or False

_____ 1. General Electric at times has established a target rate of return of 20 percent.

_____ 2. Surveys of business-pricing practices show that few firms use cost-plus pricing.

_____ 3. If marginal cost is what is being marked up, and if the markup (in absolute terms) equals $MC\left(1 - \dfrac{1}{\eta}\right)$, the firm can maximize profit.

_____ 4. If two goods are joint products, they must be produced in variable proportions.

_____ 5. If there is no external market for the transferred good, the optimal transfer price is the average cost of the product.

_____ 6. Price discrimination is unlikely to occur unless consumers can be segregated into classes and the commodity cannot be transferred from one class to another.

_____ 7. Price discrimination always occurs when differences in price exist among roughly similar products, even when their costs are not the same.

_____ 8. Price discrimination is profitable even when the price elasticity of demand is the same among each class of consumer in the total market.

_____ 9. If a monopoly practices price discrimination, it does not set marginal revenue equal to marginal cost.

_____ 10. First-degree price discrimination occurs frequently, particularly in the auto industry.

Multiple Choice

1. If the price elasticity of demand for a product equals 2, and if its producer wants to maximize profit, its marginal cost should be marked up by

   a. 50 percent.
   b. 100 percent.
   c. 150 percent.
   d. 200 percent.
   e. none of the above.

2. If the price elasticity of demand for a product equals 3, and if its producer wants to maximize profit, its price should be

   a. double its average cost.
   b. 150 percent of its average cost.
   c. double its marginal cost.
   d. 150 percent of its marginal cost.
   e. none of the above.

3. The Montana Company produces and sells two products, A and B. If they are complements, an increase in the quantity sold of product A will

   a. reduce the total revenue from product B.
   b. increase the total revenue from product B.
   c. have no effect on the total revenue from product B.
   d. be impossible to attain.
   e. none of the above.

4. The Milwaukee Corporation produces and sells two products, D and E. If they are substitutes, an increase in the quantity sold of product D will

   a. reduce the total revenue from product E.
   b. increase the total revenue from product E.
   c. have no effect on the total revenue from product E.
   d. be impossible to attain.
   e. none of the above.

5. For first-degree price discrimination to occur, a firm must have

   a. an infinite number of buyers.
   b. knowledge of the maximum prices buyers are willing to accept.
   c. a small number of buyers.
   d. both a and b.
   e. both b and c.

6. Second-degree price discrimination is

   a. more common than first-degree price discrimination.
   b. often practiced by electric and gas companies.
   c. a way for sellers to increase their profits.
   d. all of the above.
   e. none of the above.

7. To determine how a discriminating monopolist will allocate output between two classes of consumers, one must

   a. compare the marginal revenues in the classes.
   b. compare the prices in the classes.
   c. compare the slopes of the demand curves in the classes.
   d. compare the heights of the demand curves in the classes.
   e. none of the above.

Problems

1. a. Under what conditions will a firm be able and willing to engage in price discrimination?
   b. Under price discrimination, will price tend to be relatively high in markets where the price elasticity of demand is relatively high?

2. The Logan Company sells in two distinct markets, which are sealed off from each other. The demand curve for the firm's output in the one market is

$$P_1 = 200 - 10Q_1,$$

where P_1 is the price of the product, and Q_1 is the amount sold in the first market. In the second market, the demand curve for the firm's product is

$$P_2 = 100 - 5Q_2,$$

where P_2 is the price of the product, and Q_2 is the amount sold in the second market. The firm's marginal cost curve is

$$MC = 10Q,$$

where Q is the firm's entire output.

a. How many units should the firm sell in the first market?
b. What price should it charge in the first market?
c. How many units should the firm sell in the second market?
d. What price should it charge in the second market?

3. The makers of methyl methacrylate used to sell it at 85 cents per pound for commercial purposes, but for denture purposes, it was sold to the dental profession for $45 per pound. Assuming that there was no difference in quality, why would the producers of methyl methacrylate, Du Pont and Rohm and Haas, find it profitable to charge different prices? In which of these markets (the commercial market or the dental market) do you think the price elasticity of demand was lower?

4. The Montana Company estimates its average total cost to be $22 per unit of output when it produces 15,000 units, which it regards as 75 percent of capacity. It wants to earn 20 percent on its total investment, which is $175,000.

a. If it uses cost-plus pricing, what price should it set?
b. What percentage markup will it use?

5. The Dakota Company's total annual indirect costs (for all products) are estimated to be $3 million, and its total annual variable costs (for all products) are estimated to be $1.5 million. Indirect costs are allocated among the firm's products on the basis of their average variable costs.

a. If the average variable cost of product X is $14, how much would the firm add on for indirect cost?
b. What would the estimated fully allocated cost per unit be for product X?
c. If the markup for product X is 50 percent, what will its price be?

6. The Ohio Company sells a product with marginal cost equal to $9. If the Ohio Company maximizes profit, what must be the price elasticity of demand for this product if

a. the product's price is $18?
b. the product's price is $27?
c. the product's price is $13.50?

7. The California Corporation is composed of a marketing division and a production division. The marginal cost of producing a unit of the firm's product is $8 per unit, and the marginal cost of marketing it is $6 per unit. The demand curve for the firm's product is

$$P = 200 - .015Q,$$

where P is the price per unit (in dollars), and Q is output (in units). There is no external market for the good made by the production division.

a. What is the California Corporation's optimal output?

b. What price should it charge?

c. How much should the production division charge the marketing division for each unit of the product?

8. The Beiswanger Company sells a plastic toy in the United States and Europe. According to the firm's marketing department, marginal revenue is $8 per unit in both these markets. The firm's president says that it should sell more in Europe and less in the United States. The vice president of marketing disagrees.

a. Who is right? (Assume that marginal cost is the same in the United States as in Europe.)

b. Can you determine whether the price elasticity of demand is the same in both markets? Why or why not?

c. Can you determine whether the price of a toy is the same in both markets? Why or why not?

9. The Hayes Company is composed of a marketing division and a production division. The production division produces a raw material that it transfers to the marketing division. There is an external market for this raw material, the price in this market (which is perfectly competitive) being $18 per pound. The production division's average cost of production is $22 per pound.

a. The vice president of production argues that the transfer price for this raw material should be $22. Otherwise his division cannot cover its costs. Is he correct? Why or why not?

b. The vice president of marketing argues that the transfer price should be $18. Otherwise his division is paying more than it needs to. Is he correct? Why or why not?

Answers

Completion
1. inversely   2. transfer   3. price in the perfectly competitive market
4. vertical summation, marginal cost curve   5. nonnegative   6. joint, fixed
7. bundle   8. cannot, return

True or False
1. True   2. False   3. False   4. False   5. False   6. True   7. False
8. False   9. False   10. False

Multiple Choice
1. b   2. d   3. b   4. a   5. e   6. d   7. a

Problems
1. a.   The firm must be able to identify and segregate buyers into classes with different price elasticities of demand for the product, and the buyers must be unable to transfer the product easily from one class to another.
   b.   No.

2. a. Since marginal revenue in the first market equals $200 - 20Q_1$, and marginal revenue in the second market equals $100 - 10Q_2$, it follows that

$$200 - 20Q_1 = 100 - 10Q_2 = 10(Q_1 + Q_2).$$

Thus, $Q_1 = 10 - 2Q_2$, and $200 - 20(10 - 2Q_2) = 100 - 10Q_2$, which means that $Q_2 = 2$. Consequently, $Q_1 = 10 - 2(2)$, or 6.

b. $200 - 10(6) = 140$.

c. 2.

d. $100 - 5(2) = 90$.

3. Because the price elasticity of demand was different in the two markets. The dental market.

4. a. To earn 20 percent on its investment of $175,000, its profit must be $35,000. Thus, the per-unit markup must be $35,000 ÷ 15,000 = $2.33, and price must equal $22 + $2.33 = $24.33.

b. $\dfrac{\$2.33}{\$22} = 10.6$ percent.

5. a. $28.

b. $42.

c. $63.

6. a. 2.

b. 1.5.

c. 3.

7. a. Since the firm's marginal cost equals $8 + $6 = $14, and the firm's marginal revenue equals $200 - .03Q$, the profit-maximizing level of output is the one where

$$200 - .03Q = 14,$$

$Q = 6,200$.

b. Price should equal $200 - .015(6,200) = \$107$.

c. $8.

8. a. The vice president of marketing.

b. No, because marginal revenue depends both on the price elasticity of demand and price.

c. No. See the answer to part b.

9. a. No, the transfer price should be $18.

b. Yes.

CASE FIVE

Applied CAD Knowledge, Inc. (A)

John A. Seeger • Raymond M. Kinnunen

Something is seriously wrong with this planet. Look at us. I'm working a hundred and twenty hours a week or more, and not catching up. I've got these two friends—both recently divorced, like me—who aren't working at all: they're living off their girl friends, and loving it. One of them is basking in Hawaii. But here I am, busting my ass and giving my customers problems anyhow.

Some guys go on television and say, "Send money now," and people *do*. I ask my best customer to send money, and he goes bankrupt instead. What's wrong with this picture?

Jeff Stevens, President and 90% owner of Applied CAD Knowledge, Inc., was reporting on current sales and production levels to the two business school professors who comprised his Board of Directors. It was late August, and the three men sat in a booth at Bogie's restaurant. The waitress, Patty, was accustomed to these monthly meetings; she offered another round of Lite beer. "Make mine cyanide," said Stevens. "On the rocks, please."

Applied CAD, a small service bureau that designed electronic circuit boards, was experiencing the highest sales levels in its three-year history. June sales had reached $50,000—leaving a backlog of $90,000; July shipments had set a record at $58,000; August would be nearly as high. The problem facing Stevens through the summer of 1987 was a shortage of good designers to work as part-time freelancers. The surge in business saw Stevens sitting at the computer consoles himself, doing design work on second and third shifts, six or seven days a week. After eight weeks of this schedule, the strain was showing. One director asked about the longer-range sales picture, and Stevens summed it up:

Can I borrow a .45 automatic? I'd like a good game of Russian Roulette.

There's nothing on the books at all for late fall, and not much likely. Every major customer we have is in "busy phase" right now. When these designs are finished, it will be another four to six months before their next generation of product revisions. In the meantime, everybody is burned out. All I'm hoping for right now is a front porch, a rocking chair, a lobotomy and a drool cup.

THE ELECTRONICS INDUSTRY AND CIRCUIT BOARD DESIGN

The United States electronics industry in 1987 was a sprawling giant, some of whose sectors were growing while others remained in a protracted slump. In 1986, total industry size was estimated by *Electronic Business* magazine (December 10, 1985) as $100.5 billion to $182 billion. The same article projected industry revenues for 1995 to be $295.4 billion to $512 billion. The magazine concluded that its industry represented a major driving force of the American economy. The Value Line investment service reports separately on four segments of the electronics industry (see Exhibit 1).

Printed Circuit Boards

A basic part of nearly every electronic product—whichever segment of the industry produced or used it—was the printed circuit board to which a variety of electronic components were attached. These components ranged from old-fashioned resistors, capacitors, and vacuum tubes, to transistors and the most modern integrated circuit chips. All components needed some sort of platform to sit on, and some way to make connection with the other components of the circuit.

In the 1930s and 1940s, circuit boards were made from thin, non-conducting fiberboard with metal pins and sockets attached. Assembly operators wound the wire leads of the circuit's resistors, capacitors, etc. around the proper pins and soldered them in place. By the 1960s, the technology of wiring boards and assembling components had advanced to a highly automated stage. Numerically controlled machines positioned components and connected pins to one another with wires. During this decade, electronic components became increasingly miniaturized and more reliable, complex and powerful. With these technological developments, the printed circuit board (PCB) was developed; its use and technical sophistication accelerated rapidly.

In a printed circuit, the wires leading from one pin to another are replaced by electrically conductive lines "printed" or plated onto (or under) the surface of the board itself. The pins themselves are gone; wire leads from electrical components are inserted through small holes in the board and soldered on the underside. By the 1980s, components could be mounted directly on the board's surface, in contact with the printed "wires."

The increasing complexity of electronic circuits presents a problem for PCB technology. When connections were made with wires, assemblers simply attached

---

EXHIBIT 1   **Electronics Industry Revenues**
(Dollars in Amounts in Billions)

INDUSTRY SECTOR	NUMBER OF COMPANIES	1982	1983	1984	1985	1986	1987 (Est.)
Electronics	35	$16.4	$17.7	$21.6	$21.2	$22.0	$24.0
U.S. semiconductors	14	11.4	13.0	17.2	15.6	16.0	17.8
Computers/peripherals	34	78.6	88.4	104.4	110.5	115.0	127.5
Electrical equipment	25	50.9	51.2	54.9	56.5	64.7	72.0

Source: Value Line, May 8, 1987.

one end, routed the wire over the top of everything between the two pins involved, and attached the other end where it belonged. With printed circuits, however, designers are constrained to two dimensions on a flat board; they must route the line between two pins without touching any other lines, and they cannot go "over the top" without leaving the surface of the board. Furthermore, efficient design calls for the components to be tightly packed together, grouped by function. Designers frequently find that they cannot lay out a trace from one point to another without interfering with other traces.

"Multilayer" PCBs ease this problem by providing "upstairs" layers on the board, allowing the designer to go over the top. Multilayer boards contain at least three layers of traces, and sometimes more than twenty layers. Skilled designers seek to minimize the number of layers required for a given circuit, in order to reduce manufacturing costs of the board: Multilayer PCBs are far more expensive to manufacture. In 1983, multilayer boards had sales of $900 million, or 26% of the PCB market. By 1993, they are forecast to reach sales of $5.6 billion, or 41% market share. Exhibit 2 shows PCB sales and projections by type of board.

Board design was made more complicated by increasing density of components, by sensitivity of components to heat (some threw off large amounts of heat, while others would go haywire if their operating temperature was disturbed), and by radio-frequency interference (some components generated static, while others might "hear" the noise and try to process it). The layout of components on the board had tremendous impact on how well the finished product worked, as well as on its manufacturing cost.

Printed circuit boards offered many technical advantages over the previous method for fashioning circuits:

1. *Greater miniaturization*: PCBs can be highly miniaturized, allowing progressively more powerful and complex electronic circuits for smaller, lighter products.

2. *Improved performance*: product reliability is much greater than in pin-to-pin circuitry, so that applications can be made in extreme environmental conditions.

3. *Manufacturing advantages*: for high volume products, manufacturing costs are greatly reduced. PCB applications range from simple consumer products to the most powerful mainframe computers.

4. *Maintenance advantages*: PCBs allowed designers to "package" electronic systems into discrete modules which, if not functioning properly,

EXHIBIT 2   **Sales and Projections for PCBs by Type of Board**

PCB TYPE	1983		ANNUAL GROWTH RATE	1993	
	Sales in $ Millions	Market Share (%)		Sales in $ Millions	Market Share (%)
Multilevel	$ 900	25.3	20%	$5,600	41.0
Double-sided	2,000	56.1	13%	6,700	49.0
Flexible	353	10.0	10%	916	6.7
Single-sided	307	8.6	4%	454	3.3
Total	$3,560	100%		$13,670	100%

Source: Electronic Business, February 1, 1985, p. 87.

193

could be replaced without the immediate need of determining where the problem was within the board.

Frost and Sullivan, Inc., a New York market research firm, estimated (in "The Printed Circuit Board Market in the U.S.," July, 1986, quoted by permission) that the total U.S. PCB market reached $3.7 billion in sales in 1985, a decrease of 12% from 1984's production. PCBs were projected to grow to a likely $6.5 billion by 1990 and to $10.8 billion in 1995. Multi-layer PCBs were expected to be the fastest-growing type, averaging 15.7% annual growth. A little over half the market was served in 1985 by independent PCB makers, as opposed to captive suppliers, Frost & Sullivan said.

Trends in Equipment Used in Circuit Board Design

Originally (and still, for simple circuits), an engineer or technician worked from a "schematic" drawing of the circuit, which showed how the various components were connected. On a large layout table, the PCB designer manually drew in the components and linked them with black tape (or ink), to produce a "photo master" film which was in turn used to project the design photographically onto the base material of the circuit board. As circuits became more complex, the manual process bogged down.

As boards became more complex, specialized computer hardware and software began to help designers and engineers solve complex design problems. By the mid 1970s, system vendors began to offer CAD (Computer-Aided Design) systems specifically developed for PCB designing. Racal–Redac, Inc., a British firm, was the first to offer a powerful special-purpose PCB-oriented system. Based on Digital Equipment Corp.'s PDP-11 computer, the Redac product was the first to permit PCB designers to interact with the computer; designers could try various routings of

traces and see how they looked on the graphic display. This approach competed well against established systems such as Computervision, whose general-purpose equipment was priced in the $500,000 class and still lacked the interactive design capability.

By 1982, prices for PCB design systems had fallen below $100,000. New CAD equipment makers entered the field, with automated routing or documentation features that carried substantial advantages over the established Redac software. Calay and Cadnetix, as examples, introduced strong entries—neither being compatible with the Redac or Sci-Cards equipment already in the field. Racal—Redac Ltd., however, had perhaps taken the greatest strides to tailor its software to run on a variety of hardware platforms. Said Ian Orrock, Chief Executive of Redac's electronics CAD division in England, "We're all going to end up being software houses."

Another important feature of the new CAD equipment was ease of use; the older CAD/CAM systems might require months of learning time before a designer became proficient. In the late 1970s, with high equipment costs and low availability of trained designers, only the largest electronic firms designed and produced their own PCBs. Service bureaus took advantage of the market opportunity, acting as the primary design resource for smaller clients and as peak load designers for firms with in-house capacity. As electronics firms purchased and began to use the newer systems, however, they wanted service bureaus to be equipped with similar or compatible machines. Service bureaus felt the pressure to acquire the most up-to-date hardware and software available, in order to qualify as bidders on that work.

Service Bureau Operations

When a service bureau invested in CAD equipment, the sheer size of the investment created pressure to use the equipment intensively. Multi-shift operations were common, but the supply of designers to man them was severely limited. Typically, a service bureau did not hire permanent staff for all three shifts: the work load was too unpredictable. Service bureaus generally hired moonlighting designers from established electronics firms to staff their second and third shifts.

The design of printed circuit boards requires a peculiar combination of skills, primarily in spatial geometry, circuit insight, memory, and persistence. A talented designer—perhaps capable of completing a complex design in three weeks of console time—might be several times more productive than a "journeyman." In the early 1980s, talented designers willing to work odd shifts were earning over $100,000 per year; few of them had college educations.

Most customers requested separate quotations for each board; often, customers asked for bids from several service bureaus. Design clients always ran on tight schedules, Jeff Stevens observed, wanting their work to be delivered "yesterday":

Circuit board design is usually one of the last steps before a new product goes into production. Our design time is the customer's time-to-market. It's natural for them to be in a hurry.

For the design of a large, complex, 4-layered PCB a client might pay between $10,000 to $15,000. Such a project might require five to six man-weeks of labor input (two thirds of which might be designer's time); it might involve extensive communication between Applied CAD personnel and a wide variety of the client's technical personnel, and it would often require Applied CAD personnel to work through the night at various project stages to make deadlines. In such a typical project, much of Applied CAD's time would be spent sorting out and coordinating conflicting information and directions from different technical people in the client company. Stevens noted,

Even our clients themselves won't always know completely what they want. When we take their directions to their logical conclusions, problems often occur. Then we have to show them what developed. You spend a lot of time on the phone with clients, sometimes at 3 A.M. Often, I wind up making decisions for the client, so the work can go ahead; later, I have to convince the client the decision was right.

Design reliability remained a key attribute of a service bureau's reputation, since whole product lines (or engineers' jobs) might depend on the PCB design's working properly, and on its prompt delivery:

We had one job, in the old days, where a satellite was literally sitting on the launch pad, waiting for a corrected module design. The engineers had discovered a design flaw. They flew into town with the specs, and then took turns sitting behind the designer at the scope, or sitting beside their hotel room telephone, waiting to answer any questions that might come up. In this business, you have to deliver.

When the design phase of a job was finished, the computer tape or disk would be carried to a second service bureau for creation of the film photoplots needed for manufacturing. The equipment for photoplotting was far more complex and expensive than the computer systems needed for design. Only a few design shops in New England had their own photoplotting capability; they performed this work for other service bureaus and in-house design departments as well as for their own design clients.

The actual production of PCBs might be done by the client company itself or by a fabrication shop which specialized in the work. New England was home to some 80 to 100 fab shops, many of which offered

EXHIBIT 3   Low-Cost PC Board Design Software Available, Spring, 1987

COMPANY	PRODUCT	BASE PRICE	REQUIRED HARDWARE	OPERATING SYSTEM	AUTO ROUTER	AUTO-ROUTER PRICE	AUTO-PLACEMENT	COMPATIBLE NET LISTS	MAX. # OF COLORS	MAX. # OF TRACES	MAX. # OF COMPONENTS	MAX. # OF LAYERS	PACKAGING TECHNOLOGIES
Abacus Software	PC Board Designer	$195	Atari 520ST or 1040ST	GEM	•				2	1,100 Lines	250	2	
Accel Technologies	Tango-PCB	$495	IBM PC/XT or PC/AT	MS-DOS	•			Accel, Omation, Orcad	16	26,000 Lines	1,000	9	SMD
Aptos Systems	Criterion II	$4,000	ARTIST 1 CAR and IBM PC/XT or PC/AT	MS-DOS	•	$5,000	•	Aptos, Futurenet, P-CAD	16	2,000 Lines	1,000	50	SMD, ECL, Analog
Automated Images	Personal 870	$8,000	IBM PC/XT or PC/AT	MS-DOS				Applicon, Futurenet, Orcad	16			16	SMD, Hybrid
B&C Microsystems	PCB/DE	$395	IBM PC/XT or PC/AT	MS-DOS (and the Autocad Drafting package)				B&C	16				
CAD Software	Pads-PCB	$975	IBM PC/XT or PC/AT	MS-DOS	•	$750	•	Futurenet	16	4,511 nets	764	30	SMD, Fine-Line
Case Technology	Vanguard PCB	$4,250	IBM PC/AT, SUN-3 or DEC Microvax	MS-DOS, UNIX, or VMS	•	$5,500	•	Case	16	2,000 nets	1,000	256	SMD
Daisy Systems	Personal	$8,000	IBM PC/AT or Daisy PL386	DNIX				Daisy	7	14,000 Lines	14,000	255	SMD
Dasoft	Project: PCB	$950	IBM PC/XT or PC/AT	MS-DOS	•			Dasoft	6			4	SMD
Design Computation	Draftsman-EE	$1,147	IBM PC/XT or PC/AT	MS-DOS	•	$2,450			16	4,000 nets	300	20	Fine-Line
Douglas	Douglas	$395	Apple	Macintosh					2				SMD, Analog

Manufacturer	Product	Price	Hardware	Operating system		Developer		Capacity			Technology
Electronics Electronic Design Tools	CAD/CAM PROCAD	$2,495	IBM PC/XT or PC/AT and 68000 Coprocessor	MS-DOS	•	Electronic Design Tools	16	10,000 nets	3,000	56	SMD, Constant-Impedance
Electronic Industrial Equipment	Executive CAD	$11,000	IBM PC/XT or PC/AT	MS-DOS	•	Electronic Industrial Equipment	16			4	SMD, ECL
Futurenet	Dash-PCB	$13,000	IBM PC/AT and 32032 Coprocessor	UNIX	•	Futurenet	4			10	Fine-Line
Hewlett-Packard	EGS	$7,000	HP 9000	HP-UX		HP	15			255	Hybrid
Kontron	KAD-286	$10,400	IBM PC/AT	MS-DOS		Kontron	64	5,300 Lines	3,200	255	ECL, SMD, Hybrid
Personal CAD Systems	PC8-1	$6,000	IBM PC/XT or PC/AT	MS-DOS	•	P-CAD, Futurenet	16	1,000 nets	300	50	SMD
Racal-Redac	Redboard	$12,000	IBM PC/XT or PC/AT	MS-DOS	•	Racal-Redac	16	1,900 nets	511	16	SMD
Seetrax (in U.S., Circuits & Systems)	Ranger	$5,000	IBM PC/AT	MS-DOS	•	Seetrax	16	10,000 Lines	1,400	16	SMD
Softcircuits	Pcloplus	$1,024	Commodore Amiga 1000	Amigados	•		16				
Vamp	MCCAD	$395	Apple Macintosh	Macintosh	•	Vamp	2	32,000 Lines	32,000	6	SMD, Metric
Visionics	EE Designer II	$1,875	IBM PC/XT or PC/AT	MS-DOS	•		16		999	26	SMD
Wintek	Smartwork	$895	IBM PC/XT or PC/AT	MS-DOS	•	Wintek	3			6	
Ziegler Instruments (in U.S., Caddy)	Caddy Electronic Systems	$2,495	IBM PC/XT or PC/AT	MS-DOS	•	Ziegler	16			128	Analog

Source: *EDN*, March 18, 1987, pp. 140–141. Used by permission.

design as well as manufacturing services. A few large firms (Hadco at $125 million in sales) were equipped to service very large orders—100,000 or more boards of a design—but most fab shops fell in the $1–$2 million size range, with an average order size of 25–30 relatively small boards. One shop estimated its average PCB was priced at $22 each, with a setup charge of $150.

Trends in PCB Design

By the end of 1986, a number of vendors had developed PCB design packages to run on personal computers—mostly the IBM XT or AT machines. These software systems, some including automatic routing, were priced as low as a few hundred dollars or as high as $13,000, and varied widely in their features and capabilities. In-house design capability became practical for most electronics firms, although many lacked the PCB expertise that still marked the better service bureaus. Freelance designers, too, could acquire their own equipment. Exhibit 3 compares the features and prices of twenty-four such software packages.

Clients were inclined to stay with their existing service bureaus, unless they were severely burned. Good relationships between service staff and engineering personnel helped minimize communication errors, and availability of the data base from the original job allowed for revisions or modifications at much lower cost.

In the 1980s, as the cost of entering the service bureau business dropped, many new firms appeared. Jeff Stevens observed, "When I started at Redac in 1978, there were three service bureaus in New England. By 1983 there were maybe a dozen. Now there might be seventy-five, and it could reach 100 in another year." In 1987, several competing service bureaus in the area were owned by former employees of Racal–Redac, where Jeff himself had learned the business. Exhibit 4 lists the major competitors in the northeastern United States in 1986.

For the longer run, some industry analysts speculated that constant advances in miniaturizing electronic circuits might permit semiconductor technology to reduce certain whole PCBs (such as those developed for computer memory) into a single IC chip.

APPLIED CAD KNOWLEDGE, INC.: HISTORY

Jeff Stevens had learned the rudiments of circuit board design in his first job after high school graduation, as a technician in a five-person product development laboratory. Here, in 1975, one of his duties was to prepare enlarged prints of circuits, using black tape on white mylar. In another, concurrent job as a technician in an electronics manufacturing firm, he learned how the circuits themselves worked.

In 1977, Stevens left his two technician jobs for an entry-level design position with Racal–Redac in Littleton, Massachusetts. Redac operated a service bureau to complement its sales of DEC hardware and British software. As a pioneer in the field, Redac at the time boasted a near-monopoly in powerful systems dedicated to PCB design. Jeff Stevens, in a training rotation, joined Redac's service bureau as a data-entry technician.

We had three computer systems—about twenty people altogether. A system then cost about $200,000 and a lot of companies didn't have enough design work to justify buying one.

In data entry, you prepare code to represent all the terminals and components on the board. I refused to code the first job they gave me, and nearly got fired. Finally I convinced them that the job *shouldn't* be coded: the turkey who engineered it had the diodes in backward, and the circuit wasn't going to work. About a week later, they put me in charge of data entry, supervising the guy who had wanted to fire me.

EXHIBIT 4   **PC Design Service Bureaus in New England**
Design Houses (Grouped by Sales Volume in Millions of Dollars)

0–$1 Million per Year	*$1–$2 Million per Year*
Abington labs.	Automated Images, Inc.
Berkshire Design	Automated Design, Inc.
CAD Tec	CAD Services, Inc.
Cadtronix, Ltd.	Antal Associates
Computer Aided Circuits, Inc.	Multiwire of New England
Dataline PCB Corp.	Teccon
Design Services	Tech Systems & Design
Energraphics	Kenex, Inc.
Graphics Technology Corp.	Alternate Circuit Design Technology
Herbertons, Inc.	Photofabrication Technology Inc.
Het Printed Circuit Design	
High Tec CAD Service Co.	*$2–$5 Million per Year*
Jette Fabrication	Tek-Art Associates
LSI Engineering	Strato Reprographix
PC Design Company	Altek, Co.
PAC-Lab, Inc.	Eastern Electronics Mfg. Corp.
Packaging for Electronics	Datacube, Inc.
PC Design Services	Owl Electronic Laboratories, Inc.
Point Design, Inc.	
Power Processing, Inc.	*$5–$10 Million per Year*
Product Development Co.	Triad Engineering Co.
Qualitron Corp.	Photronic Labs, Inc.
Quality Circuit Design, Inc.	
Research Labs, Inc.	*$10+ Million per Year*
Scientific Calculations, Inc.	Algorex Corp.
Tracor Electro-Assembly Inc.	ASI Automated Systems, Inc.
Winter Design	Augat Interconnection Systems Group
	Racal–Redac Service Bureau

Source: Beacon Technology, "New England Printed Circuit Directory."
Copyright © 1985. Reprinted by permission.

Stevens became a designer, then a lead designer, then operations manager of the service bureau. Under his leadership, the operation dramatically improved its reputation for quality and on-time delivery, as well as its financial performance:

When I took over in October of 1981, monthly sales were $50,000 and monthly expenses were $110,000. In six months we turned it around: monthly sales were $110,000 and expenses were $50,000. There had been a tremendous amount of dead wood. We had a big bonfire with it, and went from twenty-six people to

sixteen. In some ways, it was a brutal campaign, I guess.

In June 1983, Stevens left Racal–Redac to work as a consulting designer, helping electronics firms with their CAD decisions as well as doing freelance design work. He had developed design and management expertise and established a reputation in industry circles which he could now broker directly to clients who were familiar with his previous work.

In December 1983, Jeff established Applied CAD while still working from his home in Pepperell, Massachusetts. By purchasing used computer equipment and installing it himself in his living room, Stevens was able to hold his initial investment to $35,000; the largest cost element was $28,000 for the software purchased from his former employer. (Financial data on Applied CAD's last three years of operation are shown in Exhibits 5 and 6.)

> The equipment pretty well filled up the living room, and through the summer I couldn't run it during the daytime: we didn't have enough electricity to cool it down. Winter solved that problem though; I heated the house with a PDP-11.

In late 1984, Applied CAD leased a 1,000-square-foot office suite on the ground floor of a new building near the Merrimack River in Tyngsboro, Mass. Jeff Stevens designed the interior space to hold a central computer room (with special air conditioning), a darkened "console room" for the actual design work, and a large front office. By January 1985, the computing equipment was installed and operating. The console room was furnished with two Recaro ergonometric chairs (at $1,100 each) for the designers' use; the front office held a large receptionist's desk and a sparse collection of work tables, file cabinets, and spare hardware.

EXHIBIT 5   **Balance Sheet, Applied CAD Knowledge, Inc.**

BALANCE SHEET	1985	1986	1987
Assets			
Current assets			
Cash	$128,568	$ 14,148	$ 33,074
Accounts receivable, trade	18,865	15,375	14,250
Prepaid taxes and other current assets	4,853	1,200	5,074
Total current assets	152,286	30,723	52,398
Property and equipment	174,079	190,079	203,079
Less accumulated depreciation	48,697	86,357	124,062
Total property and equipment	125,382	103,722	79,017
Total assets	$277,668	$134,445	$131,415
Liabilities and Stockholders' Equity			
Current liabilities			
Accounts payable, trade	$178,685	$ 9,025	$ 21,823
Current maturities of long-term debt	13,300		
Income taxes payable	4,008		2,303
Other current liabilities	5,000	5,373	70
Total current liabilities	149,993	14,398	24,196
Long-term debt, less current maturities	41,121	83,247	53,663
Stockholders' equity			
Common stock, no par value; authorized 15,000 shares, issued and outstanding 1,000 shares	25,000	25,000	25,000
Retained earnings	61,554	11,800	28,556
Total stockholders' equity	86,554	36,800	53,556
Total liabilities and stockholders' equity	$277,668	$134,445	$131,415

Applied CAD's Organization

Jeff oversaw all operations in his company, did all the high level marketing and sales contact work with clients, and did much of the technical design work as well. Another full-time designer was hired in May 1985 but had to be terminated in September 1986 because of persistent personal problems. Steve Jones, Jeff's data manager and former assistant at Redac, became a full-time employee in January, 1986. Among other duties, Steve covered the telephone, and performed various administrative duties. Steve had a B.S. in Engineering and, before Redac, had worked for other PCB electronics companies. In April 1987 Jeff hired John MacNamara, a former subcontract designer, on a full-time salaried basis.

In May 1987 Jeff also hired a part-time person to keep the books, write checks, and handle other office related matters. For her first three months she focused on straightening out the books and tax related items. She was also trying to find time to set up an accounting package on the per-sonal computer. The package had been purchased in August 1986 (at the request of Board members), for the purpose of generating accurate monthly statements. Since the company's founding, the Board had been asking for accurate end-of-month data on sales, accounts receivable, cash balance, backlog and accounts payable. It also wanted monthly financial statements, although Stevens himself saw little point in them: Cash flow projections served his immediate needs. The accounting package was chosen by one of the Board members, based partly on its broad capabilities. For example, it could assist in invoicing and aging receivables.

Jeff had other capable designers "on call"—available for freelance project work when the company needed them. Depending upon the market, there were time periods when Jeff could obtain the services of several contractors to meet peak work loads. In general, design contractors worked on a negotiated fixed-fee basis for completing a specific portion of a design project. In July 1987, however (after sales in June

---

EXHIBIT 6   **Income Statement, Applied CAD Knowledge, Inc.**

	1985	1986	1987
Net revenues	$328,568	$232,540	$346,627
Cost of revenue			
Salaries, wages and outside services	134,686	116,835	209,998
Research and development	14,154	7,551	13,731
Software costs	65,131	18,864	
Total cost of revenue	$213,971	$143,250	$223,729
Gross profit	114,291	89,290	122,898
Selling general and administrative expenses	72,320	143,051	77,732
Operating profit	41,971	(53,761)	45,166
Bad debt expense			(28,660)
Interest income (expense), net	2,331	3,576	(10,103)
Income before income taxes	44,302	(50,185)	6,403
Income taxes	4,508	0	0
Net income	39,794	(50,185)	6,403
Retained earnings, beginning of year	21,760	62,385	22,154
Retained earnings, end of year	$ 61,554	$ 11,800	$ 28,557

reached approximately $50 thousand and the backlog reached $90 thousand), Jeff found it difficult to attract contract designers who had free time. The backlog consisted of about fifteen boards ranging in price from $800 to $15,000. Sales in the electronics industry had turned upward and in busy times everyone was busy. Consequently, free-lance designers were committed to their own customers or employers who were also busy.

Jeff's Board of Directors consisted of Jeff and two college professors from well-known institutions in the Boston area. Since the fall of 1985 the Board had met monthly for three to four hours, usually during the first week of the month. At most meetings the Board first discussed the previous month's sales and current levels of cash, accounts receivable, backlog and payables. Other typical agenda items ranged from the purchase of new equipment and/or software, to marketing and personnel problems.

At most meetings, the Board spent considerable time discussing the current business climate and the future sales outlook. This usually led to a discussion of hiring someone to take over the marketing and sales function. It was generally agreed that such a person could not only contribute to the company's growth in sales but also free up a considerable amount of Jeff's time that could be devoted to design and operational matters. When Applied CAD was busy, however, Jeff had very little to devote to finding, hiring, and working with such a person. When the firm was not busy, Jeff's concern over the reliability of future cash flows made him hesitant to make the major salary commitment that a marketing professional would require. He was aware of the contrary pressures: "I can't get out of the 'boom–splat' syndrome," he said.

To Jeff, the "splat" came when backlogs and cash balances fell. The winter of 1987, for example, had felt to him like hitting a wall. (Exhibit 7 shows monthly totals of sales, accounts receivable, backlogs and cash balances, as estimated by Jeff at monthly Board meetings.)

Hardware and Software

After moving into his new quarters, Jeff Stevens located another PDP-11/34 computer—this one for sale at $7,000. Adding it to his shop required purchase of another Redac software package, but the added capacity was needed. Other, competing CAD systems were now available, but the decision to stick with Redac seemed straightforward to Jeff:

> Racal–Redac systems had several advantages. They were specifically dedicated to PCB design work and they had software that was brutally efficient. They were familiar to most of the free-lance designers in the area. Wide acceptance of Redac's software makes it easier to get overflow work from companies that demanded compatibility with their own equipment. Not to mention that I know this gear backward and forward, and could keep several machines busy at once.

The Redac software was originally developed in 1972, which made it very old by industry standards. Jeff pointed out, however, that because machines were slower in 1972 and had much less memory, the software *had* to be extremely efficient. Having used this software for a long time, he said, "I've been able to make process modifications to improve its efficiency, and I know all its intricacies." Jeff had developed some proprietary software for PCB design work which he believed kept him at the cutting edge of the competition. At times, he wondered about the possibilities of licensing his proprietary software to other PCB design firms. He concluded, however, that the small market for this type of software

EXHIBIT 7   **Monthly Sales and Month-End Receivables, Backlogs, Cash Levels, Applied CAD Knowledge, Inc.**
(Dollar Amounts in Thousands)

	ACCOUNTS RECEIVABLE	SALES	BACKLOG	CASH
January 1986	$18	$20	$20	$98
February	—	10	—	N/A
March	18	10	12	62
April	18	10	20	28
May	24	20	26	26
June	—	10	—	N/A
July	14	25	—	18
August	70	50	30	15
September	90	40	—	8
October	50	30	—	26
November	19	5	10	17
December	24	10	18	14
January 1987	13	3	—	7
February	40	21	—	8
March	35	28	22	6
April	32	22	37	11
May	25	22	50	5
June	50	50	90	10
July	90	58	30	10

product would probably not justify the necessary marketing and additional product development costs.

In addition to the original equipment purchased by Jeff in 1983 the company purchased a VAX Model 11/751 and a Calay Version 03 in December 1985 at a cost of approximately $170,000. (See Exhibit 8 for the cash flow statements prepared for the bank to obtain a loan.) The VAX was intended to be used as a communications and networking device and as a platform for developing new software. The Calay was a dedicated hardware system that included an automatic router which could completely design certain less complex boards without an operator. On more complex boards it could complete a major percentage of the board, leaving a designer to do the re-

mainder. In September 1986, a software upgrade to Calay Version 04 was purchased at a cost of approximately $28,000. Although bank financing was available, Jeff decided to pay cash for this equipment, to avoid raising his monthly fixed expenses. The new purchases gave Applied CAD enough machine capacity to support some $2 million in annual sales.

When the Calay machine was purchased, Jeff and the Board felt that its automatic routing capability might open a new market for the company for less complex boards. Because the Calay was virtually automatic on certain applications the final price of these boards could be much less than if they were done by hand. Because of the lower price to the customer the Calay was also appropriate for designing

EXHIBIT 8   **Cash Flow Projections as of December 16, 1985, Applied CAD Knowledge, Inc.**
(Dollar Amounts in Thousands)

	DEC 1985	JAN 1986	FEB 1986	MAR 1986	APR 1986	MAY 1986	JUN 1986	JUL 1986	AUG 1986	SEP 1986	OCT 1986	NOV 1986	DEC 1986	1986 TOTAL
Sales	25	30	30	30	30	30	30	30	30	30	30	30	30	360
Expenses*	20	24	29.5	29.5	29.5	29.5	29.5	29.5	29.5	29.5	29.5	29.5	29.5	348.5
Profit	5	6	0.5	0.5	0.5	0.5	0.5	0.5	0.5	0.5	0.5	0.5	0.5	11.5
Opening cash	141	148	102	102.5	88	88.5	89	89.5	90	90.5	91	91	91.5	
Receivables	37	17	30	30	30	30	30	30	30	30	30	30	30	
Disbursements†	30	24‡	29.5§	29.5	29.5	29.5	29.5	29.5	29.5	29.5	29.5	29.5	29.5	
Taxes‖		39#		15										
Closing cash	148	102	102.5	88	88.5	89	89.5	90	90.5	91	91	91.5	92	

*Expenses include rent, heat, light, power, salaries, contract work, telephone, etc. This level of expenses will support sales double those projected.

†Figures do not include depreciation which would only influence total profit.

‡Includes loan payment of 4K/mth.

§Includes new employees at 66K/yr.

‖Taxes based on the following assumptions: 1985 profit of 150K; 50K software expense on new equipment; 20K depreciation on new equipment; 10K misc. expenses; investment tax credit of 15K.

#25% of equipment costing 156K.

boards that would be produced in smaller quantities. Finally, Jeff and the Board felt that the manufacturer of the Calay as well as the Calay user group would supply new customer leads. Some of these expectations had been met.

The Vax, however, was not being fully used as originally intended—to allow hands-off automation of the firm's varied pieces of computing equipment, as well as providing batch data processing capacity. In its ultimate form, the VAX might actually operate the older, more cumbersome systems. It would be able to juggle dozens of design tasks between work stations and autorouters, queueing and evaluating each job, and calling for human intervention when needed. One director, visualizing robots sitting in Applied CAD's Recaro chairs, called this the "Robo-Router plan." To carry it out would require an additional investment of approximately $15,000 in hardware and another $10,000–$20,000 in programming, along with a significant amount of Jeff's time. The investment would result in very substantial cost reductions and reduced dependence on freelance designers, but it would only pay for itself under high volume conditions.

CURRENT BUSINESS OPTIONS

In August 1987, Jeff was contemplating the current business climate, his accomplishments with Applied CAD over the past three years, and the direction in which the company was headed. His major objective, and the Board's was growth. Jeff had discussed many times with the Board the need for a marketing person and a promotional brochure for the company. On occasion, he had talked with marketing people about Applied CAD's needs, but most of these prospective employees lacked the level of skills and PCB experience Jeff hoped to acquire. He had also talked with commercial artists about design of a brochure. Jeff and his Board felt that a "first class" brochure would cost $5,000–$10,000.

Marketing in the PCB business, especially among companies with sales of under $1 million, was characterized as informal. Very few companies had full-time people devoted to the marketing task; in most cases it was the owner–president who handled marketing and sales. Most small companies had their own list of faithful customers and new customers tended to come by word of mouth. In the under $1 million segment it was not uncommon for a company when extremely overloaded with work to farm out a board to a competitor. Also, certain other services, such as photoplotting, were done by shops that also did design work. Consequently, there was considerable communication among the competitors; the players seemed to know who got what jobs.

The marketing job at a company like Applied CAD consisted mainly of coordinating the advertising and a sales brochure, calling on present customers, and attempting to find new customers. Such a person needed a working knowledge of PCB design, which required experience in the industry. People with the qualifications necessary normally made a $40,000–$50,000 base salary plus commissions; frequently their total compensation exceeded $100,000 per year. Of major concern to Jeff was Applied CAD's erratic history of sales and cash balances, and the difficulty of predicting sales volume any further than two months in advance (see Exhibit 7). He balked at taking on responsibility for an executive-level salary, lacking confidence in the future. "This would probably be somebody with kids to feed or send to college," Jeff said. "How could I pay them, in slow times?"

Still, marketing appeared to be the function most critical to achieving the growth rates Jeff Stevens and his Board hoped for. It was key, also, in meeting the major potential threat posed by the recent availability of inexpensive software that could enable personal computers to design printed circuit boards (see Exhibit 3). Jeff had heard that some of that software could perform almost as well as the more expensive equipment that was being used by Applied CAD. He wondered how the advent of PC-based design might be viewed as an opportunity, not a threat.

Four possible responses had occurred to Jeff and his people: Applied CAD could ignore the PC software, adopt it, distribute it, or sell its own software to the PC users. Ignoring the new technology might work in the short run, since the complex boards designed by Applied CAD would not be the first affected; in the long run, however, failure to keep up with technology would leave more and more jobs subject to low-cost competition.

By adopting the new software for his next equipment expansion, Applied CAD could take a proactive stance. Jeff could buy a system or two to see how good they were, and hire people to work on the new systems on a freelance basis. Of course, he would need a flow of jobs to experiment with. A variation of this alternative was to sit back and wait while ready to move quickly if he saw something developing.

A third alternative, acting as a distributor for the PC software, would give Applied CAD a product to sell to prospects who insisted on doing their own design. This could establish relationships with people who might later need overload capacity.

Fourth, Applied CAD could proceed with development of its proprietary software, creating a product to sell to PC users. Jeff estimated that his Automated Design Review System could save both time and grief for other designers. In some tasks, it could cut required design time in half. In all jobs, the capability to check the finished design against the original input automatically and completely could improve quality. ADRS already existed in rough form; it was one of the elements which would make up the "Robo-Router" system, if that were implemented.

Many of these options seemed to require significant marketing skills—areas where the company was presently weak. The technical questions could be answered, if Jeff had time to work on them. But the marketing questions called for a person with extensive industry experience, broad contacts, a creative imagination, and the ability to make things happen.

Amid all the other problems facing the owner of a small business, Jeff was trying to figure out how to shape his business for the long-range future, and how to attract the kind of person he could work with to assure growth—and survival.

Applied CAD Knowledge, Inc. (B)

Raymond M. Kinnunen • John A. Seeger

In September 1987, as the summer rush slowed, Jeff Stevens began to talk seriously with Jerry King, regional Sales Manager of Calay Systems, Inc., about the marketing problems of Applied CAD Knowledge, Inc. Stevens wanted someone to become in effect a co-worker and officer of the small firm. King had been a principal in his own service bureau in the very early days of automated PCB design, and retained friendships and contacts with high level personnel in many electronics firms. (Exhibit 9 shows King's resumé.)

After a month of conversations and negotiations, including a meeting with the Board of Directors, the two men reached tentative agreement on employment terms which would give King a 3% commission on all company sales, a car allowance, and a base salary of $40,000 per year. Because the marketing person would be influential in pricing many jobs, it was important to preserve his regard for profitability; King was offered a stock interest in Applied CAD, contingent on the bottom line at the end of 1988. With a handshake of agreement, Stevens set out to reduce the terms to an employment contract letter.

The following night, Jerry King called Stevens to express his regret that he would be unable to accept the Marketing VP position, after all: he had just received an offer from AT&T, to set up Australian operations for a new venture. It was simply too good an offer to refuse, King said. A dejected Jeff Stevens reported the development at the next Board meeting; "We're back to square one," he said. "And the next 'splat' is just about to arrive."

Applied CAD's monthly sales dropped to half their mid-1987 level, and the backlog dropped to near zero. On December 8, however, Jerry King called Jeff to say he had just decided against Australia, and would like to apply again for the Marketing Vice President position, if it was still open. Jeff agreed, and the next day Jerry presented to Jeff and the Board a plan for reaching $1 million in sales in 1988, and for growing by $1 million per year in the following two years. (This plan is partially reproduced in Exhibit 10.) Concerned with the timing of cash flows, one of the directors asked how long it would take to generate enough new sales to cover their added marketing expenses. King responded, "If I couldn't provide more than enough sales to cover my pay, I wouldn't take the job."

Although not officially joining Applied CAD until January 4, Jerry spent the rest of December in joint calling, with Jeff, on customers where Calay and Applied CAD

EXHIBIT 9 **Resumé**
Jerry King

Married
Four Children
Excellent Health

EDUCATION

Fairleigh Dickenson University, Madison, New Jersey
Major: Business Administration

U.S. Navy, Electronics "A" School, Pearl Harbor, Hawaii

Continuing Education, including numerous seminars and workshops in Corporate Finance, Power Base Selling, Territory Time Management, The Art of Negotiating, Computer Graphics in Electronics, Sales Management and Marketing Techniques.

EXPERIENCE

General Business Management: Establishing policies and procedures for high volume cost efficient business operations, planning promotions for new business development, hiring, training and supervising personnel, including management level, designing and conducting management, sales, marketing and CAD/CAM training seminars internationally.

Technical Background: Twenty-one years of direct Printed Circuit Design, Fabrication and Electronics CAD/CAM marketing experience. Helped to create detailed business plans for three start-up companies including a high volume printed circuit design service bureau and raised five million dollars in venture capital used to purchase state-of-the-art CAD/CAM systems and other related equipment. Managed the development and marketing of a PCB Design Automation turn-key system which was sold exclusively to Calma/GE in 1977 and integrated with their GDS1 TRI-DESIGN system. Very strong market knowledge in Computer Aided Engineering (CAE), Computer Aided Design (CAD), Computer Aided Test (CAT), and Computer Aided Manufacturing (CAM).

ACCOMPLISHMENTS

Particularly effective in areas of personnel management, motivation and training, thereby increasing sales volume, production flow, productivity and employee morale. Significant career accomplishments in customer relations, marketing and sales leadership and management.

EMPLOYMENT HISTORY

1986–Present   Calay Systems Incorporated, Waltham, Massachusetts
Senior Account Manager

Responsible for a direct territory consisting of Northern Massachusetts, Vermont, New Hampshire, Maine and Quebec.

1985–1986   Automated Systems Incorporated, Nashua, N.H.
Eastern Regional Sales Manager

Responsible for regional design and fabrication service sales with a regional quota in excess of $5 million.

1981–1985   Engineering Automation Systems, Inc., San Jose, CA.
Western Regional Sales Manager.

Responsible for new Printed Circuit Design CAD/CAM system. Set up regional office, hired and trained sales and support staff of twelve people. Western regional sales were in excess of fifty percent of the company's business.

September 1984 Promoted to **National Sales Manager**.

1978–1981   Computervision Corporation, Bedford, Massachusetts
National Product Sales Manager.

Responsible for all electronic CAD/CAM system sales and related products. Provided direct sales management and training to the national field sales team, conducted sales training internationally, assisted in developing competitive strategy, technical support and new product development. Reported to the Vice President of North American Division.

March 1980 Promoted to **Manager, Corporate Demonstration and Benchmark Center**.

Managed team of 38 people who performed all corporate level demonstrations and benchmarks. Supported field offices with technical information and people worldwide. Reported to the Vice President of Marketing Operations.

1966–1978   King Systems, Inc., San Diego, Calfornia (A Printed Circuit Design CAD/CAM and NC Drilling Service Bureau.)
Founder, President, Chairman and Major Stockholder.

Served as Chief Executive Officer in charge of all aspects of the operation. Primary activities in sales management, direct field sales and customer relations. Responsible for financial administration, production operations and personnel administration. Assessed future needs and created business planning for increasing market share, facilities capability and penetrating new market opportunity. Developed a new concept in contract services for blanket sales to large government and commercial prime contractors.

shared some interests. In these first weeks, the "chemistry" Jeff Stevens had hoped for became readily apparent. The two men's skills complemented each other well: this would be a highly effective team, Stevens believed.

As 1988 began, King and Stevens continued to work closely together. Because Applied CAD's office layout did not provide the privacy needed for telephone prospecting, Jerry worked out of his home, joining Jeff several times per

---

EXHIBIT 10   **Excerpts from Jerry King's December 9, 1987 Presentation to the Board**

INTRODUCTION

The plan is a detailed road map for taking Applied CAD Knowledge, Incorporated (ACK) from the current sales volume to more than three million annual sales volume over the next three years. It identifies target markets, competitive environment, and sales tactics which will be used for achieving the sales projections during the plan period from January 1st 1988 through December 31st 1990. The projections show a monthly breakdown for 1988 and a yearly number for 1989 and 1990. The monthly projections were created on Lotus and provide for projected, forecasted and actual sales bookings for each month. As each month passes the actual numbers are entered and a goal status report is generated as part of the end of month reporting. At the end of each quarter a new quarter will be added so that there will always be four consecutive quarters of monthly projections.

The aggressive growth which is outlined will require significant expansion of facilities, personnel and equipment in order to maintain consistent QUALITY and ON TIME deliveries and insure REPEAT BUSINESS from established customers. It is required that the management and the Board of Directors of ACK provide the necessary production controls and capital/operating budgets to support expansion commensurate with sales volume increases over the term of the plan.

The PCB design service market can be divided into three major segments. Each of these segments will include companies that design and manufacture electronic equipment for Commercial, Industrial, Aerospace and Military vertical market areas.

Major Accounts and Government Sub-contractors (MA)

Major Accounts and Fortune 1000 companies. They present a significant opportunity for multiple board contracts and blanket purchase agreements. Any one company could fill ACK's capacity.

Primary Accounts (PA)

Primary accounts are companies that have been doing business for more than three years (not a start-up) and typically do between 5-500 million dollars in annual sales. These companies represent the most consistent level of business The type of contracts available from this market segment are usually on the level of one to four board designs per month. Typically, each board or project has to be sold separately at the project engineering level.

Venture Start-up Accounts (VA)

Venture start-up companies usually are operating on stringent budgets. They typically have no internal CAD capability and therefore must rely on outside service. The business potential for this market segment is very significant. This market represents a high risk and therefore is avoided by the major competitors leaving more opportunity for the smaller operation. It is not unusual to obtain sole source product level contracts from companies in this market.

BOOKINGS PROJECTIONS FOR APPLIED CAD KNOWLEDGE, INC. (BY JERRY KING 12/9/87)

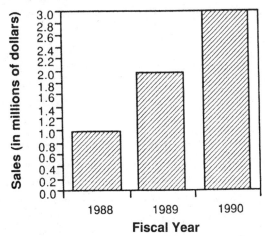

PCB DESIGN MARKET

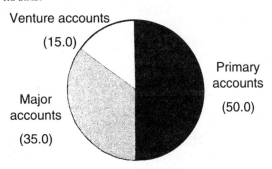

Source: Frost & Sullivan, October, 1985.

week on joint sales calls. At the January 8 meeting of the Board of Directors, the two men presented detailed sales projections for the first quarter and broader estimates for the entire year (see Exhibits 11–13). One account alone—California PrinCo—held the promise of some $250,000 in sales over the next four months. An old and

---

EXHIBIT 11   **Sales Projections Presented to the Board, January 8, 1988**
PART A: Forecast First Quarter 1988: Sales by Customer

ACCOUNT NAME	JAN 50%*	90%*	FEB 50%	90%	MAR 50%	90%	TOT 50%	TOT 90%	GRAND TOTAL
Customer A	.0	20.0	.0	8.0	20.0	.0	20.0	28.0	48.0
Prospect I	.0	7.0	.0	.0	.0	.0	.0	7.0	7.0
Prospect II	5.0	.0	2.0	.0	2.0	.0	9.0	.0	9.0
Customer B	.0	.0	12.0	.0	.0	.0	12.0	.0	12.0
Customer C	12.0	.0	.0	.0	.0	.0	12.0	.0	12.0
Customer D	.0	.0	12.0	.0	.0	.0	12.0	.0	12.0
Customer E	.0	30.0	.0	.0	20.0	.0	20.0	30.0	50.0
Prospect III	.0	.0	15.0	.0	20.0	.0	35.0	.0	35.0
Prospect IV	.0	.0	15.0	.0	20.0	.0	35.0	.0	35.0
Prospect V	.0	6.5	.0	.8	.0	3.8	.0	11.1	11.1
Customer F	.0	.0	.0	7.0	.0	.0	.0	7.0	7.0
Total	17.0	63.5	56.0	15.8	82.0	3.8	155.0	83.1	238.1

*Percentages (50% and 90%) are the estimated likelihood of receiving an order from a particular customer.

EXHIBIT 12   **Sales Projections Presented to the Board, January 8, 1988**
PART B: Forecast Fiscal Year 1988: Bookings by Product Type

	SERVICE	SOFTWARE	TOTAL	ACCUMULATIVE TOTAL
January	33	15	48	48
February	48	5	53	101
March	53	15	68	169
Quarter 1	134	35	169	
April	60	5	65	234
May	68	15	83	317
June	75	5	80	397
Quarter 2	203	25	228	
July	80	15	95	492
August	85	0	85	577
September	88	15	103	680
Quarter 3	253	30	283	
October	90	8	98	778
November	95	15	110	888
December	98	15	113	1001
Quarter 4	283	38	321	

steady customer of Applied CAD, PrinCo was nearing a decision on a major expansion in their use of circuit boards.

January sales totalled only $6,000 but many prospects seemed close to signing for large orders. At the February 19 Board meeting, Jeff and Jerry predicted sales of $100,000 per month for February and March; it appeared a 1988 sales goal of $1,000,000 might still be reachable. (Exhibit 14 shows monthly sales and backlogs through January, 1988.)

EXHIBIT 13   **Sales Projections Presented to the Board, January 8, 1988
PART C: Total Forecasted First Quarter 1988 Sales by Customer**

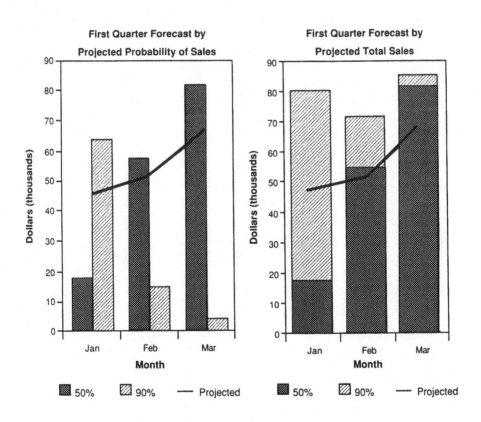

EXHIBIT 14   **Monthly Sales and Month-End Receivables, Backlogs, Cash Levels, Applied CAD Knowledge, Inc.**
(Dollar Amounts in Thousands)

	ACCOUNTS RECEIVABLE	SALES	BACKLOG	CASH
January 1986	$18	$20	$20	$98
February	—	10	—	N/A
March	18	10	12	62
April	18	10	20	28
May	24	20	26	26
June	—	10	—	N/A
July	14	25	—	18
August	70	50	30	15
September	90	40	—	8
October	50	30	—	26
November	19	5	10	17
December	24	10	18	14
January 1987	13	3	—	7
February	40	21	—	8
March	35	28	22	6
April	32	22	37	11
May	25	22	50	5
June	50	50	90	10
July	90	58	30	10
August	—	25	—	10
September	34	25	50	21
October	62	48	9	8
November	50	24	—	—
December	14	34	9	33
January 1988	8	6	—	19

Questions

1. What industry did Applied CAD Knowledge belong to? Was it perfectly competitive? A monopoly? Monopolistically competitive? Oligopolistic?

2. Was the structure of this industry changing during the 1980s? In what way? If so, to what extent was this change responsible for Jeff Stevens's problems?

3. Were barriers to entry falling during the 1980s? If so, what would you expect to be the effect on Applied CAD Knowledge?

4. Did Applied CAD Knowledge achieve satisfactory results in 1986 and 1987?

5. Are there serious principal-agent problems at Applied CAD Knowledge? If so, what are they?

6. Based on the economic state of its industry in the mid-1980s, do you think that the prices that Applied CAD Knowledge obtained for its services fell in 1986 and 1987? Was this part of the reason why results in 1986 and 1987 may not have been regarded as satisfactory?

7. Comment on Jerry King's presentations to the firm's board of directors. If you had been a member of the board, what questions would you have asked him?

CASE SIX

CATCO Electronics Corporation (USA)
Patrick L. Schul • William A. Cunningham • Lynn E. Gill

Irvin Bosworth, West Coast Distribution Manager of CATCO Electronics Corporation, stared balefully at the two letters lying before him on the table (Exhibits 1 and 2). Concerned, he poked impatiently at the intercom button.

"Linda, would you get Mr. Kano on the line for me?" Mr. Bosworth was wanting to confer with Yoshi Kano, Assistant to the President of CATCO, Inc., special staff liaison, charged with overseeing the affairs of CATCO Electronics (USA), a division of CATCO, Inc., a large multinational medical electronics firm headquartered in Osaka, Japan.

"Yoshi-san," he began, "I need to talk to you about Speedy Cargo; they're asking for a meeting to discuss a rate increase, and . . ."

"Wait a minute, Irv." Kano interrupted, "I thought we settled on agreed rates with Speedy Cargo when we met with them last year!"

"We did, Yoshi-san, but apparently times have changed, and now they're asking for not only a rate increase, but some other concessions on detention charges and the like. I've got two letters from their distribution manager, John Patrick, here on my desk explaining the situation and I've

scheduled a meeting here with John and his people for next Tuesday."

Yoshi Kano clenched his teeth. "Irv, this creates a real problem for me, especially since I gave CATCO (JAPAN) cost projections on the new budget based on the old rates. How can I go back now with different numbers? It's impossible!"

"I know, Yoshi-san," Irv replied, "it's a tough situation. But they have given us good service. I think we owe them some consideration."

"O.K., Irv, I'll take a second look at the Speedy Cargo situation. But, I'd also like to consider some alternative options. Why don't you spend the rest of the day on this. Find out what our alternatives are, then meet me in the morning at 8:00 a.m. sharp in my office to go over the matter."

On hanging up the phone, Irv remembered that his immediate boss, Wayne Smith, the West Coast Marketing Manager, had been instrumental in CATCO's decision to use Speedy Cargo. In fact, if memory served him right, Wayne was a personal friend of John Patrick of Speedy Cargo. If anyone could help solve this Speedy Cargo problem, Wayne could. Turning back to the telephone, Irv dialed Wayne Smith's number.

EXHIBIT 1   **Letter to Irvin Bosworth**

September 7, 1987

Dear Irv:

For the past 18 months, Speedy Cargo trucking has been providing container trucking services to CATCO Electronics Corporation (USA). We are located close to CATCO, and can conveniently supply CATCO with containers to unload when CATCO opens at 8:00 a.m. We securely lock CATCO's loaded containers overnight inside a burglar alarmed building to protect them from theft. Similarly, we remove all empty containers from CATCO to Speedy Cargo's yard in the evening. Speedy Cargo carries $500,000 cargo insurance on CATCO's containers. Our owner/operator drivers have been willing to work at night and on weekends on several occasions when strikes in the harbor or work delays have necessitated it. CATCO is a very important customer to Speedy Cargo, and we value our association.

Speedy Cargo's rates were guaranteed until October 1, 1987. Now Speedy Cargo must ask CATCO to adjust these rates to meet the needs of Speedy Cargo and our owner/operator drivers. During the past 12 months Speedy Cargo moved 1155 containers for CATCO. During most of this time, Speedy Cargo paid the owner/operator drivers $54 per roundtrip. On July 19th, Speedy Cargo increased the compensation to owner/operator drivers to $60 per roundtrip, or a $6 increase per container.

During 1986–87, Speedy Cargo earned a 3.5 per cent gross margin on trucking revenues of $489,404. Based on trucking industry standards, a minimum of 5% gross margin (95% operating ratio) would be expected by Speedy Cargo as a reasonable return. Adjusting for cost increases we have incurred, and to allow a reasonable rate of return, a rate of $115 per container is requested by Speedy Cargo for 1987–1988.

There is a second area that should be adjusted. Our drivers are paid the same to bring a container to the yard, and then hook up and move the container to CATCO's facility the next morning, as they are to bring the container directly to CATCO from the harbor. This is true also of empty containers taken to Speedy Cargo's yard at night. This results in an inequity for drivers who store containers in the building overnight or pull out empties from CATCO to the yard. I propose that CATCO be billed $15 for respotting containers from the yard to CATCO and from CATCO to the yard. This will compensate the drivers for the extra hook-up and for the extra driving time involved. The number of containers moved averages three in the morning and three empties at night.

For CATCO's convenience, Speedy Cargo advances certain charges and then bills CATCO for reimbursement. Examples are for container demurrage at the pier, trip permits for unlicensed chassis, and forklift charges for loose freight. Because CATCO's payment cycle is about 45 days, CATCO's has use of Speedy Cargo's working capital during that period. I propose that Speedy Cargo's bill charges advanced with a 10% surcharge to compensate us for handling the payment and for use of our money. Alternatively, CATCO's could provide Speedy Cargo with a deposit against which charges could be drawn, which could be replenished as needed.

The proposed changes in rates will allow Speedy Cargo to remain competitive in attracting the good owner/operator drivers needed to provide CATCO with excellent service. We have enjoyed working with everyone at CATCO, and look forward to a long and mutually beneficial business relationship.

Sincerely,

John C. Patrick
President

CATCO ELECTRONICS BACKGROUND

Irv Bosworth, Wayne Smith, and Yoshi Kano are all employed by CATCO Electronics Corporation, a large multinational firm based in Osaka, Japan. As indicated, Irv Bosworth is the West Coast Distribution Manager for CATCO Electronics (USA). Wayne Smith, West Coast Marketing Manager, is his immediate boss. Yoshi Kano, Assistant to the President (USA), is a special staff liaison, charged with overseeing the affairs of the United States division of the firm. (Organization charts for both CATCO (USA) and Speedy Cargo are presented in Figure 1.)

In addition to its well-known line of medical computers, the firm is a full-line producer of a diverse mix of electronics products utilized primarily in medical technological applications. Its sales worldwide are over two billion dollars, and sales in the United States are rapidly approaching the half billion mark. Like many other electronics firms, CATCO Electronics had disappointing sales in 1986–1987. However, a turn-around in the economy was expected to produce a better year for 1987–1988. Expectations were that a sales increase of between 10 and 20 percent might be realistic.

EXHIBIT 2   **Second Letter to Irvin Bosworth**

September 9, 1987

Dear Irv:

We have discussed that Speedy Cargo has been experiencing excessive waiting time at some piers to pick up or return CATCO's containers. As the economy has recovered, the volume of containers moving through the harbor has increased significantly. According to forecasts of West Coast traffic in the August issue of Handling and Shipping, these increases are expected to continue. Planned harbor expansion of container cranes and transfer facilities are several years away. The steamship companies so far have resisted keeping the piers open for more than 8 hours per day (the rail ramps are open 24 hours per day).

The result of the increased volume of containers moving through the harbors is that waiting time to pick up a full container or return an empty container has increased at certain piers and for certain steamship companies. I have attached a list of piers, pier operators, and steamships served by each pier, indicating those where we are experiencing excessive waiting (see Attachment).

Planned time to pick up a container from the harbor, deliver it to CATCO, and return the empty to the harbor is 2 1/2 hours. With this turnaround time, a Speedy Cargo owner/operator driver can make from 3 to 4 roundtrips daily for which he is compensated $60 per roundtrip, averaging $1000 per week. This barely compensates the driver for his time, fuel, maintenance, and investment in his tractor.

Recently, at certain piers it has been taking as much as 4 or 5 hours to pick up or return one container. This significantly reduces owner/operators' ability to earn a living, making them reluctant to continue pulling containers. This also requires Speedy Cargo to retain a greater number of drivers to move the same number of CATCO's containers.

Many trucking firms in the harbor area are instituting a charge for waiting in the harbor beyond 2 hours per roundtrip. Firms such as Cargo Trucking, and Well Established Freightlines have instituted this charge. Speedy Cargo proposes to institute a $25 per hour charge for time spent waiting over 2 hours for CATCO's containers. This will go to Speedy Cargo owner/operators, not to Speedy Cargo. The charge is set intentionally below what the driver could earn by completing the roundtrip with no waiting. Speedy Cargo will keep stringent control of logged times and stamped gate times to monitor waiting time charged.

Steamship companies either operate their own container transfer stations at the piers, or contract for these services from pier operators. The better steamships provide sufficient cranes and operators (longshoremen) to provide adequate service. They also own an adequate supply of maintained and licensed chassis. Other steamship companies, unfortunately, operate out of congested terminals. If a ship is being worked, cranes are not available to put containers on chassis for delivery to customers. Chassis often are not available, are in poor condition, or are not licensed. When chassis are not licensed properly, we must purchase a trip permit at a cost of $5.

Speedy Cargo often is faced with a choice of accepting a bad order chassis or waiting for a good chassis. If the drivers try to take exceptions for damages on the interchange documents, they must wait to exchange the chassis for a good chassis or pull into a repair facility for repairs. This causes excessive delays. Often, in order to service CATCO's delivery requirements, we have taken bad order chassis. When we return these chassis, exceptions for damages are inevitably taken on the interchange and Speedy Cargo is billed for repairs. We must then either try to resolve the repair charges with the steamship company, or pay the charges in order to avoid being cut off from picking up the steamship's containers. In some cases, we have asked you and our other shippers to intercede with the steamship on our behalf, because shippers have economic power over the steamships whereas we do not.

Shippers such as CATCO have a certain degree of control over waiting time in the harbor by selecting steamships that provide adequate facilities and chassis. I know that certain steamship companies providing lower prices are often accompanied by inferior service in the harbor, an inadequate supply of chassis, and poorly maintained or unlicensed chassis. It is my understanding from some of the other carriers that a few large shippers bill the steamship companies back for waiting time charged by truckers resulting from delays in the harbor. You may wish to consider negotiating this with the steamship companies that you use.

By CATCO (USA) allowing Speedy Cargo Trucking to charge for waiting time, Speedy Cargo will be able to retain and attract a sufficient supply of owner/operator drivers to provide you with the excellent service we have provided before the waiting time problem arose. We look forward to your favorable response.

Sincerely,

John C. Patrick
President

P.S. If you or Mr. Kano would like to ride with a driver for a day to witness the harbor operation first-hand, we can arrange it.

ATTACHMENT

Container Terminals

Waiting Time To Pick-Up Or Return Containers

Little or No Waiting

PIER	PORT	OPERATOR	STEAMSHIP
93	San Pedro	Private	American President
208	Terminal Island	Matson	Matson, NYK, Showa
228	Long Beach	Private	Sealand
229	Long Beach	Private	Maersk
230	Long Beach	Private	U.S. Line
232	Terminal Island	Solar International	Yang Ming
246	Long Beach	Pacific Container Terminal	TMM (Mexican), Cosco, Columbus, HK Island, Italian, Char Ching, Star Shipping, Westwood, Yugoslav Line

Intermittent Waiting

127	San Pedro	Los Angeles Container Terminal	K Line, Japan Line, Mitsui OSK, YS Line
243	Long Beach	Long Beach Container Terminal	Korea SS, Seapac OOCL, NOL

Frequent Waiting

234	Long Beach	ITS	Zim, K Line, YS Line, Japan Line, Mitsui OSK, Karlander, Hapag Lloyd, KS Line, CGM, Galleon

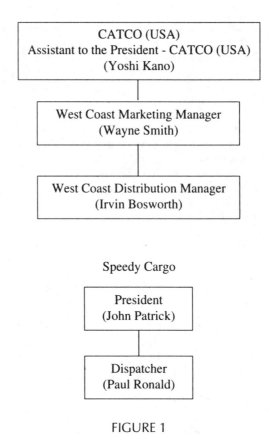

FIGURE 1

**Organizational Charts Showing Reporting Relationships in
CATCO (USA) and Speedy Cargo Trucking**

MEETING AT SPEEDY CARGO HEADQUARTERS

Paul Ronald leaped to his feet as he saw his boss, Mr. John Patrick, rushing down the hall past his office. Hurrying after him, he shouted, "Hey John! Wait up. I really need to talk to you!"

As John slowed to a fast walk, Paul continued, "We have a real problem with our drivers. I've tried to tell you about it several times before. Several drivers have quit, and when I run ads for owner operators, as soon as they find out that the job includes harbor work as well as pigs, they aren't interested. Especially when I tell them what they will be paid. We are so short of drivers, we can't handle all of the business that comes our way; and the drivers are constantly hitting me up for more money on container moves. We just can't continue like this anymore!"

"What the heck are you talking about?," shouted John angrily as he disappeared through the door to the warehouse. "We just gave those drivers an increase from $54 a round to $60 a round, and we didn't even get a rate increase from CATCO! How the heck can they expect to be paid more when I'm losing money on that account as it is? Paul, as dispatcher, you've just got to take a stronger stance with those drivers."

SPEEDY CARGO BACKGROUND

Speedy Cargo Trucking is a local shorthaul carrier certificated by the Public Utility Commission of California as a California contract carrier. However, the majority of its revenue is derived from providing specialized exempt local cartage of trailer on flatcar (TOFC) freight, better known as piggyback trailers or "pigs," and cartage of ocean containers out of the local harbors.

Trailers arrive at the railroad piggyback ramps, where they are unloaded from railroad flatcars. Speedy Cargo hauls the trailers to customers' warehouses for unloading, and then returns the empty trailers back to the railroad. The complete cycle is called a "round." Similarly, Speedy Cargo picks up empty trailers from the railroad ramp, takes them to customers to be loaded, and then delivers the loaded trailers back to the railroad where they are loaded onto flatcars for shipment to eastern points.

Speedy Cargo's harbor business consists of picking up ocean containers on chassis from the steamship companies and delivering those containers to customers for unloading at their warehouses. The empty containers are then returned to the steamship companies' wharfs in Los Angeles and Long Beach harbors. Also, in some cases, empty containers are picked up at the wharfs to be loaded for export shipping.

A third aspect of Speedy Cargo's business is a bobtail trucking operation. Speedy Cargo is a division of Lincoln Warehousing, Inc., a public warehousing firm operating over 300,000 square feet of warehousing and distribution space in Southern California. The bobtail operation exists primarily to deliver freight in the Southern California area. In addition, the bobtail trucks pick up and deliver "loose freight" (freight that is not in ocean containers or that has been unloaded from ocean containers at transit sheds located in the harbor).

Picking up loose freight in the harbor and delivering it requires that drivers load the freight onto their trucks at the transit sheds or container freight stations and also unload the freight at the customer's warehouse. The firms operating the harbor freight transit facilities charge the trucking firm picking up freight for rental of forklifts to bring the freight to the tail of the truck for loading. Forklifts are charged at $20 per hour, and on average two hours are required for loading at the transit shed. Forklift and other charges such as demurrage on freight held in the harbor beyond the "free time" are traditionally advanced by the trucking company and then billed back to customers. Depending upon the payment performance of the customer, these charges may be outstanding from 30 to 60 days. Demurrage charges are also billed by steamship companies for containers held beyond allowed free time in the harbor, usually because the containers are awaiting payment of customs duties and subsequent release by U.S. customs. These charges are also extended by the trucking company and billed back to the customer.

In certain cases, the steamship company also charges the truckline detention for containers and chassis which are held beyond free time (usually three days) for pickup in the harbor, unloading, and return of the empty to the harbor. Sometimes, the shipper holds a container too long, past the one day allowed to unload a container, and is billed for detention by the trucker. In other cases, the trucking company does not return the container from its yard to the harbor on a timely basis and must bear the cost of detention which is typically $8.50 for each day the container is held beyond free time.

In some cases, when there is a congested condition in the harbor and at certain wharfs, the trucker will not return empties in order to get more loaded containers out of the harbor for customers.

Returning an empty container may entail delays of two or more hours when volume at wharfs is too great for the cranes and available personnel to handle. The truck driver then bobtails (runs without a container attached) back to the harbor to pick up another full container, and earns revenue only on the loaded leg of the journey. Consequently, later on, an empty container must be taken from the yard to the harbor with no full container available from the return leg out of the harbor. This results in the driver running uncompensated miles. The trucker has a difficult time charging the shipper for detention on empties held in this manner, even though the detention resulted in order to provide expedited delivery service to the shipper when there is congestion at the wharf.

2nd MEETING AT SPEEDY CARGO

Later that day, John Patrick stopped at the dispatcher's office to see Paul Ronald. "I'm sorry I was so short with you, Paul," he began. "This situation with the owner operators really has me upset. I really don't know what they expect me to do. My back is against the wall with CATCO Electronics. CATCO is one of our major accounts and we would really be hurt if we lose them. The trouble is, they know it!"

"I hear what you are saying," Paul responded, "but what am I supposed to tell the owner operators? Is any chance you could explain to the folks at CATCO that we need to pay the drivers more to keep them?"

"I hope so. But, you know how hard it is to get changes through . . . what with the confusing way the Japanese make decisions. Let's put our heads together next week and see what arguments we can come up with. In the meantime, here is the year-end profit and loss for the total firm and the trucking division (Exhibit 3), the current container rates for CATCO

and the volume of business we had with them last year (Exhibit 4). Look them over, and we'll get together next week to plan our attack."

LATER THAT DAY

Later that day, John Patrick poked his head into the driver ready room and greeted Ray Nicholson, an owner operator driver who has been with Speedy Cargo Trucking for many years. Ray looked a bit solemn.

"How are you doing, Ray?"

"Not so good," Ray answered. "I've been tied up all day at Pier 234 trying to get containers out of the harbor for CATCO. The wait lines are impossible; I got two whole containers delivered. Paul really must be down on my case to stick me with that detail—I'm going broke!"

Squirming in his seat, he continued. "When I get to work pigs, I can do at least five rounds a day without busting my hump, and I average $60 per round. No way can I get by on two loads a day out of the harbor! Some days I get tied up all day for one lousy load, and on good days I can only do 3 or 4 containers a day! I need to gross at least $1,200 per week to make the payment on my tractor, pay my bills, and have something left over for my wife and kids. I'd rather just work on pigs and leave the containers for someone else!"

John looked thoughtful. "It's too bad you are having problems, Ray. Could you help me out with some cost information on handling containers? Maybe I can use it when I talk to Irv Bosworth at CATCO about our rates for next year."

A few days later, John found a cost report, prepared by Ray's accountant, on his desk (Exhibit 5). He wondered how he might be able to make use of it, or if he should invite a driver representative to go with him to the negotiations at CATCO. He made a mental note to discuss this with Paul Ronald when they meet next week.

EXHIBIT 3   **Lincoln Warehousing, Inc.**
Statement of Earnings For Year Ended August 30, 1987

	YEAR-TO-DATE	%
Revenue		
Trucking Division	$ 489,404.20	
Warehousing	6,537,821.40	
Expenses (Warehouse division only)		
Salaries	3,399,667.10	52.0
Transportation	588,403.93	9.0
Advertising	65,378.21	1.0
Over, Short, and Damage	98,067.32	1.5
Depreciation	653,782.14	10.0
Interest	915,295.00	14.0
Insurance	163,445.54	2.5
Office Expense	98,067.32	1.5
Taxes and Licenses	26,151.29	0.4
Entertainment and Travel	39,226.93	0.6
Total	$6,047,484.80	92.5
Income	490,336.61	7.5
Revenue		
Charges Advanced for Customers	$ 19,469.75	
Trucking revenue	469,934.45	
Total	$489,404.20	100.0
Expenses		
Salaries	38,920.10	8.0
Advertising	2,065.10	0.4
Automobile Expense	1,432.89	0.3
Charges Advanced for Customers	19,882.26	4.0
Owner Operators	355,016.99	72.5
Damages, Demurrage, Shortage	3,589.80	0.7
Equipment Rentals	1,178.00	0.2
Insurance	10,363.08	2.1
Office Expense	1,930.00	0.4
Postage	617.34	0.1
Rent	29,736.00	6.1
Taxes and Licenses	500.00	0.1
Telephone	5,613.35	1.1
Travel and Entertainment	1,648.11	0.3
Total	$472,493.37	96.5
Income	$ 16,910.83	3.5

225

ONE WEEK LATER

John Patrick hunched over the conference table and peered at Paul Ronald over the top of his glasses. "Well, Paul," he questioned, "where do you think we ought to head with our preparations to work this deal out with CATCO? I understand they've asked for a meeting next Tuesday to discuss the situation."

Paul rubbed his chin thoughtfully and began tentatively, "First, John, there are a few things I need to understand before we get into this thing. First off, I was surprised at how much we pay for insurance!"

"It does seem like a bunch." John agreed, "Of course that covers all of our liability insurance, as well as cargo insurance. For most shippers, we carry cargo insurance of $50,000 per container. Because the value of the cargo in most containers is less than that, we pay a minimum of $5,000 per year for cargo insurance, and then it's adjusted at the end of the year to one percent of freight billings."

"CATCO is a different matter. Because of their high value cargo, we need to carry cargo insurance in the amount of $500,000 per container. We report that separately, and that insurance policy runs 6 percent of revenue billing on CATCO's business."

"Wow! They do sock it to us on high value cargo. But I guess that the insurance cost per container is reasonable in relation to the possible loss of a container. Is it reflected in the rates? By the way, how did you ever come up with rates based on so many containers per month?"

"Well, Paul, that happened a few months before you arrived on the scene. Irv Bosworth called me in for a meeting with Yoshi Kano, their Assistant to the President in Japan. They informed me that they had a bid from a competing firm to provide ser-

---

EXHIBIT 4   **1986–87 Container Rates for CATCO Electronics (USA)**

First 60 containers per month	$92
Next 61–90 containers (monthly)	85
Over 91 containers (monthly)	55

1986–87 Containers Moved for CATCO Electronics (USA)	
October 1986	89
November	50
December	62
January 1987	71
February	86
March	120
April	84
May	99
June	144
July	142
August	119
September	89
Total	1155

EXHIBIT 5   **Analysis Of Owner-Operator Costs**

CAPACITY	3 round trips/day	
	5 days/week	
	15 trips/week	
	52 weeks/year	
	780 trips/year	
ALLOCATED COSTS		PER ROUND TRIP
Maintenance	$3,600/year	$4.61
Major Repairs	2,400/year	3.08
Insurance	3,000/year	3.85
Taxes	720/year	.92
License	2,650/year	3.40
FUEL		
	20 mile round trip	
	: 5 MPG	
	4 gallons @ $1.10	4.40
LABOR		
$10/hr × 1.42 fringe		
& taxes =	$ 14.20	
	10 hrs/day	
	$140.20	
divided by 3 trips/day	3	46.73
Amortization		
$20,000.00 tractor		
:4 years		
$ 5,000.00 amortization		
780 trips		6.41
COST FOR OWNER-OPERATOR PER ROUND TRIP $73.40		

vice on the basis of the number of containers moved, and what did I want to do about it? We were getting $92 a round before that."

"I had a meeting with the drivers to figure out what we should do—meet the price or bow out. They voted to take a cut from $60 to $54 a round to keep the business. Of course, about the only one of our 10 drivers still around that remembers that is Ray Nicholson!"

"Another thing," Paul continued. "What's this charge for rent on the statement? The trucking operations shares facilities with warehousing—how can we get socked with

a charge for rent? If we weren't in trucking, the space we use would still be there! It's not fair to charge that to us, and it makes us look not very profitable."

"I hear what you are saying," John answered in a surprised tone. "We charge the trucking operation for an acre of yard space for storing empties, for the space required to store loaded containers inside the building, and of course for office space you occupy."

"When we leased the building, we looked for one with enough yard space for our trucking operation. And, I might add, the trucking P & L statement does not include a charge for general expenses and administration. That's carried as burden in its own cost center. At our current sales volume, G & A runs about 10 percent of total sales."

The meeting continued for several hours of give and take to iron out an approach to renegotiation of next year's rates with CATCO.

2nd MEETING AT CATCO HEADQUARTERS

Irv Bosworth and Wayne Smith were both in Yoshi Kano's office 8:00 sharp the morning following their initial meeting. Irv spun the two letters from Speedy Cargo Trucking (Exhibits 1 and 2) onto Kano's desk. "Look these over when you get a chance, Yoshi-san. In the meantime, to refresh your memory, here are Speedy Cargo's current rates and the number of containers we moved last year (Exhibit 4)."

After skimming over John Patrick's two letters, Yoshi Kano responded, "Gentlemen, if I remember correctly, when Speedy Cargo took over our trucking business from Port Container Pullers last year, they agreed to meet the rate that had been proposed by Japan Overseas Trucklines, a rate of $92 per container for the first 60 containers, $85 for the next 30, and $55 for over 90 containers per month. Is this not the case?"

"This is true, Yoshi-san," Wayne responded. "But let's set the record straight. While Port did work out good for us for a few years, they went belly up on an $85 rate. While we started Speedy Cargo at a higher rate of $92 per container, we required them to carry $500,000 cargo insurance, a substantially higher level than the standard $50,000 coverage. As you know, this request was based on our experience of having a container stolen out of Port Container's yard. John Patrick told me the insurance coverage costs Speedy Cargo an extra $7 per container, which they tacked onto what we were paying Port. Of course, after we hit them with the proposal from

Japan Overseas, that cost just got folded into the rate. Apparently they're just not able to provide the necessary service under these rates and conditions. All I hear about is the troubles they're having getting all of our containers out of the harbor, how congested some of the wharfs are and the trouble Speedy Cargo has attracting and keeping good drivers. That's really their major problem."

Pointing his finger out at Wayne, Kano angrily replied, "Wayne, you and I both know that Japan makes all the decisions about what steamship lines to use. We simply abide by their decisions at this end. I'm sick of hearing that excuse!"

"Look Wayne," Kano continued, "I don't mean to fly off the handle like this. But you know the pressure we have been getting from both ends over this new Just-in-Time inventory technique. The whole industry, including our customers, are insisting we provide more frequent deliveries in smaller quantities. Our biggest customer, Logon Manufacturing, Inc., is shoving this whole JIT thing down our throat, and Japan agrees with them. They keep referring to us as 'partners in production', but they want this extra service with almost no price increase. Japan feels that the entire industry will force JIT on all suppliers and we might as well gear up for the change."

Irv looked confused. "I know our sales force has been throwing around this Just-in-Time thing, but I'm not sure what it is or how it will affect us."

"I've been aware of this problem," stated Kano. "We Japanese live by the JIT philosophy but Americans are just now beginning to see the light. That's why I asked Bill Kanban, our West Coast Head of Operations, to prepare a report on JIT and how it will impact on our company. You should have that report (Exhibit 6) by this afternoon. In the meantime, let's get back to our problem at hand."

Irv responded, "I really wonder if their 10 drivers are enough to take care of us, especially when the end of the month rolls

EXHIBIT 6   **Memo from Bill Kanban**

TO: All West Coast Managers
FROM: Bill Kanban, Head of Operations
SUBJECT: Just-in-Time
DATE: September 9, 1987

In response to a request from Yoshi Kano, this memo is an attempt to briefly describe the Just-in-Time inventory philosophy now being implemented by most of our major customers. Also included is the impact this will mean to our operations. JIT has been utilized extensively by Japanese firms, including our parent company.

The basic philosophy behind JIT is that inventory is waste. Under JIT, orders are placed on relatively fixed schedules from suppliers, but in smaller and more frequent orders. The orders should arrive JUST IN TIME to be used in production. Inventory holding costs are to be eliminated or minimized.

In order for JIT not to simply be an excuse to push inventory back on us, our customers will work closely with us on their production needs. Since the majority of our sales are to firms located in Silicon Valley, our effective delivery radius is only 150 miles or 4 hours one way. As a result we feel we can safely guarantee 2 deliveries per day within a 1 1/2 to 2 hour time window, as opposed to our traditional 2 deliveries per week. With our proposed changes in transportation equipment, including using a mixture of our own and for-hire trucks, costs of providing this service should not increase above the 5 to 7 per cent range. Our first customer that will go to this schedule is D.K. Systems, who have indicated that they would be willing to renegotiate prices up to a 10% increase if we can live up to these performance standards. If our research is correct on our additional costs, this is a potential 3 to 5 percent increase in profitability. This is, however, a big if. As you know, over 90% of our sales come from 3 products—medfax communicators, digital blood delivery monitors, and medtech desktop computers. But, our shipments from Japan are full containers of only one item. Thus, to fill a complete order, no matter how big or small, will normally require 3 separate containers. It is not that uncommon to have to hold up several orders and trucks waiting for a container to be delivered from the port. Whatever the reason for the delay, this costs us money. Our drivers are teamsters and they cost us $21.76 per hour including fringes regardless of whether they are driving or not because the order is not ready. Given what the detention combined with waiting time costs are for the regulated carriers we use, their time sitting around drinking coffee is $13.79 per hour.

With our new proposed JIT delivery schedule this simply cannot happen. Therefore, the only insurance we can use is inventory, which runs counter to the JIT philosophy. More important, it is much more costly, and cost increases were not figured in when we arrived at the above estimates. Each container is worth about $500,000 to $750,000 and our inventory carrying costs run about 25 percent, as can be seen from the accompanying attachment. Japan only ships full containers, and we cannot store less than full containers for any length of time—due to our warehouse limitation. Any safety stock that we would contemplate keeping would be in container minimums.

I am aware of the problem expressed by Speedy Cargo concerning delay times at the docks. The same problem exists at the Japanese ports. I have spoken with Chet Haire who handles all outgoing shipments from the parent company. He is negotiating with On Time freight forwarders to handle the scheduling of all shipments, and promises that this problem will be taken care of in the next couple of months. However, it would be wise if we checked this out with whatever carrier we decide to use.

To sum up, I am confident that we can handle the transition to a JIT system within the costs outlined above. The "weakest link", as I see it, is the level and consistency of container deliveries from the ships. If this is resolved, then implementing a JIT system can be done efficiently.

around and we get our usual end-of-the-month peak inflow of containers. Good Lord, we might have 40 containers in one ship and the merchandise is already sold when it arrives! We need to get all that merchandise to the distribution center and shipped to make our month's end sales quota, and you know what CATCO (JAPAN) says when we don't. Paul Ronald, the Speedy Cargo dispatcher, always gives me a bunch of bull about CATCO being "Number One," but when we have a full warehouse crew ready to unload freight and the containers don't arrive as planned, I really wonder! I just want all our merchandise delivered on time, with no headaches!"

"I know we used Well Established Freightliners for many years prior to switching over to Port. Are they still around, Irv?" Kano queried.

"As a matter of fact, I talked to Glenn Canary over at Well Established yesterday. He indicated they would be more than willing to take on the business, but their rates are way out of line at $125 per container. I know they give great service; they own their own trucks you know; but they just can't compete with nonunion carriers."

"Anyone else?" pressed Kano.

"Well, I talked to Lenny Solox over at Solox Trucklines. I was favorably impressed with this guy. He wanted the business and would provide it for $92 per container. As far as getting the job done, he said he could get all the drivers we wanted . . . no problem."

"Solox also uses owner operators and not their own trucks. Lenny used to work for Well Established before he started his own firm. They have been in business for about 2 years now. Since both Solox and Speedy Cargo use the same source of drivers, I wonder how Lenny can guarantee drivers where John Patrick is having so much trouble. You know how the trucking business has been around here since deregulation. We've got more firms to pick from and rate discounts are rampant. However, a lot of these new trucklines are only around for a couple of years or less before they go belly-up. Their cash flow is so bad they resort to buying freight, even at a loss, just to have the cash coming in."

Wayne interrupted, "After Irv and I talked the other day about this problem, I called up Beth Logan over at Medco Systems, one of our competitors. She is their traffic manager and we have known each other for quite a while. They have used Speedy Cargo, Well Established and Solox for their deliveries, and Beth has kept a record of their performance on some vendor quality program she has for her personal computer. After a little sweet talking—"

"And a $135.00 dinner charged on your company VISA," laughed Irv.

EXHIBIT 7   **Vendor Quality Report Summary**

	SPEEDY CARGO	SOLOX	WELL ESTABLISHED
Average Transit Time	7	5	7
Truck Availability	5	5	9
Price	8	9	4
Reliability	7	4	7
Loss & Damage	7	5	8
Special Services	6	6	8
Claims Settlement	5	3	7
Bill Accuracy	6	4	8

"Yes," agreed Wayne, "Things I do for CATCO. Anyway, she agreed to give me a very abbreviated summary of their quality assessment of three carriers."

As Wayne passed out the report (Exhibit 7), he continued, "Although the report is somewhat general, I think it gives us an idea of how the three truckers rank relative to each other, at least as far as Beth sees it. It won't answer our problems for us, but it's the best I could get for $135.00. At least it gives us a basis on which to compare services."

Looking over the figures, Kano responded, "Wayne, I believe we are in a tough situation here. While I recognize the need for developing stronger continuity with our vendors, I am still very reticent to change the budget figures unless it's absolutely necessary. You must recognize my situation. However, given our discussion here, I do believe that we need to at least meet with Speedy Cargo to discuss their concerns. Before we meet, however, I want you and Irv to put your heads together and take a closer look at the inherent validity and impact on our operations of the Speedy Cargo proposals before we get to the table."

Questions

1. Is CATCO Electronics a perfectly competitive firm? A monopolist? Is Speedy Cargo a perfectly competitive firm? A monopolist?

2. Does Speedy Cargo engage in price discrimination?

3. If Speedy Cargo moves over 91 containers in a particular month for CATCO Electronics, does its revenue per container for those containers exceeding 91 cover its costs?

4. What are the costs and benefits to Yoshi Kano of changing the budget figures? Are they different from the costs and benefits to CATCO Electronics of such a change?

5. With the existing rates, is Speedy Cargo likely to continue operations?

6. If you were Yoshi Kano, would you approve the rate increase for Speedy Cargo? Why or why not?

7. If you were John Patrick, would you continue to deliver cargo for CATCO Electronics if CATCO refuses to approve the rate increase? Why or why not?

Part Five

RISK ANALYSIS AND CAPITAL BUDGETING

CHAPTER 14

Risk Analysis

Chapter Profile

The probability of a particular outcome is the proportion of times that this outcome occurs over the long run if this situation exists over and over again. Expected profit is the sum of the amount of money gained (or lost) if each outcome occurs times the probability of occurrence of the outcome.

A decision tree represents a decision problem as a series of choices, each of which is depicted by a decision fork or a chance fork. A decision tree can be used to determine the course of action with the highest expected monetary value. As an example, we took up the decision of whether or not to drill an oil well.

The expected value of perfect information is the increase in expected monetary value if the decision maker could obtain completely accurate information concerning the outcome of the relevant situation (but he or she does not yet know what this information will be). This is the maximum amount that the decision maker should pay to obtain such information. Using methods described in this chapter, one can calculate the expected value of perfect information.

Risk is often measured by the standard deviation or coefficient of variation of the probability distribution of profit. Whether a decision maker wants to maximize expected profit depends on his or her attitudes toward risk. The decision maker's attitudes toward risk can be measured by his or her utility function.

To construct such a utility function, we begin by setting the utility attached to two monetary values arbitrarily. Then we present the decision maker with a choice between the certainty of one of the other monetary values and a gamble where the possible outcomes are the two monetary values whose utilities we set arbitrarily. Repeating this procedure over and over, we can construct the decision maker's utility function.

One way to adjust the basic valuation model for risk is to use certainty equivalents in place of the expected profit figures in equation (14.7) in the text. Based on the decision maker's utility function, one may be able to construct indifference curves showing the certainty equivalent corresponding to each uncertain outcome.

Another way to introduce risk into the valuation model is to adjust the discount rate. Based on the decision maker's utility function, one may be able to construct indifference curves between expected rate of return and risk. Using such indifference curves, one can estimate the risk premium (if any) that is appropriate.

Uncertainty refers to a situation where the relevant probabilities cannot be estimated. Many rules, including the maximin rule, have been proposed as aids to decision making under conditions of uncertainty. According to the maximin rule, the decision maker should choose the course of action where the worst possible outcome is least damaging. There are important problems in this rule, as well as others proposed to handle the situation of uncertainty.

Questions

Completion

1. If a decision maker's utility function is _____ the decision maker maximizes expected monetary value.

2. The Millrose Company stores spare parts at two warehouses, one in Scranton and one in Cleveland. The number of defective and acceptable spare parts at each warehouse is given below.

| | *Number of spare parts* | | |
Warehouse	Defective	Acceptable	Total
Scranton	200	800	1,000
Cleveland	50	450	500

   If one of the 1,500 spare parts kept by the firm is chosen at random (i.e., if each spare part has a 1/1,500 chance of being chosen), the probability that it will be defective is _____ .

3. In the previous question, the probability that the chosen spare part will be at the Scranton warehouse is _____ .

4. In question 2, the probability that the chosen spare part will be *both* defective and at the Scranton warehouse is _____ .

5. In calculating the expected value of perfect information, it is important to recognize that the decision maker (does, does not) _____ know what this information will be.

6. When a decision maker applies the maximin rule, he or she assumes that nature (or whatever force determines the outcome of the situation) dictates that if any course of action is taken, the _____ outcome will occur.

7. Whether a decision maker wants to maximize expected profit depends on his or her attitude toward _____ .

8. A _____ fork is a juncture representing a choice where the decision maker is in control of the outcome.

9. A _____ fork is a juncture where "chance" controls the outcome.

10. If the decision maker's utility function is linear, she (will, will not) _____ maximize expected profit.

True or False

_____ 1. The maximization of expected utility results in the same decisions as the maximin rule if the utility function is linear.

_____ 2. Under conditions of uncertainty, it is easy to formulate optimal general rules for decision makers; they should maximize expected utility, using the known probabilities of the relevant outcomes.

_____ 3. Risk and uncertainty are indistinguishable.

_____ 4. According to the subjective definition of probability, the probability of a particular outcome is the proportion of times that this outcome occurs over the long run if this situation exists over and over again.

_____ 5. One problem with the maximin rule is that it ignores the maximum amount that the decision makers can lose.

_____ 6. If James Johnson is indifferent between the certainty of a $50,000 gain and a gamble where there is a 0.4 probability of a $40,000 gain and a 0.6 probability of a $60,000 gain, the utility he attaches to a $50,000 gain equals $0.4U(40) + 0.6U(60)$, where $U(40)$ is the utility he attaches to a $40,000 gain, and $U(60)$ is the utility he attaches to a $60,000 gain.

_____ 7. If a firm accepts a particular gamble, there is a 0.3 chance that it will gain $1 million and a 0.6 chance that it will lose $2 million. Based on this information, one cannot calculate the expected monetary value of this gamble to the firm.

_____ 8. If John Jeffries is a risk averter, his utility function is linear.

_____ 9. If Mary Solomon is a risk lover, her utility function is linear.

_____ 10. Martin Bush is willing to accept greater risks only if he obtains a higher expected rate of return. Thus, he is a risk averter.

Multiple Choice

1. If a decision maker is indifferent to risk, and if the expected value of perfect information is $40,000, the decision maker should be willing to pay the following for perfect information:

   a. $35,000.
   b. $45,000.
   c. $55,000.
   d. $65,000.
   e. $75,000.

2. If a decision maker is a risk averter for values of monetary gain above $10,000, then he or she

   a. must be a risk averter for values of monetary gain below $10,000.
   b. must be risk neutral for values of monetary gain below $10,000.
   c. must be a risk lover for values of monetary gain below $10,000.
   d. must be either a or b.
   e. none of the above.

3. William Moran rolls a true die. If the die comes up a 2, he receives $6,000; if it does not come up a 2, he pays $1,000. The expected monetary value of this gamble to him is

   a. $1,167.
   b. $833.
   c. $167.
   d. -$167.
   e. -$833.

4. William Moran's utility function is $U = 10 + 3M$, where U is utility, and M is monetary gain (in dollars). He will prefer the certainty of a gain of $20 over a gamble where there is a 0.3 probability of a $9 gain and a 0.7 probability of

   a. a $31 gain.
   b. a $29 gain.
   c. a $27 gain.
   d. a $25 gain.
   e. none of the above.

5. In the previous question, if William Moran has a 0.4 probability of receiving $100 and a 0.6 probability of losing $200, the expected utility of this gamble is

   a. -70.
   b. -80.
   c. -230.
   d. -250.
   e. none of the above.

6. The difference between the expected rate of return on a specific risky investment and that on a riskless investment is called

   a. the risk-adjusted discount rate.
   b. the risk premium on this investment.
   c. the investment's level of risk.
   d. all of the above.
   e. none of the above.

Problems

1. The Deming Company must determine whether or not to add a new product line. If the new product line is a success, the firm will increase its profits by $1 million; if it is not a success, its profits will decrease by $0.5 million. Deming's managers feel that the probability is 0.6 that the new product line will be a success and 0.4 that it will not be a success.

   a. If Deming's managers are risk neutral, should they add the new product line?
   b. How would you determine whether they are risk neutral?
   c. What is the expected value of perfect information to them?

2. A newspaper publisher in a small town must decide whether or not to publish a Sunday edition. The publisher thinks that the probability is 0.7 that a Sunday edition would be a success and that it is 0.3 that it would be a failure. If it is a success, he will gain $200,000. If it is a failure, he will lose $100,000.

   a. Construct the decision tree for this problem, and use it to solve the problem, assuming that the publisher is risk neutral.
   b. What is the expected value of perfect information?
   c. How would you go about trying to determine whether the publisher is in fact risk neutral?

3. A Tucson restaurant owner must decide whether or not to expand his restaurant. He thinks that the probability is 0.6 that the expansion will prove successful and that it is 0.4 that it will not be successful. If it is successful, he will gain $100,000. If it is not successful, he will lose $80,000.

   a. Construct the decision tree for this problem, and use it to solve the problem, assuming that the restaurant owner is risk neutral.
   b. List all forks in the decision tree you constructed, indicate whether each is a decision fork or a chance fork, and state why.

4. In the previous problem, would the restaurant owner's decision be altered if he felt that

   a. the probability that the expansion will prove successful is 0.5, not 0.6?
   b. the probability that the expansion will prove successful is 0.7, not 0.6?
   c. What value of the probability that the expansion will prove successful will make the restaurant owner indifferent between expanding and not expanding the restaurant?

5. The president of the Hawaii Company says that she is indifferent between the certainty of receiving $100,000 and a gamble where there is a 0.5 chance of receiving $250,000 and a 0.5 chance of receiving nothing. In the following graph, plot three points on her utility function.

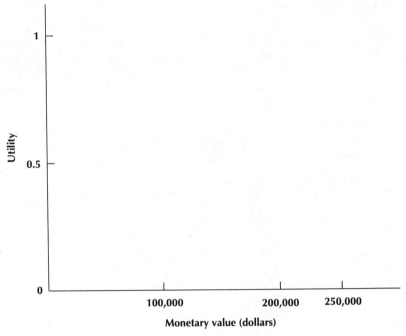

6. The utility function of the president of the Manhattan Company is shown below.

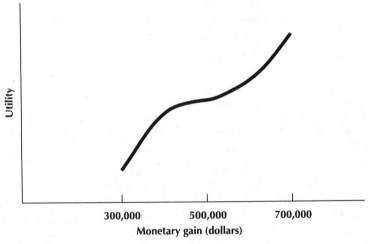

a. Is he a risk averter at all levels of monetary gain?
b. Is he a risk lover at all levels of monetary gain?
c. Does he prefer the certainty of gaining $400,000 over a gamble where there is a 0.5 probability of gaining $300,000 and a 0.5 probability of gaining $500,000?

7. If each card in a standard 52-card deck of playing cards has the same probability of being drawn, what is the probability that a single card that is drawn will be

a. a red 9?
b. a black ace?
c. a black card?
d. neither a red card nor a queen?
e. a queen, king, or ace?

8. a. The Rosetree Corporation is considering the purchase of a firm that produces tools and dies. Rosetree's management feels that there is a 50–50 chance, if Rosetree buys the firm, that it can make the firm into an effective producer of auto parts. If the firm can be transformed in this way, Rosetree believes that it will make $1 million if it buys the firm; if it cannot be transformed in this way, Rosetree believes that it will lose $2 million. What is the expected monetary value to Rosetree of buying the firm?

   b. In fact, the Rosetree Corporation decides to purchase the firm described in the previous question. Does this mean that Rosetree's management is (i) risk neutral, (ii) a risk averter?

9. The utility function of the president of the Howe Company can be represented by the following equation:

$$U = 10 + 2M,$$

where U is utility, and M is monetary gain (in thousands of dollars). He has the opportunity to invest $25,000 in a small electronics firm. He believes there is a 0.5 probability that he will lose his entire investment and a 0.5 probability that he will gain $32,000.

   a. If he makes the investment, what is his expected utility?
   b. Should he make the investment?

10. An appliance firm must decide whether or not to offer Roland Whelan a job. If Whelan turns out to be a success, the firm will increase its profits by $100,000; if he turns out not to be a success, the firm's profits will decrease by $80,000. The firm feels that the chances are 50–50 that he will be a success.

   a. What is the expected value of perfect information?
   b. What is the expected monetary value to the firm if it does not hire Whelan?
   c. What is the expected monetary value to the firm if it hires Whelan?

11. A firm must decide whether or not to go forward with an R and D project to develop a new process. If the project is successful, it will gain $5 million; if it is not successful, it will lose $1 million. Suppose that the firm has no idea of what the probabilities of success or failure may be. If the maximin rule is applied, should the firm go forward with the R and D project? Why or why not?

12. a. The Contact Engineering Company must decide whether or not to buy a piece of equipment. If it buys this equipment, and if the price of ammonia increases by more than 10 percent in the next year, it will make $3 million; if it buys the equipment and the price of ammonia does not increase by this amount in the next year, it will lose $2 million. If it does not buy the equipment, it gains (and loses) nothing, regardless of what happens to the price of ammonia. Construct a table showing the firm's profits if each possible outcome occurs, given that the firm takes each possible course of action.

b. What decision should the Contact Engineering Company make, if it applies the maximin rule? What criticisms can be made of this rule?

13. William McCarthy's indifference curve between expected rate of return and risk is shown below:

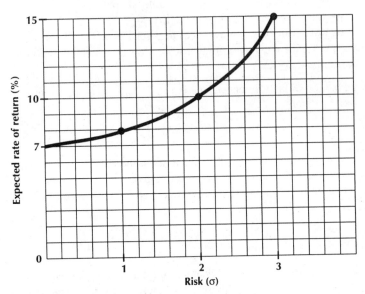

a. For him, what is the risk premium for an investment where σ = 3?
b. If σ = 2, what is the risk-adjusted discount rate?
c. What is the riskless discount rate?

Answers

Completion
1. linear   2. 250/1,500 = 1/6   3. 1,000/1,500 = 2/3   4. 200/1,500 = 2/15
5. does not   6. worst   7. risk   8. decision   9. chance   10. will

True or False
1. False   2. False   3. False   4. False   5. False   6. True   7. True
8. False   9. False   10. True

Multiple Choice
1. a   2. e   3. c   4. e   5. c   6. b

Problems
1. a. Yes.
   b. Construct the utility function of the decision maker.
   c. $200,000.

2. a.

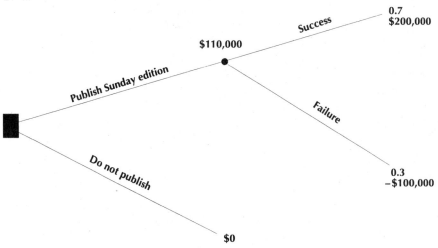

He should publish the Sunday edition.

b. .7($200,000) + .3(0) − $110,000 = $30,000.

c. Construct his utility function.

3. a.

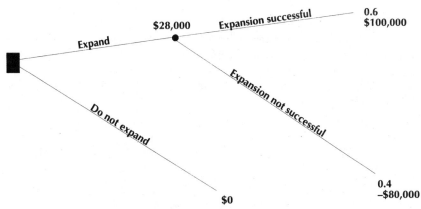

Since the expected monetary value if he expands is 0.6 ($100,000) +
0.4 (−$80,000) = $28,000, he should expand the restaurant.

b. The first fork on the left is a decision fork since the restaurant owner decides
whether or not to expand. The next fork is a chance fork, since "chance"
decides whether or not the expansion is successful.

4. a. No.

b. No.

c. 4/9.

5. Let zero be the utility of receiving nothing, and 1 be the utility of receiving $250,000. Then, since she is indifferent between the certainty of receiving $100,000 and the gamble described in the problem, the utility of receiving $100,000 must equal

$$0.5(1) + 0.5(0) = 0.5.$$

Thus, three points on her utility function are given below.

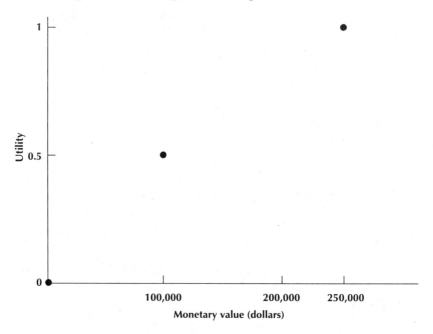

6. a. No.
   b. No.
   c. Yes.

7. a. 1/26.
   b. 1/26.
   c. 1/2.
   d. 6/13.
   e. 3/13.

8. a. 0.5($1 million) + 0.5(−2 million) = −$0.5 million.
   b. (i) No, since it would have chosen not to purchase it if it were risk neutral.
      (ii) No, since it would have chosen not to purchase it if it were risk averse.

9. a. The utility of −$25,000 equals 10 + 2(−25) = −40. The utility of +$32,000 equals 10 + 2(32) = 74. His expected utility equals 0.5(−40) + 0.5(74) = 17.
   b. Since the expected utility if he makes the investment (17) exceeds the expected utility if he does not make it (10), he should make it.

10. a. 0.5($100,000) + 0.5(0) – $10,000 = $40,000.
    b. zero.
    c. 0.5($100,000) + 0.5(–$80,000) = $10,000.

11. No, because the maximum loss if it goes ahead with the project is $1 million, whereas the maximum loss if it does not go ahead with it is zero.

12. a.

	Price of ammonia increases by more than 10%	*Price of ammonia increases by 10% or less*
	(Profits of Contact Engineering Company)	
Contact buys equipment	+$3 million	–$2 million
Contact does not buy equipment	zero	zero

    b. It should not buy the equipment. It assumes that the worse outcome will occur, if each action is taken. This may be far too pessimistic.

13. a. 8 percent.
    b. 10 percent.
    c. 7 percent.

CHAPTER 15

Capital Budgeting

Chapter Profile

The investment selection process is composed of four steps. (a) The firm must generate proposals for alternative investment projects. (b) For each of these proposed projects, it must estimate cash flows for the project. (c) It must evaluate each of the proposed projects and select those to be implemented. (d) It should review the projects after implementation.

For each proposed project, the difference between the cash flows with and without the project should be estimated each year on an after-tax basis. Indirect effects of the project on parts of the firm's activities seemingly far removed from the investment should be taken into account if the firm's cash flows are impacted.

If the outlays for an investment project all occur in the current year, the net present value of the project equals

$$\sum_{t=1}^{n} F_t / (1 + k)^t - I ,$$

where F_t equals the cash flow in year t, and I equals the investment outlay. If a project's net present value is greater than zero, it should be accepted; if not, it should be rejected.

Another measure of the profitability of a proposed project is its internal rate of return, which is defined as the interest rate that equates the present value of the net cash flows from the project to its investment outlay. Generally, if a firm accepts projects where the internal rate of return exceeds the firm's cost of capital, the results are the same as if the net present value criterion is used. (However, recall note 4 of Chapter 15 of the textbook.)

The cost to the firm of debt capital is the rate of return that must be paid to the investors. New long-term debt is often issued by firms at (or close to) par. If so, the after-tax cost of debt capital is the coupon interest rate times $(1 - t)$, where t is the firm's marginal tax rate.

The cost of equity capital is the equilibrium rate of return required by the investors in the firm's common stock. Assuming that the firm's dividends per share will increase at a constant compound annual rate of g, the cost of internal equity is $(D_1/W) + g$, where D_1 is the annual dividend paid next year, and W is the price per share of the firm's stock. The capital asset pricing model can also be used to estimate the cost of equity capital.

In calculating the net present value of a project, the firm should base the interest rate, k, on the weighted cost of capital, which is the weighted average of the costs of debt and equity capital, the weights being the proportions of debt and equity financing in the firm's desired financial structure.

The interest rate, k, should also be modified to reflect the riskiness of the project, as well as the attitudes of the firm's decision makers with regard to risk. The ways such modifications can be made have already been described in Chapter 14.

Questions

Completion

1. The decision maker should carry out any investment project with a _____ present value.

2. Mr. Smith buys a bond for $1,000. If the bond pays interest of $50 per year indefinitely, the interest rate is _____ percent. If the price of the bond increases to $1,500, the interest rate is _____ percent. If the price of the bond falls to $500, the interest rate is _____ percent.

3. If the interest rate is 10 percent, a dollar received a year from now is currently worth _____ , and a dollar received 2 years from now is currently worth _____. Thus, a business venture that will pay you both a dollar a year from now and a dollar 2 years from now is currently worth _____ .

4. If the present value of a dollar received 2 years from now is 85.7 cents, the interest rate must be _____ percent. If the interest rate is more than _____ percent, one dollar received 20 years from now is worth less than 15 cents now.

5. A _____ expenditure is a _____ outlay that is expected to result in a flow of future cash benefits (extending beyond one year in the future).

6. The first step of the investment selection process is to generate _____ for investment projects.

7. The cash flows used in evaluating an investment project should be the difference between the cash flows _____ and _____ the project.

8. To calculate the internal rate of return, we find the value of _____ that sets the project's net present value equal to _____.

9. The _____ is the relationship between risk and expected return for all stocks in the market.

10. _____ risk is due to cyclical changes in the economy and other broad movements that affect all stocks.

True or False

_____ 1. If an investment yields $100 per year indefinitely into the future, and the interest rate is 10 percent, the present value of this investment is $500.

_____ 2. If the firm maximizes profit, it will accept investments where the interest rate exceeds the rate of return.

_____ 3. If a firm borrows money to buy equipment at an interest cost that is less than the rate of return from the equipment, it will lose money.

_____ 4. Capital budgeting refers to decisions concerning a firm's choice of investment projects.

_____ 5. The stock market as a whole has a beta of zero.

_____ 6. Firms frequently assume that if they do not invest in new equipment, their profits will stay at current levels.

_____ 7. The cost of internal equity is $D \div (W + g)$, where D is the annual dividend, W is the price per share of the firm's stock, and g is the annual compound rate at which the firm's dividends per share increase.

_____ 8. Noncash items like depreciation are irrelevant in evaluating investment projects.

_____ 9. Estimates of incremental cash flow depend on what the alternative is, if the investment project is not carried out.

_____ 10. There may be no unique value of the internal rate of return.

Multiple Choice

1. The Mangrum Company buys a painting for $1,000 in 1996. If maintenance of the painting is costless, and if the interest rate is 0.10, how much must it sell the painting for in 1999 if the present value of the investment in the painting is to be nonnegative?

   a. At least $(1.10)^3 \times \$1,000$.
   b. At least $(1.30) \times \$1,000$.
   c. At least $1,000.
   d. At least $\$1,000 + (.30)^3 \times \$1,000$.
   e. None of the above.

2. The Mangrum Company can pay $50 now (for the coming year) and $50 a year from now (for the next year) for a service that protects against termites. Alternatively, it can pay $100 now (for the coming two years) for the service. The firm should be indifferent between these two alternatives if the rate of interest is

   a. zero.
   b. 2 percent.
   c. 5 percent.
   d. 10 percent.
   e. none of the above.

3. In the previous question, if the rate of interest is 10 percent, the cost of the second alternative exceeds that of the first alternative by

   a. zero.
   b. $4.55.
   c. −$5.00.
   d. $500.
   e. none of the above.

4. In question 2, if the rate of interest is 8 percent, the firm should be indifferent between the first alternative and paying _____ now (for the coming two years) for this service.

   a. $96.00.
   b. $96.30.
   c. $100.00
   d. $104.00.
   e. none of the above.

5. . Suppose the rate of return on alternative investments is 6 percent, and that a particular asset will yield $1,500 per year indefinitely. The asset is worth

   a. $9,000.
   b. $25,000.
   c. $90,000.
   d. $250,000.
   e. $100,000.

6. If a firm maximizes profit, the rate of return of the least productive project that is accepted by the firm must be _____ the interest rate at which the firm can borrow.

   a. less than
   b. 1/2
   c. greater than or equal to
   d. twice
   e. less than or equal to

7. The cost of internal equity is $\frac{D_1}{W} + g$, where

   a. D_1 is the annual profit of the firm.
   b. W is the price of the firm's product.
   c. g is the annual rate of increase of the firm's dividends per share.
   d. all of the above.
   e. none of the above.

Problems

1. The following excerpt from congressional testimony by executives of the Armstrong Cork Company describes the procedure it used to decide which investment projects to undertake.

    The more important aspects of the Armstrong Cork Company system can be summarized as follows:

    1. The economics of proposed capital appropriation requests are examined by the controller's office in consultation with the interested staffs like central engineering, research, industrial engineering, economic and marketing research, purchasing, and so forth, before presentation to top management.
    2. The basic evaluation is made in return on investment terms.
    3. An evaluation of risk is made, based on the length of time required to recover the cash to be expended.
    4. Management relies on these valuations in making appropriation decisions.
    5. Follow-up reports of the in-process status and actual results of capital appropriations granted are made annually by the controller's office to top management, which, in turn, discuss the results with the accountable persons.

    "Return on investment" or, as we use the phrase, "return on capital employed" (ROCE), is nothing more than the ratio of net profit after tax to total book assets. In the Armstrong Cork Company, ROCE is accepted as the basis for measuring operating management performance; the success or failure of all our individual and collective efforts to improve operations is reflected in our ROCE results. . . .

    All matters related to financing are reserved to a staff vice-president. The determination of what shall be financed is reserved, depending upon the amounts involved, for the executive committee of our board of directors or the board itself. In practice, the board of directors and its executive committee control "what shall be financed" almost entirely through our system of capital appropriation requests. This control of capital expenditures automatically controls the basic level of working capital. The general level of cash, accounts receivable, and inventories required by operations is determined basically by the types of businesses in which we operate. Since we are primarily a manufacturing company, the types of businesses we operate are established by the plant, property, and equipment we buy. Therefore, the board of directors and its executive committee, in controlling such purchases, indirectly but effectively control the types of business we operate and, consequently, the basic levels of cash, accounts receivable, and inventories.

    Our procedures for reviewing capital appropriation requests are designed specifically to fit the needs of our organization. They do this by profit and loss statements expressed in terms of ROCE. We place our emphasis on accuracy of perspective rather than on accuracy of detail. Our aim is to discover the best of the many potential expenditures.

    We don't attempt to provide the figure that makes approval or disapproval of a request automatic. The figures we develop are relative, not absolute. One of the most valuable results of our system will never be measured since it is the elimination of projects of low ROCE potential from consideration before an undue amount of valuable technical and management effort is expended upon them.[6]

---

[6] This description pertains to the situation a number of years ago.

a. Does this procedure attempt to accomplish the same objective as the present-value rule? Explain.

b. What differences can you detect between this procedure and the present-value rule?

2. A government program involves the training of disadvantaged teenagers. The cost of training each person is $8,000. With this training, he or she makes $500 more each year than he or she otherwise would. If this income differential is an adequate measure of the social benefit, and if the interest rate is 10 percent, is this program worthwhile?

3. The Winston Company is considering a $3 million investment in a new piece of equipment. If this investment is accepted, the company's cash inflow will be reduced by $3 million this year; its production costs are expected to fall by $450,000 per year over the next five years, and its inventory costs are expected to fall by $875,000 over the next five years. The piece of equipment will be depreciated over five years, using straight-line depreciation. The firm's marginal tax rate is 34 percent.

a. Determine the incremental after-tax cash flow each year from this investment.

b. If the marginal tax rate were 48 percent, not 34 percent, what would be the incremental after-tax cash flow each year?

c. If the cost of capital is 10 percent, what is the net present value of this investment, if the firm's marginal tax rate is 34 percent?

4. The Salem Corporation is considering the purchase of a new machine that costs $30,000, and that will reduce labor costs by $17,500 per year for the next four years. Its marginal tax rate is 34 percent.

a. If the discount rate is 15 percent, should the firm buy this machine?

b. If the discount rate is 8 percent, should the firm buy this machine?

5. The Trenton Company's common stock sells currently at $80 per share. Its dividend per share is expected to be $8 next year. In the past decade, its dividend per share has been increasing at a 10 percent annual rate, and this growth rate is expected to continue in the future.

a. What is the Trenton Company's cost of equity capital?

b. If the firm's common stock were to sell for $100, not $80, what would be its cost of equity capital?

c. If the dividend per share were to increase at 5 percent, not 10 percent (and if the common stock price were $100), what would be its cost of equity capital?

6. The Hartford Company wants to estimate its cost of equity capital. The beta for its stock is 0.9, the risk-free rate of return is 7 percent, and the rate of return on the average stock is 12 percent.

a. What is this firm's cost of equity capital?

b. If its beta were 1.2 rather than 0.9, what would be its cost of equity capital?

c. If its beta were 1.5 rather than 0.9, what would be its cost of equity capital?

7. The Riverside Corporation issues new long-term debt at par—that is, at $1,000 per bond. The coupon interest rate is 10½ percent. The company's marginal income tax rate is 34 percent.

   a. What is the firm's after-tax cost of debt?
   b. If the company's marginal income tax rate were 48 percent rather than 34 percent, what would be the firm's after-tax cost of debt?

8. The Buffalo Company is considering the purchase of a new truck, which would result in a $25,000 incremental after-tax cash outflow this year and a $8,000 incremental after-tax cash inflow for each of the next four years.

   a. What is the internal rate of return from this investment?
   b. If the cash outflow were $30,000 rather than $25,000 this year, what would be the internal rate of return?

9. The Evanston Company's after-tax cost of debt capital is 10 percent, and its cost of equity capital is 15 percent. What is its weighted cost of capital if

   a. the proportion of debt financing in the firm's desired financial structure is 40 percent and the proportion of equity financing in the firm's desired financial structure is 60 percent?
   b. these proportions are 30 and 70 percent, rather than 40 and 60 percent?

10. The Marble Orchard Bank is considering a large investment in new data-processing equipment. The effect on the bank's after-tax cash flow would be as follows:

Year	Effect on cash flow (million of dollars)
1993	−10
1994	3
1995	4
1996	3
1997	2
1998	1

   a. If the bank's cost of capital is 10 percent, what is the present value of the investment?
   b. If the bank's cost of capital is 12 percent, what is the present value of the investment?

Answers

Completion
   1. positive   2. 5, 3 1/3, 10   3. 90.9 cents, 82.6 cents, 173.5 cents
   4. 8, 10   5. capital, cash   6. proposals   7. with, without
   8. the interest rate, zero   9. security market line   10. Systematic

True or False

1. False 2. False 3. False 4. True 5. False 6. True 7. False
8. False 9. True 10. True

Multiple Choice

1. a 2. a 3. b 4. b 5. b 6. c 7. c

Problems

1. a. In crude terms, both seem to attempt to promote the wealth (or something like it) of the firm. The firm's executives are supposed "to use the capital they are allocated by the board to obtain the best possible return on it." However, this decision-making procedure does not focus directly on the wealth of the firm and is not the same as the present-value rule.

   b. Armstrong Cork used the ratio of net profit (after tax) to investment as a measure of the desirability of an investment project, whereas the present-value rule uses the present value of the investment project.

2. If the benefit continued indefinitely, its present value would be $500 \div 0.10$, or $5,000. This is an overestimate, since the benefit will not continue indefinitely. Since the cost is $8,000, the investment is not worthwhile. (Note that these figures are hypothetical, and that no judgment should be made concerning the effects of actual or proposed government programs.)

3. a.

Year	Incremental after-tax cash flow (million of dollars)
0 (this year)	-3
1	$(1 - .34)(.725) + 3/5 = 1.0785$
2	1.0785
3	1.0785
4	1.0785
5	1.0785

   b.

Year	Incremental after-tax cash flow (million of dollars)
0	-3
1	$(1 - .48)(.725) + 3/5 = 0.977$
2	0.977
3	0.977
4	0.977
5	0.977

c. t	Net cash flow (millions of dollars)	$\dfrac{1}{(1 + .10)^t}$	Net cash flow $\dfrac{}{(1 + .10)^t}$
1	1.0785	.9091	.98046
2	1.0785	.8264	.89127
3	1.0785	.7513	.81028
4	1.0785	.6830	.73662
5	1.0785	.6209	.66964
		Sum	4.08827

Thus, $\displaystyle\sum_{t=1}^{5} \frac{F_t}{(1+k)^t} - I = 4.08827 - 3 = 1.08827$ millions of dollars.

4. a. If the firm buys the new machine, the incremental after-tax cash flow in each of the next four years equals $(\$17,500 - \$7,500)(1 - .34) + \$30,000/4 = \$14,100$. Thus, the net present value equals

$$\$14,100 \left(\frac{1}{1.15} + \frac{1}{1.15^2} + \frac{1}{1.15^3} + \frac{1}{1.15^4} \right) - \$30,000 =$$

$$\$14,100 \,(.8696 + .7561 + .6575 + .5718) - \$30,000 =$$

$$\$14,100 \,(2.8550) - \$30,000 = \$10,255.$$

Since it exceeds zero, it appears that the firm should buy the machine.

b. The net present value equals

$$\$14,100 \left(\frac{1}{1.08} + \frac{1}{1.08^2} + \frac{1}{1.08^3} + \frac{1}{1.08^4} \right) - \$30,000 =$$

$$\$14,100(3.312) - \$30,000 = \$16,699.$$

Since it exceeds zero, it appears that the firm should buy the machine.

5. a. $\dfrac{8}{80} + .10 = .20$. Thus, the cost of internal equity seems to be about 20 percent.

b. $\dfrac{8}{100} + .10 = .18$. Thus, the cost of internal equity would be about 18 percent.

c. $\dfrac{8}{100} + .05 = .13$. Thus, the cost of internal equity would be about 13 percent.

6. a. $.07 + 0.9(.12 - .07) = .115$.
   b. $.07 + 1.2(.12 - .07) = .13$.
   c. $.07 + 1.5(.12 - .07) = .145$.

7. a. $.105(1 - .34) = .0693$. The firm's after-tax cost of debt is 6.93 percent.
   b. $.105(1 - .48) = .0546$. The firm's after-tax cost of debt is 5.46 percent.

8. a. $25{,}000 = \left(\dfrac{1}{1+k} + \dfrac{1}{(1+k)^2} + \dfrac{1}{(1+k)^3} + \dfrac{1}{(1+k)^4} \right) 8{,}000$

$$\dfrac{25}{8} = 3.125 = \left(\dfrac{1}{1+k} + \dfrac{1}{(1+k)^2} + \dfrac{1}{(1+k)^3} + \dfrac{1}{(1+k)^4} \right).$$

Looking at Appendix Table 2 of the text (in the row where $n = 4$), we see that k is about 11 percent.

b. $\$30{,}000 = \left(\dfrac{1}{1+k} + \dfrac{1}{(1+k)^2} + \dfrac{1}{(1+k)^3} + \dfrac{1}{(1+k)^4} \right) 8{,}000$

$$\dfrac{30{,}000}{8{,}000} = 3.75 = \left(\dfrac{1}{1+k} + \dfrac{1}{(1+k)^2} + \dfrac{1}{(1+k)^3} + \dfrac{1}{(1+k)^4} \right).$$

Looking at Appendix Table 2 (in the row where $n = 4$), we see that k is between 2 and 3 percent.

9. a. $.40(.10) + .60(.15) = .13$. Thus, the weighted cost of capital is 13 percent.

   b. $.30(.10) + .70(.15) = .135$. Thus the weighted cost of capital is 13.5 percent.

10. a.

Time (t)	Cash flow (millions of dollars)	$\dfrac{1}{(1+.10)^t}$	Cash flow $(1+.10)^t$
0	−10	1.0000	−10.0000
1	3	.9091	2.7273
2	4	.8264	3.3056
3	3	.7513	2.2539
4	2	.6830	1.3660
5	1	.6209	0.6209
		Sum	0.2737

The present value of the investment is .2737 millions of dollars.

b.

Time (t)	Cash flow (millions of dollars)	$\dfrac{1}{(1+.12)^t}$	Cash flow $(1+.12)^t$
0	−10	1.0000	−10.0000
1	3	.8929	2.6787
2	4	.7972	3.1888
3	3	.7118	2.1354
4	2	.6355	1.2710
5	1	.5674	.5674
		Sum	−0.1587

The present value of the investment is −.1587 millions of dollars.

CASE SEVEN

The Carriage House Inn: A Family Corporation
Michael D. Everett

In the summer of 1987 Margo Filmore, a new generally trained MBA and consultant with a major bank and trust company in a large U.S. city, pondered her first assignment. What recommendations should she make to the heirs of The Carriage House Inn, Incorporated, a medium sized family corporation, which included a prosperous 70 room motel, six unit apartment building, and a residence converted into a small office building? She apparently faced two basic questions and some serious data problems. First, what constituted the best economic recommendations in terms of keeping or selling various segments of the corporation? Second, what recommendations would best fit the overall preferences of the heirs and keep peace in the family?

The lack of good managerial accounting and financial data for each segment of the corporation compounded the problem. The family corporation only had traditional financial report accounts which lumped the three businesses, or segments, and fixed and variable costs together for tax reporting purposes (Exhibit 1). Although Margo could understand the output of commonly used accounting, financial, and statistical techniques, she would have to review some of them (Exhibit 2) and obtain help from other staff members to develop appropriate models.

CORPORATE BACKGROUND

Through interviews with the surviving children Margo familiarized herself with the history of the family business and preferences of family members. In the early 1950s the Boyds with their four young children, Mary, Robert, Sally, and Jan, built a small stucco motel on a major commercial artery in the affluent, rapidly growing suburbs of a large U.S. city. The venture prospered with a 35-room one-story structure built in a U shape with a nicely landscaped courtyard. The business represented a total family. Mr. Boyd had the instincts and risk preferences for shrewd investments. Mrs. Boyd shared in the decision making and did most of the actual management of the motel, which they called the Carriage House Inn. The children and extended family helped in the physical labor from painting rooms to making beds.

By the mid 1950s the Carriage House Inn faced a major threat from a proposed interstate highway. This would shift traffic from a state highway, just half a mile from the motel, to an interchange about 3 miles away. Mr. Boyd joined with other local businesses in the area to fight the interstate, but lost. After it was completed, they were surprised to find that business actually improved.

Thus, gradually through the 1960s the family rebuilt the motel into a "modern," two-story brick structure which doubled its size to 70 rooms. The motel continued to prosper and generate substantial excess cash flow. For various reasons, including the desire to avoid marginal personal tax rates of over 50 percent, the Boyds incorporated and reinvested their excess profits into related businesses. First, they converted their old residence, which faced onto the major artery, into a small office building. Then they built a six-unit apartment building on an unused portion of the property facing a side street. As part of their estate planning the parents placed the corporation into a trust for their children.

When Mr. Boyd passed away Mrs. Boyd continued to successfully manage the motel in cooperation with the estate trustees until her death in the mid 1980s. Robert and his wife, who lived in the area, took considerable interest in the motel and became involved in its management in the early 1980s. During Mrs. Boyd's final illness all the children took turns caring for her and managing the motel. After her death the children continued to cooperate and take turns managing the motel and other businesses. For Mary, Sally, and Jan this required traveling to the city every month and staying a week or more. Robert and his wife wanted to keep the motel and seriously considered quitting their jobs to manage it full time for the extended family.

Mary, Sally, and Jan remained torn between sentimental attachment to the Carriage House Inn and keen appreciation for the problems and risk involved in owning a motel, apartment, and office building, particularly while trying to oversee their management from a distance. They wanted to protect long time, loyal employees and return to their old home from time to time. On the other hand, the assets invested in the corporation could help supplement the sisters' current income and retirement programs and send their children through college. Numerous brokers had wanted to handle the properties, although no serious negotiations or setting of prices had occurred. Traveling to the city each month constituted a major disruption to their families and professional careers.

If they kept all or some of the businesses and appointed Robert to manage them, they agreed that the family would form a board of directors to supervise the management and make final decisions on major projects. They also agreed they would pay Robert and his wife the $90,000 they were now (1987) paying a resident supervisor plus themselves for rotating in to manage the motel.

ACCOUNTING DATA

The 1987 financial report accounting data projected for 1988 (Exhibit 1) indicated the corporation was making a good income. The Trust lawyers believed they could convert the old family corporation into an S corporation to avoid double taxation (i.e. taxation of profits as corporate income and then dividends as personal income). If so, the children would pay taxes at their personal marginal rate—probably 33 percent for federal taxes in 1988 and 8 percent for state taxes. Margo, nevertheless, wondered how much income the heirs could realize if they sold the corporation and invested the proceeds in broadly based financial instruments such as mutual stock funds which had been yielding 10 to 30 percent per year in the bull market of the 80s. Also, were all the businesses making money or were gains in some off-setting losses in others?

Her managerial economics course had used a very basic value or profit maximizing model which focused on all the relevant revenues and costs of a decision. Her managerial accounting course had provided a basic accounting framework for estimating these relevant revenues and costs by segments or businesses. Thus, Margo decided to try converting the financial report accounts, used mainly for tax purposes, to managerial cost accounts both on an accrual (upper part of Exhibit 2) and cash flow basis (lower part). Once she had her electronic spreadsheet programmed she could use it for other consulting projects such as advising the family on management decisions should they decide to keep the Carriage House and other businesses.

With Robert's help she separated out the VARIABLE and UNDISTRIBUTED (or programmed) costs for the three major businesses (motel, apartments, office building) from detailed financial report accounts and other records. They could trace most of the motel's variable costs for renting a room such as maid and laundry service and a rough estimate for utilities. They could not trace out minor repairs and wear and tear costs for the rooms, however, and had to leave them in the UNDISTRIBUTED SEGMENT COST category. These latter costs contained programmed cost for management, desk clerks, advertising, and maintenance of common facilities.

Then Margo and Robert went to work on the fixed costs. DEPRECIATION came from past tax returns. They estimated that this legal depreciation for tax purposes

EXHIBIT 1   **Summary of the Carriage House Inn's Financial Report Accounts Projected for 1988 (Dollars/Year)**

MOTEL INCOME		
Gross Motel Income	712,921.60	
Bad Debts, Refunds, and Motel Tax	34,944.41	
Motel Net Income		677,977.19
OTHER INCOME		
Office Building Income	23,426.00	
Apartment Income	32,549.00	
Total Other Income	55,975.00	
GROSS CORPORATION INCOME		733,952.19
OPERATING EXPENSES		
Gross Payroll	197,245.82	
Total Utilities	62,732.97	
Total Services	98,436.72	
Other Operating Expenses	26,421.40	
Total General and Administrative	40,963.98	
Depreciation	65,794.00	
TOTAL CORPORATION EXPENSES		491,594.89
PRETAX CORPORATE INCOME		242,357.30
Federal Income Tax (.33)	79,977.91	
State Income Tax (.08)	19,388.58	
POST TAX INCOME		142,990.81

roughly reflected the wearing out and replacement cost of the physical capital. For the MARKET VALUE OF ASSETS for each business, Margo utilized the average of appraisals the trust company appointed realtors had made using recent sales of comparable properties and construction costs.

Robert could not supply the appropriate discount rates to calculate the OPPORTUNITY COST OF ASSETS. Thus, Margo asked the trust company appointed realtors their opinion. They said over the last several years the discount rate for economy motels had averaged around 14 percent nationally but that home mortgage rates had dropped to around 10 percent currently and the prime rate to around 9 percent. Thus, Margo used a 12 percent discount rate for the motel and 10 percent for the house converted to an office building and apartments as a rough estimate so they could go ahead and fill in the rest of the accounts.

They were able to convert the NET SEGMENT MARGIN (NSM) to taxable income, taxes, and cash flow with a few simple adjustments (bottom of Exhibit 2). They continued to assume an S corporation and used the tax rates from Exhibit 1. The lawyer handling the trust had assured her that estate taxes would remain essentially the same whether the family kept or sold any of the assets or the entire corporation. Margo and a Bank accountant, Bill Wise, also experimented with various cash flow payoff measures such as return on assets, net present value over several years, and present value of the assets. This, however, required a number of assumptions about growth of the land values versus depreciation and after tax discount rates, noted on the spreadsheet.

Although the cash flow for each business and the NSM for the motel looked

good, no clear decision emerged. Jan, who had some business training and knew the discount rate should contain a component for risk, felt that 12 percent was far too low. Sally added that their conservative mutual funds had been yielding nearly 20 percent for the last four years. Robert argued that the NSM should include expected growth in the land values of the businesses. He said including this growth would show the motel could cover all its costs even with higher discount rates. Mary, who had an engineering background pointed out that the cash flow did not include repair, renovation, and rebuilding of worn out buildings and equipment which could easily cost several hundred thousand dollars.

Margo agreed they needed better estimates of discount rates, physical depreciation, potential growth rates for land values, and even returns on broadly based financial investments. Therefore, she studied the real estate consultant's report in more detail, and talked with family members again and key informants to learn more about local market conditions. She also consulted with the Bank's financial and investment experts.

COMPETITIVE ENVIRONMENT

Despite the optimism which the accounting reports generally provided, a complete analysis required estimates of future revenues and costs. These depended not only on the growth in the suburban area and entry of competitors into the market but also on the costs of maintaining and improving the land and buildings.

The apartments and house converted to an office building had adequate demand given the growth and prosperity in the area. The apartments enjoyed full occupancy with tenants who generally paid their rent

EXHIBIT 2   **Projected 1988 Managerial Cost and Cash Flow Accounts by Major Segment and for the Overall Corporation (Dollars/Year)**

	MOTEL	OFFICE	APT	OVERALL CORP
REVENUE	677,977	23,426	32,549	733,952
LESS VARIABLE	160,753	1,768	2,336	164,857
OPERATING CONTRIBUTION MARGIN	517,224	21, 658	30,213	569,095
LESS UNDISTRIBUTED SEG COST	248,683	4,530	7,731	260,944
CONTRIBUTION TO FIXED COSTS	268,541	17,128	22,482	308,151
LESS FIXED COSTS				
DEPRECIATION	58,541	2,764	4,489	65,794
OPPORTUNITY COST OF ASSETS	204,000	22,000	30,000	256,000
EQUALS ASSETS IN SEGMENT	1,700,000	220,000	300,000	2,220,000
TIMES DISCOUNT RATE	0.12	0.10	0.10	0.115
NET SEGMENT MARGIN (NSM)	6,000	(7,636)	(12,007)	(13,643)
(Contribution to corp overhead and profits)				
FOR CASH FLOW ADD BACK IN				
OPPORTUNITY COST OF CAPITAL	204,000	22,000	30,000	256,000
TO NET SEGMENT MARGIN	6,000	(7,636)	(12,007)	(13,643)
EQUALS TAXABLE INCOME	210,000	14,364	17,993	242,357
LESS TAXES (.41)	86,100	5,889	7,377	99,367
PLUS DEPRECIATION	58,541	2,764	4,489	65,794
EQUALS NET CASH FLOW (CF)	182,441	11,239	15,105	208,785
CASH FLOW PAYOFF MEASURES				
NET MARKET VALUE OF ASSETS	1,700,000	220,000	300,000	2,220,000
ESTIMATED GROWTH OF ASSETS	0.00	0.00	0.00	0.00
(assume growth in land values equals depreciation of buildings)				
TOTAL RETURN-C + GROWTH	182,441	11,239	15,105	208,785
TOT AFTER TAX RET ON ASSETS	0.107	0.051	0.050	0.094
AFTER TAX DISCOUNT	0.082	0.066	0.067	0.078
NET PRESENT VALUE FOR 5 YRS	174,370	(13,262)	(20,867)	140,241

After tax disc = disc rate $\times$ (1 – [taxes/(taxable inc + depre)])

Since motel cash flow is on an after tax basis, the return to other possible investments also should be on an after tax basis. However, we add depreciation back into taxable income because alternative investments in financial instruments would not have depreciation to reduce taxable income.

on time and stayed several years. A well established real estate firm had leased the house for an office and seemed content to stay there for many years. Land values had been increasing 3 to 5 percent a year in real terms over the last 20 years as the area grew and prospered. The future, however, remained unclear. Were land values inflated now? How long might a possible recession adversely affect land values? The buildings and equipment, moreover, were aging and probably would require extensive repair in the foreseeable future. A five percent physical depreciation rate could swamp potential increases in the land values.

The motel had survived turbulent markets but now perhaps confronted even greater uncertainties. During the 1970s and early 1980s the corporation had weathered challenges from new luxury motels in the area, the oil price increases, reduced travel and inflation, and a deep recession. In spite of the national economic problems, the suburban areas had prospered. Major corporate headquarters had located within several miles while high quality housing developments and commercial growth had continued along the major artery.

As the larger, more luxurious full service motels with restaurants and indoor swimming pools moved into the general area, however, the Carriage House Inn became classified as a limited service economy motel. It provided a clean, friendly family environment, coffee, juice, and sweet rolls for breakfast, and an outdoor swimming pool in a nicely landscaped environment for an average $32 per room sold in 1987. As the mother would say, "With fewer costly frills and a virtually paid-off, low interest mortgage, we can easily underprice those new motels."

The Carriage House Inn also enjoyed a loyal clientele of repeat business representatives during the week and relatives visiting families in the local community during holidays and summer vacations. Its listing in the American Automobile Association's (AAA) guidebooks generated significant off the roads business. Although the motel was located over three miles from the nearest interstate highway and over half a mile from the nearest limited access state highway, it had enjoyed a phenomenal 83 percent occupancy rate for the last 10 to 15 years. The motel industry generally averages about 65 percent occupancy.

Nevertheless, in the later 1980s and for the 1990s the Carriage House Inn faced several new threats. Nationwide the economy motel segment was becoming overbuilt. Rumors persisted that a major motel chain was planning to build an economy motel with a restaurant at the off ramp of the limited access state highway about half a mile from the Carriage House Inn. The motel's plant and equipment were aging and within the foreseeable future might require some major renovation and style changes, which easily could cost one to two hundred thousand dollars, to keep the motel competitive. Robert's preliminary negotiations with several banks indicated they would charge about 16 percent on major renovation loans.

Nelson Ledbetter, a financial analyst with the Bank, filled Margo in on the national economic situation and financial markets. Conservative financial instruments such as broadly based mutual funds and even insured savings accounts had yielded high rates of return averaging from nearly 10 to over 20 percent for the last four years. As the expansion out of the deep 1982 recession got longer, however, more economists were predicting lower consumer spending and perhaps another recession. Interest rates started moving back up in mid 1987 while oil prices, which had dropped sharply in 1986, were recovering and might increase overall inflation. These movements could adversely affect an inflated stock and bond market. Nelson pointed out that historically (1926 to 1985) Standard and Poor's index of 500 stocks had averaged almost a nominal 10 percent and real 7 percent return. He also indicated that over the last few years the bank had used about a 14 percent discount rate for small to medium sized motels like the Carriage House Inn.

Margo still remained uneasy about using discount rates to incorporate all the risk the motel faced. From her statistics courses she remembered a distinction between average and individual risk. She also wanted to estimate the impact of competition from new local economy motels on the Carriage House's occupancy rates, revenues, NSM, and cash flow. She needed some marketing research data to estimate these potential impacts.

MARKET RESEARCH DATA

Several months earlier Robert and his wife had done a survey of the Carriage House Inn's customers to see what they wanted in terms of rates, service, amenities, decor, and other motel characteristics. The motel staff had asked a cross section of guests to fill out the survey one typical week. In general the guests indicated that they were satisfied with the Carriage House. They like the clean, neat rooms, friendly family atmosphere, and the relatively low rates for the area. Many, however, were also very enthusiastic about major renovations. A number suggested putting a hot tub by the swimming pool like the larger hotels. One lady even gave extensive suggestions for new wallpaper and drape designs on the back of her questionnaire. Of course, virtually all of the guests wanted low room rates.

Although this survey supported Robert's position that the motel could remain competitive and keep its customers and high occupancy rate with major renovation, Margo remained a little uneasy. One of her marketing courses had stressed that consumers usually could not tell how they weigh product or service characteristics. Thus, more sophisticated market research studies ask consumers to rate products with different characteristics. Then the studies use these ratings to estimate the average weights

customers put on the characteristics. Robert and his wife, moreover, had a vested interest in the data.

Thus, Margo asked Jim Brady, a marketing research staff member, to help her do another survey. They developed a short questionnaire asking Carriage House customers to rate the attractiveness of different motel style-price options in the immediate area (Exhibit 3). The motel staff had about 30 representative customers fill out the questionnaire. These customers mainly represented repeat traveling sales people and persons visiting relatives in the area. Off-the-road customers traveling through the area constituted a minority of the Carriage House clients. This gave almost 100 usable ratings of different style-price combinations.

Theoretically, the average rating for each style-price combination would give a rough estimate of the occupancy for the Carriage House or a similar motel. For example, Jim calculated the average rating for the Carriage House under assumption 1 in the questionnaire (the present style-price combination with no other economy motels in the immediate area) at 9.2 out of a possible 10. This suggested that about 92 percent of the existing customers would return. The actual Carriage House Inn summer occupancy rate during the week exceeded 90 percent.

Next, Jim ran a multiple regression analysis on the data under assumption 2 in the questionnaire (a new economy motel in the area). He used RATING as the dependent variable and PRICE and STYLE as the independent variables (Exhibit 4). Both PRICE and STYLE were measured in the same units (1, 2, 3 = low, moderate, high). Thus, their coefficients indicated how heavily customers might weigh them. He used these weights to compute ratings for the Carriage House, given different combinations of STYLE and PRICE for it and its potential competitors. For example, the regression model predicted that with a new economy motel nearby, the RATING for the Carriage House would equal 5.3

EXHIBIT 3   **Questionnaire**

Valued Guests:

We would appreciate your ratings of several possible motel styles and prices in this immediate area. Assuming you have the following motel options, please rate the probability you would stay in each option.

1. First assume that the present situation continues to exist with the Carriage House Inn as the only economy motel within several miles of this highway exit. The motel continues to have its same prices, service, and upkeep. How would you rate your probability of staying at the Carriage House Inn on a scale from 0 to 10 where 10—you are sure you would stay, 0—you are sure you would not stay, and 5—a fifty-fifty chance you would stay?

2. Now assume that two other economy motels exist in this immediate area near the highway exchange along with the present Carriage House. One of these motels resembles the Carriage House but has undergone major renovation and redecoration to modernize it. It has service similar to the Carriage House. The other economy motel is a new structure with a restaurant and similar quality furniture as the Carriage House but of course new. The following boxes indicate the various style-price options these motels might have. Please write a number from 0 to 10 in each box to indicate your probability of staying in a motel with that style-price combination, given the availability of the other style-price combinations listed. Use each rating number only once. Again 0—the lowest rating possible, and 5—an intermediate rating.

MOTEL STYLE-PRICE OPTIONS

	AVERAGE ROOM RATE	(1) CARRIAGE HOUSE AS IT IS NOW	(2) A SIMILAR MOTEL WITH RENOVATION	(3) A NEW ECONOMY MOTEL WITH A RESTAURANT
(1)	$35			
(2)	$40			
(3)	$45			

(i.e. 4.7 + 2.1 (1) − 1.5 (1)). Renovating the Carriage House, however, would raise its RATINGS, particularly if prices remained relatively low. Margo could compare these hypothetical RATINGS to the present Carriage house RATINGS (assumption 1) and at least try to ascertain any possible trends in occupancy with different STYLES, PRICES, and competition.

FINAL DECISION MAKING

Margo remained somewhat bewildered with the various accounting and financial techniques and data estimates. It seemed that each technique gave a partial analysis, leaving out some key variables and not agreeing with the other techniques. Different data assumptions, moreover, led

EXHIBIT 4   **Regression Model of Motel Ratings As a Function of Style and Price**

*** MULTIPLE LINEAR REGRESSION ***

DEPENDENT VARIABLE: RATING   81 VALID CASES

COEFF OF DETERM: 0.0659705   ESTIMATED CONSTANT TERM: 4.70370
MULTIPLE CORR COEFF: 0.812222   STANDARD ERR OF ESTIMATE: 1.53489

ANALYSIS OF VARIANCE FOR THE REGRESSION:

SOURCE OF VARIANCE	DEGREES OF FREEDOM	SUM OF SQUARES	MEAN OF SQUARES	F TEST	PROB
REGRESSION	2	356.241	178.120	75.6065	0.0000
RESIDUALS	78	183.759	2.35589		
TOTAL	80	540.000			

VARIANCE	REGRESSION COEFFICIENT	STANDARDIZED COEFFICIENT	STANDARD ERROR	T	PROB
STYLE	2.11111	0.667592	0.208872	10.1072	0.0000
PRICE	-1.46296	-0.462630	0.208872	-7.00411	0.0000

to widely different results. She finally decided to try to fall back on that very basic economic model and list all the relevant changes in total revenue and total cost the family would experience by keeping the Carriage House Inn. She could then change data assumptions and at least range the NET SEGMENT MARGIN and perhaps other payoff measures in Exhibit 2.

First she just ranged the discount rate to account risk. This generated a range of NET SEGMENT MARGINS for the motel. As a check she left the DISCOUNT RATE constant and ranged each possible revenue and cost category. For example, she put in a low and high occupancy rate in the spreadsheet. This generated a range of REVENUES, VARIABLE COSTS, and OPERATING CONTRIBUTION MARGINS. Next she ranged depreciation to reflect assumptions about future repair costs and possible renovations. Finally, she accounted for possible growth in land values by adding in a dollar amount to NET SEGMENT MARGIN from most pessimistic

to most optimistic. If she had time, she could incorporate these ranges into the CASH FLOW and CASH FLOW PAYOFF MEASURES. She could also utilize more formal uncertainty approaches such as that described in the text.

Questions

1. In contrast to our discussion in the textbook, this firm contains three quite distinct businesses. Is it possible to allocate all the firm's costs to one and only one of these three businesses? If not, what are the difficulties?

2. To what extent can the data in Exhibit 1 resolve the questions Margo Filmore (and the heirs) faced?

3. In Exhibit 2, why did Margo Filmore subtract the opportunity cost of assets to get the contribution of each segment of the corporation to corporate overhead and profits?

4. Which segments of the firm seem to represent a sound business investment in terms of 1988 estimated payoffs or returns?

5. What do the expected future market environment and market research data suggest about the future competitive position of the Carriage House Inn?

6. How important in this decision are forecasts of future land values and the costs of possible major repairs?

7. Using the simulation techniques described in the text, Margo Filmore found that the probability distribution of the motel's net segment margin was as follows:

Net segment margin	Probability
Less than –$74,280	.025
–$74,280 to –$27,720	.135
–$27,720 to $18,840	.340
$18,840 to $65,400	.340
$65,400 to $111,960	.135
$111,960 and over	.025

Interpret these results, and indicate whether—and, if so, how—they throw light on the decision to be made.

Part Six

GOVERNMENT— BUSINESS RELATIONS AND THE GLOBAL ECONOMY

CHAPTER 16

Government and Business

Chapter Profile

Commissions regulating public utilities often set price at a level at which it equals average total cost, including a "fair rate of return" on the firm's investment. One difficulty with this arrangement is that, since the firm is guaranteed this rate of return (regardless of how well or poorly it performs), there is no incentive for the firm to increase its efficiency. Although regulatory lag results in some incentives of this sort, they often are relatively weak.

There has been a great deal of controversy over the practices of the regulatory commissions. Many economists have viewed them as lax or ill-conceived. In many areas, like transportation, there has been a movement toward deregulation. In the airline industry, this movement has been particularly dramatic.

The socially optimal level of pollution (holding output constant) is at the point where the marginal cost of pollution equals the marginal cost of pollution control. In general, this will be at a point where a nonzero amount of pollution occurs. To establish incentives that will lead to a more nearly optimal level of pollution, the government can establish effluent fees and enact direct regulations, among other things.

In 1890, the Sherman Act was passed. It outlawed any contract, combination, or conspiracy in restraint of trade and made it illegal to monopolize or attempt to monopolize. In 1914, Congress passed the Clayton Act, and the Federal Trade Commission was created. A more recent antitrust development was the Celler-Kefauver Anti-Merger Act of 1950.

The real impact of the antitrust laws depends on the interpretation placed on these laws by the courts. In its early cases, the Supreme Court put forth and used the famous rule of reason—that only unreasonable combinations in restraint of trade, not all trusts, required conviction under the Sherman Act. The situation changed greatly in the 1940s when the court decided that Alcoa, because it controlled practically all of the nation's aluminum output, was in violation of the antitrust laws. In the early 1980s, two major antitrust cases—against American Telephone and Telegraph and the IBM Corporation—were decided.

The patent laws grant the inventor exclusive control over the use of an invention for 17 years (after June 1995, 20 years from initial filing) in exchange for his or her making the invention public knowledge. The patent system enables innovators to appropriate a larger portion of the social benefits from their innovations than would be the case without it, but they frequently have only a limited effect on the rate at which imitators appear. Nonetheless, firms continue to make extensive use of the patent system.

The socially optimal level of pollution (holding output constant) is at the point where the marginal cost of pollution equals the marginal cost of pollution control. An external economy occurs when an action taken by a firm or individual results in uncompensated benefits to others. An external diseconomy occurs when an action taken by a firm or individual results in uncompensated costs or harm to others.

Questions

Completion

1. Commissions often set price at the level at which it equals _____ , including a fair return.

2. The government (can, cannot) _____ convict firms of violation of the antitrust laws merely by showing that the firms fixed prices or attempted to do so. The government (does, does not) _____ have to show what the effects were.

3. The Standard Oil case, decided in 1911, resulted in _____. The American Tobacco case, decided in 1911, resulted in _____ . The U.S. Steel case, decided in 1920, resulted in _____ . All of these cases were tried under Section _____ of the _____ .

4. The IBM case alleged that IBM has had monopoly power in the market for _____. This case was tried under Section _____ of the _____ .

5. While many economists favor the market _____ approach to antitrust policy, the majority favor the market _____ approach to evaluating undesirable monopolistic characteristics.

6. The market _____ shows the percentage of total sales or production accounted for by the biggest four firms.

7. The _____ outlawed any contract, combination, or conspiracy in restraint of trade and made it illegal to monopolize or attempt to monopolize.

8. At the socially optimal level, the cost of an extra unit of pollution equals the cost of _____ pollution by an extra unit.

9. Patent protection has increased imitation costs by a (larger, smaller) _____ percentage in the pharmaceutical industry than in the electronics industry.

10. The more an industry cuts down on the amount of wastes it discharges, the _____ are its costs of pollution control.

11. The more untreated waste an industry dumps into the environment, the _____ the cost of pollution.

True or False

_____ 1. Because price levels have been rising in the past forty years, most regulatory commissions use replacement cost to value a firm's assets.

_____ 2. Regulatory lag results in rewards for efficiency because, if a regulated firm is efficient, the lag automatically is reduced and profits increase.

_____ 3. A firm with a 60 percent market share frequently is permitted to go untouched by the antitrust laws, while at the same time two firms with 10 percent of a market sometimes are forbidden to merge.

_____ 4. Whether or not price fixing is illegal depends on the price fixers' share of the market; if their share is small enough, price fixing is not illegal under U.S. law.

_____ 5. If firm A acquires the stock or assets of a competing corporation, this may be illegal based on Section 7 of the Clayton Act, as amended by the Celler-Kefauver Act.

_____ 6. In recent years, horizontal mergers have often been disallowed by the courts, but all vertical mergers have been permitted.

_____ 7. The antitrust laws have as yet had no significant effect on business behavior and markets.

_____ 8. The U.S. patent laws grant the inventor exclusive control over the use of his or her invention for thirty years.

_____ 9. The patent system and the antitrust laws tend to push in opposite directions.

_____ 10. A firm's size is not necessarily a good indicator of the extent of its monopoly power.

_____ 11. National defense is not a public good.

_____ 12. In large part, environmental pollution is due to external economies.

Multiple Choice

1. It is illegal in the United States for rival firms

   a. to agree to fix prices.
   b. to restrict or pool output.
   c. to share markets on a predetermined basis.
   d. all of the above.
   e. only a and b.

2. It is illegal in the United States for a firm

   a. to set its price equal to that of one of its competitors.
   b. to merge with a larger firm.
   c. to charge one customer a different price than another under any circumstances.
   d. to license its patents.
   e. none of the above.

3. The most important reason why economists oppose monopoly is that, as compared with perfect competition, monopolies

   a. reap higher profits.
   b. charge higher prices.
   c. result in a misallocation of resources.
   d. are unlikely to be philanthropic.
   e. none of the above.

4. In the United States in 1968, about half of all manufacturing assets were controlled by

   a. 100 corporations.
   b. 500 corporations.
   c. 1,000 corporations
   d. 5,000 corporations.
   e. 10 corporations.

5. If firms enter into exclusive and tying contracts that substantially lessen competition, this is illegal according to the

   a. Sherman Act, Section 1.
   b. Sherman Act, Section 2.
   c. Clayton Act.
   d. Federal Trade Commission Act.
   e. Celler-Kefauver Act.

6. If a firm enters into a contract in restraint of trade, this is illegal based on the

   a. Sherman Act, Section 1.
   b. Sherman Act, Section 2.
   c. Clayton Act.
   d. Federal Trade Commission Act.
   e. Celler-Kefauver Act.

7. In 1958, the Antitrust Division sued Bethlehem Steel and Youngstown Sheet and Tube to stop a proposed merger between them. This case was brought under the

   a. Sherman Act, Section 1.
   b. Sherman Act, Section 2.
   c. Robinson-Patman Act.
   d. Federal Trade Commission Act.
   e. Celler-Kefauver Act.

8. The patent system is defended on the grounds that

   a. it increases the incentive for invention.
   b. it increases the incentive for innovation.
   c. it hastens the disclosure of inventions.
   d. all of the above.
   e. none of the above.

9. Which of the following is *not* a public good?

   a. a smog-free environment.
   b. national defense.
   c. blood donated to the Red Cross.
   d. the Apollo space program.
   e. all of the above.

Problems

1. Consider an electric power plant that has the marginal cost curve shown below. Suppose that this plant's demand curve varies over time. For simplicity, assume that there is a peak period (when air conditioners are running and lights are on) and an off-peak period (at night). The demand curve during each period is shown below:

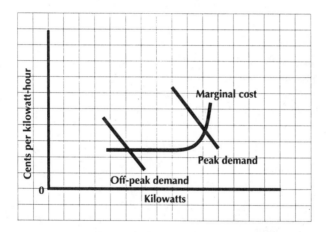

   a. Should the electric power plant charge a higher price during the peak period than during the off-peak period? Why or why not?
   b. In the 1970s, a number of regulatory commissions instituted higher rates for electric utilities during the summer than during the winter. Is this sensible, based on your answer to part a?
   c. In 1978, the Public Utility Regulatory Policy Act required electric utilities to implement time-of-day pricing or to "show cause" why such pricing should not be implemented in their service areas. Time-of-day pricing calls for higher electricity rates during the times of day when the use of electricity is relatively high than during those when it is relatively low. Does time-of-day pricing tend to promote efficiency?

2. In one of the most famous antitrust suits of this century, the government charged Du Pont, the large chemical firm, with "monopolizing, attempting to monopolize and conspiracy to monopolize interstate commerce in cellophane . . . in violation of Section 2 of the Sherman Act." Du Pont produced 75 percent of the cellophane sold in the United States.

a. Considering Du Pont's share of the cellophane market, was it clear that the company was in violation of Section 2 of the Sherman Act?

b. The Supreme Court pointed out that, "despite cellophane's advantage, it has to meet competition from other materials in every one of its uses. . . . The overall result is that cellophane accounts for 17.9 percent of flexible wrapping materials." How can one tell whether cellophane had to meet competition from other materials, and how stiff this competition was?

c. The Supreme Court decided that Du Pont was not in violation of the Sherman Act. In reaching this decision, it pointed to the high cross elasticity of demand existing between cellophane and other flexible packaging materials like Pliofilm. Why is this of relevance?

3. In the early 1960s, the Aluminum Company of America wanted to acquire the Rome Cable Corporation, but this merger was challenged by the government. The 1958 market shares, based on alternative market definitions, are given below:

Definition	Alcoa	Rome
	(percent)	
Bare aluminum conductor wire and cable	32.5	0.3
Insulated aluminum conductor wire and cable	11.6	4.7
Combined aluminum conductor wire and cable	27.8	1.3
All bare conductor wire and cable (aluminum and copper)	10.3	2.0
All insulated conductor wire and cable	0.3	1.3
Combined insulated and bare wire and cable (all metals)	1.8	1.4

Is it obvious that the merger should have been stopped? Do you think that the courts stopped it?

4. In the early 1960s, Continental Can Company wanted to merge with the Hazel-Atlas Glass Company. Continental, the second-largest producer of tin cans in the United States, sold about one-third of all tin cans. Hazel-Atlas, the third largest bottle maker, sold about one-tenth of all glass bottles.

Do you think that the definition of the relevant line of commerce was important in this case? Do you think that the courts prevented the merger?

5. There are several firms that produce a particular product. Their sales in 1996 are as follows:

Firm	Sales (millions of dollars)
A	100
B	50
C	40
D	30
E	20
F	5
G	5

a. What is the concentration ratio in this industry?

b. Would you regard this industry as oligopolistic? Why or why not?

c. Suppose that firm A merges with firm G. What now will be the concentration ratio in this industry?

d. Suppose that, after they merge, firms A and G go out of business. What now will be the concentration ratio in this industry?

6. A producer of table salt does not set the same price for all buyers. Instead, the price varies inversely and substantially with the size of the customer's order. The differences in price are not due to cost differences. The buyers are retail stores, and the large buyers can resell the salt at a lower price than can the small buyers. Is the salt manufacturer's pricing illegal? If so, what law does it violate?

7. We list a number of U.S. laws below, after which we list a number of antitrust provisions. In the blank space before each provision, put the letter corresponding to the U.S. law containing this provision.

   A. Sherman Act, Section 1
   B. Sherman Act, Section 2
   C. Clayton Act
   D. Federal Trade Commission Act
   E. Celler-Kefauver Act
   F. Robinson-Patman Act

   _____ a. It is illegal to enter into a contract, combination, or conspiracy in restraint of trade.

   _____ b. It is illegal to discriminate among purchasers to an extent that cannot be justified by a difference in cost.

   _____ c. It is illegal to use unfair methods of competition.

   _____ d. It is illegal to attempt to monopolize trade.

   _____ e. It is illegal to attempt to enter into exclusive and tying contracts.

   _____ f. It is illegal to attempt to discriminate among purchasers, where the effect might be to drive competitors out of business.

   _____ g. It is illegal to attempt to employ unfair or deceptive acts or practices.

   _____ h. It is illegal to attempt to acquire the stock of competing corporations.

8. Some states, such as Oregon and Vermont, have passed laws that all carbonated-beverage containers must carry a minimum refundable deposit.

   a. According to the director of communications services for American Can Company, "What *is* happening in Oregon is that consumers are paying $10 million more a year for beer and soft drinks than they did before the bottle bill became law. Retail price increases . . . have far exceeded those in neighboring states." Why do you think this was true?

   b. According to this executive of American Can Company, "Oregon [and Vermont] consumers are denied their free choice of container." Is this true? According to William Baumol and Wallace Oates, this amounts to "a denial of . . . the freedom to pollute unpenalized." Do you agree?

9. According to one study of the Delaware River, the extra social costs involved in going from one level of pollution abatement to another are shown below. Also shown are the extra benefits to society in going from one level of pollution to another. (All figures are in millions of dollars.)

Transition	Extra cost	Extra benefit
From abatement level 1 to 2	35	200
From abatement level 2 to 3	20	20
From abatement level 3 to 4	130	10
From abatement level 4 to 5	245	25

a. If abatement level 1 is currently being achieved, is it socially worthwhile to advance to abatement level 2? Why or why not?

b. Is it socially worthwhile to advance to abatement level 3? Why or why not?

c. Is it socially worthwhile to advance to abatement level 4? Why or why not?

d. Is it socially worthwhile to advance to abatement level 5? Why or why not?

10. In 1965, the Ohio Valley Electric Corporation sued Westinghouse and General Electric for damages. According to Ohio Valley Electric, it had been overcharged for electrical equipment it purchased during a period when the electrical equipment producers conspired to raise prices. In the subsequent trial, it built its case in considerable part on the following graph, which shows the relationship between average order prices and book prices during 1948 to 1963.[*]

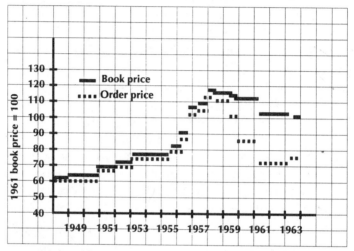

[*] *Source:* R. Sultan, *Pricing in the Electrical Oligopoly* (Boston: Harvard University, 1974).

a. The book price was the published price issued by General Electric and other electrical equipment producers. The average order price was the average price actually negotiated for such equipment. Does it appear that this equipment was frequently sold below its book price?

b. There was evidence that the electrical equipment producers had held meetings to control prices before 1959. Is the relationship between average order price and book price different in the post-1959 period than in the earlier years?

c. According to the Ohio Valley Electric Corporation, in the absence of a conspiracy, the actual order price would have borne the same relationship to the book price in the early 1950s as in the early 1960s. Specifically, it would have been about 75 percent of the book price. Is this necessarily true?

11. The overwhelming majority of families in the United States have television sets.

a. For these families, is a television program a nonrival good? That is, can one consumer enjoy this good without other consumers getting less of it?

b. Is it possible for firms to exclude some of these families from viewing certain programs?

c. Who pays for ordinary TV programs?

d. Must there be any commercials on "pay TV"?

12. "Public goods have marginal costs of zero. In other words, they can be provided as cheaply for one as for all. Consequently, it is foolish to attempt to compare the benefits of public goods with their costs. Any public good is worth producing because it benefits so many people." Comment and evaluate.

Answers

Completion

1. average total cost   2. can, does not   3. dissolution of Standard Oil, dissolution of American Tobacco, acquittal, 2, Sherman Act   4. electronic computers, 2, Sherman Act   5. performance, structure   6. concentration ratio 7. Sherman Act   8. reducing   9. larger   10. greater   11. greater

True or False

1. False   2. False   3. True   4. False   5. True   6. False   7. False 8. False   9. True   10. True   11. False   12. False

Multiple Choice

1. d   2. e   3. c   4. a   5. c   6. a   7. e   8. d   9. c

Problems

1. a. Many economists favor such a pricing policy. One advantage is that it would help to even out the amount of electricity utilized at various periods of time.
    b. Yes, if the demand for electric power is greater in the summer than in the winter.
    c. Yes.

2. a. No, because it was not clear that cellophane alone was the relevant line of commerce.
    b. One relevant measure is the cross elasticity of demand between cellophane and other flexible packaging materials.
    c. Because it indicates how closely these other materials can substitute for cellophane.

3. It was not obvious. The Supreme Court ruled against the merger, whereas the district court permitted it.

4. The district court said cans and bottles were separate lines of commerce, but the Supreme Court emphasized the competition between cans and bottles. The Supreme Court ruled against the merger.

5. a. 220/250 = 88 percent.
    b. Yes, because the concentration ratio is so high.
    c. 90 percent.
    d. 140/145 = 97 percent.

6. Yes. The Robinson-Patman Act.

7. a. A.
   b. C.
   c. D.
   d. B.
   e. C.
   f. F.
   g. D.
   h. E.

8. a. Because of increased costs of handling, sorting, washing, returning, and refilling bottles, according to this executive.
   b. The issue is too complex to permit a very brief answer, but many economists would agree with Baumol and Oates.

9. a. Yes, because the benefit exceeds the cost.
   b. No, because the benefit does not exceed the cost.
   c. No, because the benefit does not exceed the cost.
   d. No, because the benefit does not exceed the cost.

10. a. Yes.
    b. Yes.
    c. No. For example, increased competition among electrical equipment producers could result in a decrease in the ratio of actual order price to book price.

11. a. Yes, because once the program is put on the air, an extra family can watch it without depriving others of the opportunity to do so. In other words, once the program is broadcast to some viewers, others can watch it at no (or trivial) extra cost.
    b. Yes. A means has been devised to "scramble" the signal so that, unless a viewer's TV set is equipped to unscramble it, the viewer cannot get the program. Viewers rent this equipment or operate it by means of coins. This is called "pay TV."
    c. Advertisers pay for the broadcasts in order to air their commercials. In addition, listeners pay something, if they don't like commercials!
    d. No, because the viewers pay directly for the broadcasts.

12. It is not true that any public good is worth producing. The efficient output of a public good can be determined by summing the individual demand curves vertically and by finding the intersection with the supply curve. In many instances, the efficient output may be zero.

CHAPTER 17

Managerial Economics: Taking a Global View

Chapter Profile

The exchange rate is the number of units of one currency that exchanges for a unit of another currency. To a large extent, exchange rates currently are set by supply and demand. The value of a country's currency (relative to other currencies) tends to fall if its inflation rate or its economic growth rate is comparatively high or if its interest rates are comparatively low.

Specialization and trade depend on comparative, not absolute advantage. A nation is said to have a comparative advantage in those products where its efficiency relative to other nations is highest. Trade can be mutually beneficial if a country specializes in the products where it has a comparative advantage and imports the products where it has a comparative disadvantage.

The principle of comparative advantage can be used to predict (within limits) the pattern of world trade. If markets are relatively free and competitive, producers will automatically be led to produce in accord with comparative advantage. If a country has a comparative advantage in the production of a certain good, it will turn out—after the price of the good in various countries is equalized and total world output of the good equals total world demand—that this country is an exporter of the good under free trade.

A tariff is a tax imposed by the government on imports, the purpose being to cut down on imports in order to protect domestic industry and workers from foreign competition. Tariffs benefit the protected industry at the expense of the general public. Quotas are another barrier to free trade. Tariffs and quotas are sometimes justified on the basis of national security and other noneconomic considerations. Moreover, tariffs and other forms of protection are sometimes adopted to protect infant industries, to prevent a country from being too dependent on only a few industries, and to carry out other such national objectives. In recent years, some economists have begun to argue that countries should adopt strategic trade policies.

Many companies must decide whether (and if so, where) to build facilities abroad. Whether or not a firm locates a plant in a particular country depends on the size of the market in that country, the country's investment climate, and the availability of skilled labor there. If a firm decides to build a plant overseas, there is a time-cost trade-off.

International technology transfer is of great importance to many firms. There are four principal ways by which technology can be transferred across national borders: export of goods, direct investment in wholly owned subsidiaries, licensing, and joint ventures. In recent years, more and more firms have been forming strategic alliances with firms in other countries (as well as those in their own countries).

Questions

Completion

1. If a firm decides to build a plant overseas, there is often a trade-off between _____ and _____.

2. The principal channels by which technology can be transferred across national borders are _____, _____, _____, and _____.

3. If the United States exports corn to Italy, this results in an (increase, decrease) _____ in the price of corn in Italy. If Italy exports wine to the United States, this results in an (increase, decrease) _____ in the price of wine in Italy.

4. Both a _____ and a _____ generally increase the price of an imported good. Two ways in which governments try to help protect their domestic industries are by _____ and _____.

5. _____ will help to indicate whether a country has a comparative advantage or disadvantage in producing a commodity. If there is a comparative advantage, after the price of a good in various countries is equalized and total world output of the good equals total world demand for it, a country will tend to (export, import) _____ the good under free trade and competition. (For simplicity, transportation costs are ignored.)

6. In some cases firms have established overseas branches to control foreign sources of _____. In other cases they have invested overseas in an effort to _____ their competitive position. Very frequently firms have established foreign branches to exploit a _____ lead.

7. A firm with a technological edge over its competitors often prefers to exploit its technology in foreign markets through wholly-owned _____ rather than through _____ or other means.

8. If the rate of interest is higher in Japan than in Great Britain, investors will sell _____ and buy _____ in order to switch from the lower-yielding British securities to the higher-yielding Japanese securities. Consequently the pound will tend to _____ relative to the yen.

9. If the French economy is growing more rapidly than other economies, French (exports, imports) _____ are likely to grow more rapidly than its (exports, imports) _____. Thus, French demand for foreign currency will grow (more, less) _____ rapidly than the amount of foreign currency supplied. Consequently the French franc is likely to _____.

10. The 1974 Trade Act and the 1988 Omnibus Trade and Competitiveness Act gave the President considerable leeway in deciding what _____ action to take against foreign trade practices that are regarded as _____.

True or False

_____ 1. One reason why U.S. firms found it so difficult to compete with foreign rivals during the early 1980s was the big increase then in the value of the dollar relative to other currencies.

_____ 2. Quotas can be even more effective than tariffs in keeping foreign goods out of a country.

_____ 3. International differences in resource endowments and in the relative quantity of various types of human and nonhuman resources are important bases for specialization.

_____ 4. The purpose of a tariff is to cut down on imports in order to protect domestic industry and workers from foreign competition.

_____ 5. If Chile could produce each and every good and service with 80 percent as much of each and every input as Argentina, Chile would have a comparative advantage over Argentina in all goods and services.

_____ 6. Export subsidies and other such measures frequently lead to countermeasures. For example, to counter foreign export subsidies, the U.S. government imposes duties against such subsidies on goods sold here.

_____ 7. If Italians demand more Bordeaux wine, Roquefort cheese, and other French goods and services, this will cause both the demand curve and the supply curve for French francs to shift to the right.

_____ 8. When foreign trade practices are determined to be unfair, the President can retaliate against goods and services other than those cited in the complaints.

_____ 9. Whether or not a firm locates a plant in a particular country has been shown to be independent of the size of the market in that country.

_____ 10. Many strategic alliances involve the sharing of technological information.

Multiple Choice

1. Direct investment is often preferred by firms as a channel for international technology transfer if

    a. they can obtain the necessary resources.
    b. they believe that other methods of transfer will give away valuable know-how to foreign producers who are likely to become competitors.
    c. they fear that the country where the investment will occur is likely to appropriate private assets.
    d. both a and b.
    e. all of the above.

2. A shift to the right in the demand for German marks will occur if

    a. German interest rates are relatively high and German inflation is relatively low.
    b. German interest rates are relatively low and German inflation is relatively high.
    c. both German interest rates and German inflation are relatively low.
    d. both German interest rates and German inflation are relatively high.
    e. none of the above.

3. If the German mark depreciates from 50 cents to 45 cents, the dollar price of a German product selling in Germany for 150 marks

    a. falls by $10.
    b. falls by $7.50.
    c. falls by $5.00.
    d. increases by $7.50.
    e. none of the above.

4. The purpose of a tariff is to

    a. reduce imports to protect domestic industry and workers from foreign competition.
    b. produce revenue to pay for shipping costs.
    c. reduce costs.
    d. all of the above.
    e. none of the above.

5. Country A can produce 1 ton of food or 4 tons of coal with 1 unit of resources. Country B can produce 2 tons of food or 5 tons of coal with 1 unit of resources.

    a. Country A will export food and import coal.
    b. Country B will export food and import coal.
    c. Country A will neither import nor export food.
    d. Country B will neither import nor export coal.
    e. None of the above.

6. One difference between tariffs and quotas is that only tariffs

   a. reduce trade.
   b. raise prices.
   c. provide the government with revenue.
   d. reduce the standard of living of the nation as a whole.
   e. none of the above.

7. If Canada specializes in wheat and England specialized in Scotch whiskey and if wheat is on the vertical axis and Scotch whiskey is on the horizontal axis, Canada's trading possibilities curve is flatter (that is, closer to being a horizontal line) if

   a. the price of a fifth of Scotch whiskey is low relative to the price of a bushel of wheat.
   b. the price of a bushel of wheat is low relative to the price of a fifth of Scotch whiskey.
   c. the typical Canadian consumer prefers a fifth of Scotch to a bushel of wheat.
   d. the typical English consumer prefers a fifth of Scotch to a bushel of wheat.
   e. none of the above.

8. Critics of strategic trade policies worry that

   a. special-interest groups will use such policies to advance their own interests.
   b. the criteria for identifying which industries should be protected are vague.
   c. free trade is completely obsolete.
   d. both a and b.
   e. all of the above.

9. Among the most important factors influencing where a firm locates a foreign plant are

   a. the size of the local market.
   b. the country's investment and political climate.
   c. the availability of skilled labor.
   d. the availability of relevant know-how.
   e. all of the above.

10. Firms often prefer licensing over direct investment as a channel of international technology transfer when

   a. the foreign market where the direct investment would occur is small.
   b. the firm with the technology lacks the resources required for direct investment.
   c. there are important advantages through cross-licensing.
   d. both a and b.
   e. all of the above.

Problems

1. The Buchanan Company plans to construct a new plant in Mexico. The cost (in millions of dollars) of building the plant equals

$$C = 8 - 2t + .1t^2, \quad (1 \le t \le 3)$$

where t is the number of quarters (3-month periods) taken to construct it. It is impossible to construct it in less than one quarter, and the firm is committed to construct it in no more than three quarters. The discounted profit (gross of the cost of building the plant) is estimated to equal

$$R = 20 - 1.6t, \quad (1 \le t \le 3)$$

where R is in millions of dollars.

   a. To minimize the cost of building the plant, how many quarters should the firm take to construct it?

   b. To maximize profit, how many quarters should the firm take to construct it?

2. a. If Germans want to import a product from the United States, and if the product costs $5 in the United States, how much will it cost in Germany if the exchange rate is 3 marks = 1 dollar? If the exchange rate is 4 marks = 1 dollar? If the exchange is 2 marks = 1 dollar?

   b. The quantity of the product (in part a) demanded in Germany is related to its price (in marks) in the way indicated below. The table below shows the desired expenditure by Germans on this product at various levels of the exchange rate. Fill in the blanks.

Exchange rate	Dollar price of good	German price of good (marks)	Quantity demanded	Total desired expenditure (in dollars)
4 marks = 1 dollar	5	_____	500	_____
3 marks = 1 dollar	5	_____	1,000	_____
2 marks = 1 dollar	5	_____	1,200	_____

   c. Plot the relationship between the price of a dollar (in marks) and the quantity of dollars demanded by the Germans to buy the product in parts a and b. (Use the graph on the next page.)

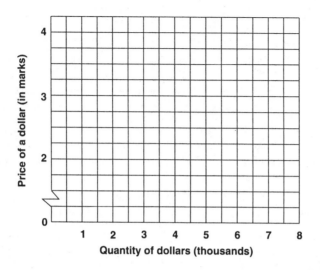

3. a. U.S. consumers want to import a product from Germany. The following table relates to the demand for this good in the United States. It shows the desired expenditure on this product by Americans at various levels of the exchange rate. Fill in the blanks.

Exchange rate	German price of good (marks)	Dollar price of good	Quantity demanded	Total desired expenditure (in dollars)
4 marks = 1 dollar	12	_____	2,000	_____
3 marks = 1 dollar	12	_____	1,250	_____
2 marks = 1 dollar	12	_____	500	_____

b. Plot in the graph in problem 2c the relationship between the price of a dollar (in marks) and the quantity of dollars supplied by Americans to buy the product in part a.

c. If the only international trade between Germany and the United States is that described above, what will be the equilibrium exchange rate?

d. In the situation described in part c, would there be a shortage or surplus of marks if the price of a mark were 30 cents?

4. Countries A and B have not traded with each other because of political differences. Suddenly, they reconcile their political differences and begin to trade. Cigars are relatively cheap, but beef is relatively expensive in country A. Beef is relatively cheap, but cigars are relatively expensive in country B.

a. When these countries begin to trade, will the demand for cigars produced in country A increase or decrease? Will the price of cigars increase or decrease in country A?

b. Will the demand for cigars produced in country B increase or decrease? Will the price of cigars increase or decrease in country B?

c. Will the demand for beef produced in country A increase or decrease? Will the price of beef increase or decrease in country A?

    d. Will the demand for beef produced in country B increase or decrease? Will the price of beef increase or decrease in country B.

    e. Will the demand for resources used in country A to produce cigars increase or decrease? Will the demand for resources used in country B to produce beef increase or decrease?

    f. Will the demand for resources used in country B to produce cigars increase or decrease? Will the demand for resources used in country A to produce beef increase or decrease?

5. Suppose that Germany and the United States are the only producers and consumers of a particular machine tool. The demand and supply curves for this machine tool in the United States are as follows:

Price (dollars)	Annual quantity demanded (thousands)	Annual quantity supplied (thousands)
500	9.5	6.5
1,000	9	7
1,500	8.5	7.5
2,000	8	8

    a. In the absence of foreign trade, what would be the equilibrium price of this machine tool in the United States?

    b. How many of these machine tools would be sold in the United States?

6. In the case of the machine tool in problem 5, the demand and supply curves for this machine tool in Germany are as follows:

Price (expressed in dollar equivalent of German price)	Annual quantity demanded (thousands)	Annual quantity supplied (thousands)
200	4	4
500	3.5	4.5
1,000	3	5
1,500	2.5	5.5

    a. In the absence of foreign trade, what would be the equilibrium price of the machine tool in Germany?

    b. How many of these machine tools would be sold in Germany?

7. Suppose that free trade between Germany and the United States begins with respect to the machine tool in problems 5 and 6 and that the market in both countries is competitive. For simplicity, assume that the costs of transporting the machine tools from one country to another are negligible.

    a. Under these circumstances, what would be the equilibrium price of this machine tool?

    b. How many of these machine tools would be produced in the United States? In Germany?

    c. How many of these machine tools would be bought in the United States? In Germany?

8. Suppose that the U.S. government establishes a quota of 1,000 machine tools per year on imports from Germany of the machine tool discussed in problems 5 to 7.

   a. What would be the equilibrium price of the machine tool in the United States? In Germany?
   b. How many of the machine tools would be produced in the United States? In Germany?
   c. How many of the machine tools would be bought in the United States? In Germany?

9. Only two firms, the Milton Company of the United Kingdom and the Frost Company of the United States, are capable of producing a new product. Because the Frost Company has a head start in developing the product, it will decide first whether to produce it. The following table shows the payoff matrix for the two firms.

Possible strategies for Milton	Possible strategies for Frost	
	Produce the product	Do not produce the product
Produce the product	Milton's profit: −$5 million Frost's profit: −$5 million	Milton's profit: $10 million Frost's profit: zero
Do not produce the product	Milton's profit: zero Frost's profit: $10 million	Milton's profit: zero Frost's profit: zero

   a. What will be the decision of the Frost Company?
   b. What will be the decision of the Milton Company?
   c. How can the British government influence this decision?
   d. What are the risks to the British government if it influences the decision according to your answer to part c?

10. Only two countries (Peru and Paraguay) can produce two products, C and D. Labor is the only input in producing these products. Each country can produce the following amount of each product with a day of labor:

	Product C (tons)	Product D (tons)
Paraguay	3	2
Peru	2	1

   a. Does Peru have an absolute advantage in the production of product C? Product D?
   b. Does Paraguay have an absolute advantage in the production of product C? Product D?
   c. Does Peru have a comparative advantage in the production of product C? Product D?
   d. Does Paraguay have a comparative advantage in the production of Product C? Product D?

Answers

Completion
1. the time it takes to build the plant, the cost of the plant   2. export of goods, direct investment in wholly owned subsidiaries, licenses, joint ventures
3. decrease, increase   4. tariff, quota, tariffs, quotas   5. Market forces, export
6. raw materials, defend, technological   7. subsidiaries, licensing   8. British pounds, Japanese yen, depreciate   9. imports, exports, more, depreciate
10. retaliatory, unfair

True or False
1. True   2. True   3. True   4. True   5. False   6. True   7. False
8. True   9. False   10. True

Multiple Choice
1. d   2. a   3. b   4. a   5. b   6. c   7. a   8. d   9. e   10. e

Problems
1. a.   10 quarters (although this would violate the firm's commitment).
   b.   2 quarters.
2. a.   15 marks. 20 marks. 10 marks.
   b.

German price of good (marks)	Total desired expenditure (in dollars)
20	2,500
15	5,000
10	6,000

   c.

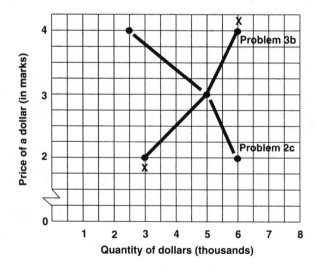

3. a.

Dollar price of good	Total desired expenditure (in dollars)
3	6,000
4	5,000
6	3,000

b. See answer to problem 2c.
c. 3 marks = 1 dollar
d. More marks would be demanded than supplied. There would be a shortage of marks.

4. a. Increase, increase
   b. Decrease, decrease
   c. Decrease, decrease
   d. Increase, increase
   e. Increase, increase
   f. Decrease, decrease

5. a. $2,000
   b. 8,000 per year

6. a. $200
   b. 4,000 per year

7. a. $1,000
   b. 7,000, 5,000
   c. 9,000, 3,000

8. a. $1,500, $500
   b. 7,500, 4,500
   c. 8,500, 3,500

9. a. Produce the product.
   b. Do not produce the product.
   c. Subsidize production of the product by Milton.
   d. The United States might retaliate.

10. a. No, no
    b. Yes, yes
    c. Yes, no
    d. No, yes

CASE EIGHT

Revving Up for Relief: Harley-Davidson at the ITC
Dorothy Robyn with assistance from Don Lippincott

Only the Harley when ridden down a straight highway makes a rider smile. Nothing else feels or sounds quite like it, and when you ride a Harley, nothing needs explaining. It's all said. You feel good, just looking at it.

Cycle World, May 1980

On September 1, 1982, Harley-Davidson, the U.S.-headquartered motorcycle manufacturer, petitioned the federal government for temporary relief from high levels of Japanese heavyweight motorcycles and motorcycle components. Harley claimed that the Japanese had exported a great many more heavyweight motorcycles to the U.S. than market demand warranted and, to reduce unprecedented inventories, were selling models at prices so low that Harley could not compete. Harley sought a "temporary respite from imports to regain its competitiveness and attain a strong market position over the long-term."

The body to whom Harley made its petition was the U.S. International Trade Commission. Created in 1916 as the U.S. Tariff Commission, the ITC is an independent, quasi-judicial entity charged with investigating possible injury from imports to U.S. producers and workers. The six commissioners—appointed by the president for non-renewable nine-year terms—also make policy recommendations to the president concerning specific remedies (e.g., tariffs, quotas, and orderly marketing agreements), if warranted.

Even before the evidence from Harley-Davidson and its Japanese competitors was in, the decision facing the ITC looked to be a tough one. In the fall of 1982, gloomy forecasts of a deepening U.S. recession had combined with a postwar-high 10.4% unemployment rate to intensify already widespread protectionist sentiment. American antagonism toward imports was mounting steadily, and proposed remedies were directed especially toward Japan and its skyrocketing trade surplus. At the same time, the Reagan administration, less than two years old, had voiced strong support for free trade, and Reagan had already overruled one ITC recommendation to extend existing trade protection.

This case was written for use at the John F. Kennedy School of Government, Harvard Universtiy. (0987) Copyright © 1986 by the President and Fellows of Harvard College. Reprinted with permission of the Kennedy School of Government Case Program, Harvard University.

Harley-Davidson and the U.S. Motorcycle Market.[1]

Established in Milwaukee in 1903 by William Harley and the three Davidson brothers, Harley-Davidson had become all but "synonymous with the word motorcycle" after half a century of operations. In 1955, for example, Harley had 60–70% of the (largely heavyweight) American market, with sales of roughly $20 million. Britain's BSA, Triumph, and Norton companies and the Italian Moto-Guzzi served the rest of that market, which—with motorcycle ownership constant at around 500,000—was largely stagnant between 1950 and 1960.

In 1959, two Japanese producers—Honda and Yamaha—entered the U.S. market. Honda, which with sales of $55 million was already the world's largest motorcycle manufacturer, established a U.S. subsidiary (other foreign producers relied on distributors) and began offering very small, lightweight motorcycles. Technically superior to anything comparable produced in the U.S., these cycles sold for under $250 retail, compared to $1,000 to $1,500 for the bigger American and British machines. A marketing effort backed by heavy expenditures on advertising ("You meet the nicest people on a Honda") sought to counter the unsavory image of "bikers."

Honda's strategy (subsequently adopted by other Japanese producers), combined with demographic changes that increased the number of 14 to 24 year olds by half between 1960 and 1970, produced a radical change in the size and shape of the U.S. motorcycle market. Sales rose from 40,000-50,000 units in 1960 to well over a million in 1974, by which time more than 2.4% of all Americans owned motorcycles. Lightweight models—a negligible part of the market in 1960—dominated it by 1966; while they lost ground to middleweight models

in the late 1960s and early 1970s, Japanese manufacturers were by then producing motorcycles of that size as well. In short, by 1974, Japanese producers were dominating a market shared by U.S. and European companies only 15 years earlier.

Because the overall U.S. market for motorcycles grew so dramatically, Harley prospered throughout most of this decade and a half of change. By 1970, its market share had dropped below 5%, but Harley was marking its seventh consecutive year of revenue growth, and sales exceeded $50 million. In 1973, Honda, Suzuki, and Kawasaki entered the over-750cc market segment, and in 1974, Kawasaki—then the leading Japanese producer of heavyweight motorcycles—opened a plant in Lincoln, Nebraska designed to produce up to 100,000 bikes per year. While Harley's share of the heavyweight market plummeted from 99.6% in 1972 to 44% in 1975, the company's fraction of the total U.S. market for motorcycles grew continuously during that time.

In 1978, faced with mounting Japanese inventories and price cuts, Harley petitioned the ITC for relief from Japanese motorcycles of all sizes, alleging that imports were being sold, or were likely to be sold, at less than fair value, in violation of the Antidumping Act of 1921. The ITC determined unanimously that while such dumping may indeed have occurred, Harley had not been injured—as evidenced by the fact that the company had been consistently profitable from 1972–77 and that the demand for heavyweights was growing.

By late 1982, Harley's condition had deteriorated. Three years earlier, Honda of America had begun domestic production in Marysville, Ohio. With a work force of some 450, the Ohio plant was turning out 50,000 motorcycles annually, including Honda's top-of-the-line models.

---

[1]This section draws heavily on the following: Harvard Business School, *Note on the Motorcycle Industry-1975*, (#578–210); and *Harley Davidson/Marketing Strategies for Motorcycles-1977*, (#9-584-032).

Kawasaki was by then employing roughly 350 workers in its Nebraska plant to produce 1000cc heavyweights. Harley's sales had slipped from just over 50,000 in 1979 to just over 30,000 in 1982, and its share of the large cycle market had dropped from 21% to 14% in the same three-year period. Once again, Harley turned to the ITC.

Harley filed its 1982 complaint under Section 201 of the 1974 Trade Act, which—unlike those sections of the law under which the overwhelming majority of relief petitions before the ITC are filed—does not require proof of an unfair foreign trade practice (e.g., pricing below cost, or "dumping") or government subsidy to be affirmed. Section 201 is known as the "escape clause" since it allows countries—under special circumstances—to impose temporary import relief which would normally not be permissible for signatories to the General Agreement on Tariffs and Trade (GATT), an international framework of rules designed to promote free trade. Congress intended this clause to provide "additional time to permit a seriously injured domestic industry to become competitive under relief measures, and, at the same time, to create incentives for the industry to adjust, if possible, to competitive conditions in the absence of long-term restrictions." However, to receive tariff or quota relief under 201, not only must an industry demonstrate serious injury (or the threat of such injury) from increasing imports competing directly with its products, but no other cause (such as the general economic climate, poor management, etc.) can be considered a more important cause of injury:

> The Commission shall . . . make an investigation to determine whether an article is being imported into the United States in such increased quantities as to be a substantial cause of serious injury, or the threat thereof, to the domestic industry producing an article like or directly competitive with the imported article.

THE DEBATE OVER INJURY

Harley-Davidson

When the ITC convened a hearing on November 30, 1982, Harley opened its case by attempting to show that it was the only U.S. producer of heavyweight motorcycles. This definitional point was important because by excluding production and sales figures of Kawasaki USA and Honda of America, Harley could make a stronger case for injury to the domestic industry.

Although the ITC had ruled in 1978 that Kawasaki USA was a domestic producer, Harley argued that the U.S. operations of Kawasaki and Honda "are not true motorcycle manufacturing facilities because [they] are limited to the assembly of motorcycle components, which are largely of Japanese origin, and the manufacture of minor components." Moreover, since the domestic content of the final products was less than 50%, Harley maintained, they should be considered foreign imports.

A second definitional argument was that the term "heavyweight" should include 750cc engines and motorcycles (industry sources generally limited the term to engines and motorcycles with displacement greater than 750cc). Harley spokesmen maintained that the 750cc models—manufactured exclusively by Japanese producers—were "like and directly competitive with" Harley's (larger) models, consistent with the language of Section 201. Harley-Davidson chairman Vaughn L. Beals cited a recent trade press study that included new owners of a particular Harley 1000cc model; 43% of those questioned said they had also considered a 750cc model (see Exhibit 1).

EXHIBIT 1   Engine Size of Other Motorcycles Considered

	TOTAL BUYERS	BMW R100 BUYERS	HARLEY-DAVIDSON XLH/XLS 1000 BUYERS	HONDA GL 1100 BUYERS	KAWASAKI KZ 550 BUYERS	SUZUKI GS 550 BUYERS	SUZUKI GS 1100 BUYERS	YAMAHA XJ 750 BUYERS
Less than 400cc	3 %	5 %	3 %	5 %	2 %	3 %	1 %	3 %
400–499cc	5	–	1	1	9	18	–	1
500–599cc	23	3	4	2	59	54	2	10
600–699cc	16	2	17	2	22	45	1	15
700–799cc	30	12	43	7	38	21	12	69
800–899cc	5	10	4	6	3	2	1	11
900–999cc	15	17	16	8	8	1	44	16
1,000–1,199cc	45	80	54	72	18	8	83	30
1,200cc or more	11	22	12	30	1	3	9	6
Total	*	*	*	*	*	*	*	*
Average engine size	865cc	1,045cc	925cc	1,100cc	690cc	640cc	1,040cc	835cc

Base: Buyers who considered other makes.
*Totals exceed 100% due to multiple responses.

Source: Ziff-Davis Publishing Co. survey (1982), presented as testimony before the US International Trade Commission, Investigation No. TA-201-47.

EXHIBIT 2 **U.S. Sales of Heavyweight Motorcycles: Total, Harley-Davidson, Japanese, and Total Imports 1977–1982**
(Sales in Units; Market Share in Percent)

	TOTAL		HARLEY-DAVIDSON		JAPANESE		TOTAL IMPORTS	
	SALES	MARKET SHARE	SALES	MARKET SHARE	SALES	MARKET SHARE	SALES	MARKET SHARE
1977	200,174	100.0	41,972	21.0	143,052	71.5	158,202	79.0
1978	209,789	100.0	44,469	21.2	152,993	72.9	165,320	78.8
1979	253,824	100.0	51,760	20.4	190,000	74.9	202,064	79.6
1980	238,892	100.0	40,567	17.0	192,643	80.6	198,325	83.0
1981	246,712	100.0	41,321	16.7	200,353	81.2	205,391	83.3
1982[1]	220,000E	100.0	31,500E	14.3E	185,640E	84.4E	188,500E	85.7E
1982 Jan.-Sept.	193,557	100.0	26,648	14.8	162,311	83.9	164,909	85.2

E = Estimated

[1]Estimated by Harley-Davidson based on 9 months data and seasonal adjustment factors.

Source: R. L. Polk registration data, presented in testimony before the US International Trade Commission, Investigation No. TA-201-47.

Moving from definitional to substantive arguments, Harley addressed the criteria for 201 relief:

1. Dramatic Increases in Imports Have Occurred. Citing new motorcycle registration data (a proxy for retail sales), Harley claimed that U.S. sales of Japanese heavyweight machines had gone from 143,052 in 1977 to 200,353 in 1981—a 40% increase (see Exhibit 2). Taking into account projected 1982 sales, the Japanese would be able to claim 84% of the U.S. heavyweight market, up from 71.5% in 1977. Looking just at 790+cc motorcycles imported fully assembled from Japan, Department of Commerce data indicated that between 1977 and 1982 U.S. inventories had increased by more than 152,000 units (see Exhibit 3).

2. Imports Have Caused Serious Injury. Although the total U.S. heavyweight motorcycle market increased by 23% between 1977 and 1981, Harley spokesmen argued, Harley-Davidson's sales showed a net decline of 2%. Sales in 1982 were projected to reach only 31,500 units, a 25% drop from their 1977 level, and a 39% drop from their peak sales level in 1979. This loss of sales and market share was responsible for tremendous declines in production and capacity utilization, profits, and employment—the very definition of economic injury under Section 201.[2]

EXHIBIT 3 **Estimated Changes in U.S. Inventories of Heavyweight Japanese Motorcycles (790cc and Over), Based on U.S. Imports for Consumption and U.S. Registrations (Units)**

	U.S. REGISTRATIONS OF JAPANESE MOTORCYCLES (790+CC)[*]	IMPORTS FOR CONSUMPTION FROM JAPAN[†]	ESTIMATED INVENTORY INCREASE[‡]
1977	30,378	38,615	8,237
1978	45,048	68,768	23,720
1979	62,383	88,379	25,996
1980	84,924	123,237	38,313
1981	71,479	116,011	44,532
1982 (Jan.-Sept.)	81,169	92,732	11,563
Total inventory increase, 1977–September 1982			152,361

[*]Total registrations of Japanese heavyweight motorcycles, less estimated registrations of U.S.-assembled motorcycles and registrations of motorcycles with engine displacements between 700cc and 790cc.
[†]TSUA number 692.5075.
[‡]Calculated as imports less registrations

Source: R. L. Polk registration data. U.S. Department of Commerce (IM146), presented in testimony before the U.S. International Trade Commission, Investigation No. TA-201-47.

---

[2]Among the symptoms of economic injury to domestic producers that the ITC is required by law to consider are: (a) significant idling of productive facilities; (b) inability to operate at a reasonable profit; and (c) significant unemployment or underemployment.

As evidence of idling facilities, Harley cited "dramatic" production declines from 1980 to 1982, and a steep drop in its capacity utilization—from 85% in 1980 to 51% in 1982. To demonstrate unprofitability, Harley provided (proprietary) tables showing operating losses in the millions for 1981 and 1982 as well as concomitant cutbacks in capital investment, engineering, and R&D. A banker from Harley's chief lender, Citicorp, testified that the motorcycle manufacturer had been a successful corporation for over 80 years with unparalleled, "almost fanatical customer support." He maintained that no one could have predicted the unprecedented importation of Japanese motorcycles into the U.S. "far in excess of demand" and the "drastic price reductions" of the Japanese firms that were threatening the company's lifeblood. Although Harley management appeared to be doing everything it could to stay afloat, he warned, the company's "very survival [was] threatened":

> As a result of its disproportionate loss of sales, [Harley] is in an overadvanced situation. In other words, we are extending credit to Harley-Davidson in excess of the amounts available under the formula terms of the loan agreement. . . .

Under the circumstances, a lender is entitled to declare the borrower in default under the loan agreement. Our continuing support of Harley-Davidson, therefore, is extraordinary.

With respect to unemployment, which Harley termed the "most devastating effect" of the increased imports, grim statistics indicated that roughly 36% of its work force—or 1,159 employees—had lost their jobs during the preceding nine-month period (see Exhibit 4). Other evidence included temporary plant closings and reduction of management salaries and benefits during the past year.

3. Imports Have Been a "Substantial Cause" of Injury. As prima facie evidence that imports had been a "substantial cause" of its injury, Harley underscored the simultaneity of the decline of its own market share with the rise in the Japanese percentage. By way of explanation, Harley's chief economic consultant, Stanley Nehmer, pointed to the pattern of price suppression by Japanese producers.

> Although demand was exceptionally strong in 1979, Japanese producers kept their prices low enough to increase

EXHIBIT 4   **Total Number of Employees Engaged in United States (Harley-Davidson) Production and Sale of Heavyweight Motorcycles (700+ cc) (1977–1982)***

YEAR	HOURLY	SALARIED	TOTAL
1977	1903	1097	3000
1978	2054	1189	3243
1979	2204	1262	3476
1980	2148	1321	3469
1981	2167	1153	3320
1982[†]	1216	945	2161

*Year end total.
†July.

Source: Harley-Davidson

their market share. In 1980, however, when confronted with a drop in the level of demand from the previous year, Japanese producers cut import prices and instituted aggressive dealer and consumer incentive programs, so that they increased both their share of U.S. sales and their sales volume. Conversely, Harley-Davidson suffered a 22 percent loss of volume, and a sharp drop in market share that year. These trends have continued in 1981 and 1982, and the Japanese have steadily gained market share and volume.

As further evidence of price-cutting, Nehmer cited Commerce Department data showing that between 1977 and 1982, the "average unit value" of imports from Japan of motorcycles of 790cc and above had declined both in current dollars and in real (1977) dollars (see Exhibit 5):

The Japanese price cutting strategy appears to have become especially aggressive during 1982 [when] for the first time since 1979–80, overall market

demand has declined. . . . [I]n spite of the downturn in the market, imports . . . are literally flooding the market.

The impact of these price cuts on Harley's market share had been dramatic, Nehmer concluded (see Exhibit 6).

This impact had been seriously aggravated, moreover, by the introduction of Japanese models that virtually copied elements of Harley styling, its traditional area of distinction. Harley Chairman Vaughn Beals cited several trade publication articles including one describing a conversation with a Japanese designer in the industry:

One Japanese stylist told me, "We are very conscious of beauty. We know what looks right to the Japanese, but in areas of Western design, such as motorcycles, we are not so sure of ourselves. So we tend to copy what others are doing successfully such as Harley-Davidson. We hire European stylists because we assume they know better than we do what Westerners like."

EXHIBIT 5   **Heavyweight Motorcycles from Japan: Quality, Value, and Average Unit Value of U.S. Imports for Consumption of Motorcycles with Engine Displacement of 790cc and Over, 1977–1981 and First Nine Months of 1981 and 1982**

	QUANTITY (UNITS)	VALUE* (CURRENT DOLLARS)	AVERAGE UNIT VALUE (CURRENT DOLLARS)	AVERAGE UNIT VALUE[†] (1977 DOLLARS)
1977	38,615	64,300,850	1,665	1,665
1978	68,768	133,740,290	1,945	1,804
1979	88,379	185,180,121	2,095	1,749
1980	123,237	241,080,179	1,956	1,439
1981	116,011	235,865,402	2,033	1,369
1981 (Jan.-Sept.)	81,491	168,053,244	2,062	1,389
1982 (Jan.-Sept.)	92,732	168,620,970	1,818	1,184

*Customs value basis.
[†]Deflated using U.S. Producer Price Index, index based on 1977 = 100.

Source: U.S. Department of Commerce (IM146), Bureau of Labor Statistics, Producer Price Index, presented in testimony before the U.S. International Trade Commission, Investigation No. TA-201-47.

EXHIBIT 6 **Indices of Harley-Davidson's Market Share and the Average Unit F.O.B. Value of Imports from Japan of 790+cc Motorcycles, 1977–1982 (1977 = 100)**

*Deflated to 1977 dollars using the *Producer Price Index*.
†1982 figures annualized based on 9 months' seasonally adjusted data.

Source: R. L. Polk registration data and the Bureau of Labor Statistics, Producer Price Index, presented in testimony before the U.S. International Trade Commission, Investigation No. TA-201-47.

As part of this strategy of duplication, Beals claimed, the Japanese had introduced the "dresser" or long-distance touring bike, and the "V"-configuration engine—the "heart" of the Harley motorcycle, the thing that "automatically conveys [its] masculine image . . . its sleek look." Harley consultant Stanley Nehmer addressed the economic implications of this strategy.

These models were first introduced by the Japanese in 1980, and accounted for only a small share of total 1980 sales [see Exhibit 7]. With the introduction of a series of new Japanese V-configuration and "dresser" models in 1981 and 1982, however, these "Harley-type" motorcycles have obtained a substantial and growing share of the total heavyweight market, almost totally at Harley-Davidson's expense.

4. Imports Have Been the Most Important Cause of Injury. Finally, Harley advocates argued that high interest rates, unemployment, and other macroeconomic factors had been a much less important source of injury than Japanese imports. Had Harley maintained its 1979 market share (20.4%) during 1980–82, Nehmer calculated, it would have sold an additional 41,892 motorcycles. Of this falloff in sales relative to

299

EXHIBIT 7   **Relative U.S. Market Shares Held by Various Heavyweight Motorcycles, 1977–1982**

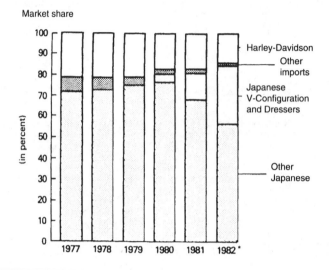

*1982 Estimate based on 9 months' data and seasonal adjustment factors.

Source: R. L. Polk registration data, presented in testimony before the U.S. International Trade Commission, Investigation No. TA-201-47.

1979 levels, 27.1% (or 11,337 units) was attributable to declining overall demand, and 72.9% to increased import sales (see Exhibit 8).

Harley stressed that it was pursuing an aggressive recovery plan, including quality control, an advanced inventory system, and plans to develop a new "family" of lower-end heavyweights. In the first year of this program, Harley boasted, it had doubled the number of defect-free shipments and lowered its break-even point from 53,000 to 35,000 cycles sold per year. However, without immediate import relief, Harley's chairman cautioned, the "prospects for completing these vital programs, quite frankly, are bleak."

Japanese Producers

Unanimously contesting the validity of the Harley petition were U.S. subsidiaries of the "Big Four" Japanese cycle producers: Honda, Kawasaki, Suzuki, and Yamaha. The Japanese companies challenged Harley's definition of terms as well as its substantive claims regarding injury.

On the question of who qualified as a domestic producer, the Japanese manufacturers disputed Harley's less-than-50%-local-content rule as legally irrelevant and underscored the sizable capital investment by Honda of America and Kawasaki USA, who together employed more than 800 American workers.

The "Big Four" also sought to redefine which of their products should be included in the injury claim. First, they argued that 750cc cycles were not "like or directly competitive with" Harley products— limited to 1000cc and 1340cc cycles—as required by Section 201. Price was the major explanation, they maintained: 1982 dealer costs for the lowest priced 1000cc

EXHIBIT 8 **Importance of Increasing Imports Relative to Declining Demand as an Explanation for the Decline in Harley-Davidson's Sales of Heavyweight (700+cc) Motorcycles Since 1979**

	1979	1980	1981	1982*	CUMULATIVE 1980–1982 LOST SALES
Total heavyweight motorcycle sales in the United States	253,824	238,892	246,712	220,000E	–
Sales of Harley-Davidson motorcycles in the United States	51,760	40,567	41,321	31,500E	–
Projected sales of Harley-Davidson motorcycles at 1979 market share[†]	–	48,734	50,329	44,880E	–
Total decline in Harley-Davidson motorcycles sales from 1979 levels	–	11,193	10,439	20,260E	41,892
Net decline in Harley-Davidson's sales due to increased import sales	–	8,167	9,008	13,380E	30,555
Net decline in Harley-Davidson's sales due to declining demand	–	3,026	1,431	6,880E	11,337
Share of decline in Harley-Davidson's sales due to increased import sales (percent)	–	73.0	86.3	66.0E	72.9
Share of declining Harley-Davidson sales due to declining demand (percent)	–	27.0	13.7	34.0E	27.1

E = Estimated.

*Estimated on the basis of January–September 1982 data and seasonal adjustment factors presented in the Polk Report.

[†]Projection made based on Harley-Davidson 1979 market share of 20.4 percent. Harley-Davidson's market shares in 1977 and 1978 were 21.0 and 21.2 percent, respectively.

Source: testimony before the U.S. International Trade Commission, Investigation No. TA-201-47.

bike were $500 greater than for the most expensive 750cc cycle, and dealer markups only accentuated the disparity.

Such a pricing pattern indicates that producers have positioned their models to appeal to the broadest range of consumers, while minimizing the competitive overlap between engine categories. It appears, therefore, that any competition between producers would take place within each engine size category but not to any significant degree between categories.

The Japanese producers also cited a consultant's survey of motorcycle owners which found a very low incidence of cross-pricing between Harley and bikes in the 700–899cc range.

Second, Japanese producers maintained that their importation of power train components was in no way injurious to the U.S., since no domestic industry for such components existed, nor would one exist in the absence of imports. Moreover, the importation of power train components reflected current practice by domestic producers throughout the motor vehicle industry.

As to the question of injury, the Japanese producers made two fundamental arguments. Japanese-brand cycles weren't competitive with Harleys; even within the same (large) engine size category, the two markets were distinct. Consistent with that, Harley's financial troubles were not caused by Japanese competition; rather, they stemmed from the 1981–82 recession and associated unemployment.

Absence of Competition

Looking just at the 1000cc and larger bikes, Japanese producers compared "dealer net prices" for Japanese and Harley brands across four models: dressed tourers, standard tourers, cruisers, and sportsters. Harley's were consistently more expensive—on average, by $1600, $1800, $1500, and $400 for the four models respectively. Harley's and Japanese models were in "distinctly separate market segments," they concluded.

As additional evidence of non-competitiveness, Japanese producers cited performance characteristics compiled by *Cycle Guide* for selected Harley and Japanese-brand cruisers and dressed tourers. In both instances, the Japanese bikes recorded superior characteristics in seven important categories, including top speed, fuel consumption, braking, and price (see Exhibit 9). In the dressed tourers, the superior Honda GL1100A listed for $6600 versus $7900 for the Harley FLH Classic. In the cruisers, the Kawasaki Z1100 Spectre listed for $4300 versus $7300 for the Harley FXRS. The Japanese concluded that, given the superior technical performance and significantly lower cost to the consumer, "There would appear to be no reason for a rational purchaser to select a Harley . . . [and that] head-to-head competition [w]ould have eliminated Harley from the market long ago."

Finally, Japanese producers pointed to a consultant's survey which revealed that only 55 of 262 (21%) Harley owners polled said they had priced a Japanese alternative, and only 80 of 794 (10.1%) Japanese cycle owners had priced Harleys. This was true despite the fact that a large number of dealers sold both Harleys and Japanese bikes, and shoppers had only to walk across the floor. Thus, the Japanese concluded, Harley owners were indeed "a breed apart."

EXHIBIT 9   **Comparative Performance Characteristics of Selected Harley-Davidson and Japanese Brand Motorcycles, 1982**

	DRESSED TOURERS		CRUISERS	
	HONDA GL1100A	H-D FLH CLASSIC	KAWASAKI Z1100 SPECTRE	H-D FXRS
Engine displacement (cc)	1,085	1,339	1,090	1,339
Quarter-mile time (seconds)	13	15	12	14
Speed end of quarter-mile (mph)	99	82	110	93
Top speed (mph)	139	101	142	109
Weights (lbs)	724	752	553	594
Fuel consumption (mpg)	40–50	32–42	36–44	40–47
Stopping distance from 60 mph (in feet)	145	180	132	124
Suggested list price	$6,600	$7,900	$4,300	$7,300

Source: *Cycle Guide*, November, 1982, p. 4, as presented in testimony before the U.S. International Trade Commission, Investigation No. TA-201-47.

Harley-Davidson's Sales Performance

Economic conditions, not Japanese competition, were the primary cause of Harley's injuries, the "Big Four" maintained: Heavyweight motorcycles are a "big-ticket luxury consumer product," and their purchase is therefore highly sensitive to changes in the general economy. Using quarterly employment data, the Japanese producers' chief economic consultant, John Reilly of ICF, Inc., found that 73% of the variation in Harley sales between 1979 and 1982 was explained by the level of blue collar employment (see Exhibit 10). (Use of semi-annual employment data produced an even higher proportion of variation explained.) By comparison, the level of sales of Japanese-brand motorcycles explained less of the variation in Harley sales (see Exhibit 11).

THE DEBATE OVER IMPORT RELIEF

Harley's Proposal

To allow for recovery from the injury imports had caused, Harley requested a five-year increase in the existing 4.4% tariff on imported 700cc and larger heavyweight motorcycles and power train components:

48% for the first three years, 40% in the fourth year, and 30% in the fifth year. The American manufacturer sought to restore the approximate price differential between Japanese and Harley heavyweights that existed in 1979. Using statistics on "average unit value" of 790cc and larger imports, Harley computed that the real value of imports had dropped by $883 between 1979 and 1982; stated differently, a tariff rate of 48% was necessary to restore import values to their 1979 level (see Exhibit 12). (Harley lacked data on 700cc–790cc cycles, but maintained that a comparable price decline had occurred in that segment of the market.)

The effect of the proposed tariff on sales of existing Japanese models would be delayed due to the "massive" size of current inventories, Harley recognized. But the tariff would immediately limit the ability of Japanese producers to introduce low-priced new models aimed at the upscale niche, with direct benefits to Harley-Davidson: increased sales, a reduction in costly rebate and dealer support programs, and a renewal of creditors' confidence.

In addition to improving its own bottom line, Harley argued, the proposed import relief should provide other benefits to the

---

EXHIBIT 10 **Proportion of Variation (R^2) in Harley-Davidson Sales Explained by Blue-Collar Employment**

PERIOD	NUMBER OF DATA POINTS	R^2	T STATISTIC*	D-W STATISTIC
$Q_1 77$–$Q_2 82$	22	0.54	4.93	1.6
$Q_1 78$–$Q_2 82$	18	0.59	4.80	1.7
$Q_1 79$–$Q_2 82$	14	0.73	5.65	2.3
$Q_1 80$–$Q_2 82$	10	0.63	3.70	2.5
$Q_1 81$–$Q_2 82$	6	0.69	3.01	3.2

*The T Statistic in each case indicates a confidence level of 95% or better that the regression is valid.

Source: ICF Inc. (December 13, 1982), presented a post-hearing submission to the U.S. International Trade Commission, Investigation No. TA-201-47.

EXHIBIT 11   Proportion of Variation (R^2) in Harley-Davidson Sales Explained by Sales of Japanese Motorcycles

SALES OF JAPANESE-BRAND MOTORCYCLES SPECIFIED AS INDEPENDENT VARIABLES

PERIOD	NUMBER OF DATA POINTS	700cc AND LARGER		900cc AND LARGER		1000cc AND LARGER	
		R	R^2	R	R^2	R	R^2
$Q_1$77–$Q_2$82	22	0.14	0.02	-0.13	0.02	0.26	0.07
$Q_1$78–$Q_2$82	18	0.13	0.02	-0.21	0.04	0.29	0.08
$Q_1$79–$Q_2$82	14	0.30	0.09	-0.19	0.04	0.47	0.22
$Q_1$80–$Q_2$82	10	0.44	0.20	0.37	0.14	0.54	0.30
$Q_1$81–$Q_2$82	6	0.45	0.20	0.49	0.24	0.44	0.19

SALES OF JAPANESE-BRAND MOTORCYCLES SPECIFIED AS INDEPENDENT VARIABLES

PERIOD	NUMBER OF DATA POINTS	700cc AND LARGER		900cc AND LARGER		1000cc AND LARGER	
		R	R^2	R	R^2	R	R^2
1st half 77–1st half 82	11	0.06	0.00	-0.24	0.06	0.19	0.03
1st half 78–1st half 82	9	0.03	0.00	-0.35	0.12	0.20	0.04
1st half 79–1st half 82	7	0.21	0.04	-0.39	0.16	0.41	0.17
1st half 80–1st half 82	5	0.56	0.32	0.46	0.21	0.60	0.36

Source: ICF Inc. (December 13, 1982), presented as a post-hearing submission to the U.S. International Trace Commission, Investigation No. TA-201-47.

EXHIBIT 12   **Calculation of the Average Increase in the Tariff Rate Needed to Restore the Prices of Imported Heavyweight Motorcycles to Their 1979 Level***

Actual average unit value of imports in 1979	$2,124
Projected average unit value of imports in 1982 (2,124 × 1.28[†])	$2,719
Actual average unit value of imports for the first nine months of 1982	$1,836
Difference between projected and actual value	$883
Percentage point increase in tariff rate needed to bring the actual unit value to the projected unit value	48

*Based on the average unit value of imports of 790cc and above heavyweight motorcycles.
[†]Percentage increase in the U.S. PPI between 1979 and January–September, 1982.

Source: Testimony before the U.S. International Trade Commission, Investigation No. TA-201-47.

U.S. economy as well. Most important, Harley could re-employ workers it had been forced to lay off—1,159 of them during the first seven months of 1982. Harley's U.S. secondary suppliers would also benefit from the company's increased production. And although U.S. consumers would face higher retail prices for motorcycles in the short run, the proposed import relief should encourage competition, and hence lower prices, in the long run. The benefits of current low import prices were less than it would seem, moreover, Harley explained, because they were based chiefly on excessive inventories:

> Whereas Harley-Davidson's experience suggests that sales can be maintained adequately with six months worth of dealer inventories, available information suggests that the Japanese have approximately one and a half to two years of inventories on hand. This implies that the importers and dealers of Japanese motorcycles have at least one year of *excess* inventories, the annual carrying costs of which may be as high as $400–$500 per unit. These carrying costs represent a deadweight loss to the economy.

Japanese Producers' Response

In a post-hearing brief, Japanese cycle producers challenged Harley's case for a steep import tariff. The challenge was twofold. First, the proposed remedy wasn't justified: Harley's analysis of the tariff (48%) necessary to restore Japanese cycle prices to their 1979 level was flawed. Second, even if such a steep tariff were necessary to restore 1979 prices, the adverse economic impact it would have—on consumers, dealers, and workers—was unacceptably large.

Flawed Analysis

Harley's analysis of Japanese motorcycle prices—which was based on the declining value of imported cycles between 1979 and 1982 (see Exhibit 12) was flawed in three respects, Japanese producers argued. First, "import values" (i.e., f.o.b. values) of Japanese cycles understated the price dealers paid, which is "what should be of concern to Harley-Davidson." Second, import-value data excluded 750cc motorcycles, which accounted for more than half of all sales of Japanese 700cc and larger cycles.

Third, import data by definition ignored domestic content—in particular that of Honda's most expensive motorcycles, which had been produced in the U.S. since 1981—and hence distorted the trend in the real value of Japanese-brand heavy-weights.

The "Big Four" producers offered, as an alternative, data drawn from their consultant's survey of Japanese manufacturers. Figures for 1977–82 on the volume of cycles shipped annually to dealers and the price to dealers of the average cycle in each shipment, expressed both in current dollars and in constant 1967 dollars (see Exhibit 13), provided the basis for a series of calculations designed to dispute Harley's findings.

First, using 1967 dollars as the measuring rod, the Japanese producers calculated the decline in Japanese-brand cycle prices between 1979 and 1982—that is, the amount necessary to restore prices to their 1979 level, Harley's stated goal. This amount—$46, or $141 in 1982 dollars[3]—was far less than Harley's comparable figure of $883.

The Japanese brief then calculated the tariff rate necessary to increase the average price of an imported 1982 Japanese motorcycle, as specified by Harley ($1,836), by $141. The result: 7.7% (see Exhibit 14). To pass that same amount on to dealers, the Japanese concluded using their own data on dealer costs, would result in a 4.7% price increase to dealers (see Exhibit 14).

Finally, the Japanese brief repeated those same calculations using a base period of 1977–1979, on the grounds that the 1979 base year chosen by Harley was the year in which real prices of Japanese motorcycles to dealers reached their peak. Those calculations indicated that to restore 1982 prices to their 1977–79 level would require a tariff rate of 4.5% and a price increase to dealers of 2.7% (see Exhibit 15).

EXHIBIT 13   **Average Prices of Shipments of Japanese Brand 750cc and Larger Motorcycles to Dealers, 1977–1981, and January–September 1982 (in Current Dollars and in Constant 1967 Dollars)**

PERIOD	UNITS SHIPPED	TOTAL VALUE ($ 000)	AVERAGE UNIT PRICE	PPI INDUSTRIAL PRODUCTS	AVERAGE UNIT PRICE* ($1,967)
1977	164,537	314,720	1,913	195.1	981
1978	168,691	364,033	2,158	209.4	1,031
1979	185,050	453,054	2,448	236.5	1,035
1980	217,346	580,345	2,670	274.8	972
1981	223,909	635,172	2,837	304.1	933
1982 (9 months)	150,338	454,937	3,026	306.1	989

*(Average unit price ÷ PPI) × 100 = unit value ($1967).

Source: ICT analysis based upon questionnaire responses by Honda, Kawasaki, Suzuki, and Yamaha. The shipments and shipment values reported in the Honda of America Manufacturing producer questionnaire were for transfers of motorcycles to America Honda, which sells the motorcycles to dealers. The data reflect America Honda's actual shipments to dealers and shipment values of motorcycles produced domestically by Honda American Manufacturing, as reported to ICF by American Honda. Presented to U.S. International Trade Commission, Investigation No. TA-201-47.

[3](1) $1,035–$989 = $46. (2) ($46) (306.1/100) = $141.

EXHIBIT 14   **Tariff Rate and Price Effects Based upon the Harley-Davidson Method Applied to a Correct Calculation of the Change in the Real Price of Japanese-Brand 750cc and Larger Motorcycles Between 1979 and January–September 1982 (in 1982 Dollars)**

Average unit value of 1982 imports from Japan*	$1,836
Price increase required to restore 1979 real unit value	$141
Tariff Rate [($141 ÷ $1,836)(100)]	7.7
Average 1982 price to dealers	$3,026
Average price increase to pass tariff cost on to dealers†	$141
Percent price increase to dealers	4.7

*The calculations in Exhibit 14 are based upon an average import value of $1,836 for 1982 as specified by Harley-Davidson. Based upon questionnaire responses, the USITC reported average 1982 import unit value of $2,123.
†The importer and the dealer would incur an inventory carrying cost on the amount represented by the tariff. For the purpose of simplification, such costs, which would amount to about eight dollars per unit, have been omitted from the analysis.

Source: ICF, Inc. Presented to U.S. International Trade Commission, Investigation No. TA-201-47.

EXHIBIT 15   **Tariff Rate and Price Effects Based upon a 1977–1979 Base Period (in 1982 Dollars)**

Actual unit value of 1982 imports from Japan	$1,836
Price increase required to restore 1977–1979 real unit value	$83*
Tariff rate [($83 ÷ $1,836)(100)]	4.5
Average 1982 price to dealers	$3,026
Average price increase to pass tariff cost on to dealers	$83
Percent price increase to dealer	2.7

*Japanese producers obtained the $83 figure as follows:
1. For 1977–79, the average price of Japanese-brand motorcycles sold to dealers was $1,016 in 1967 dollars (derived from Exhibit 2).
2. Restoration of the 1982 average import price to the 1977–79 level would require a price increase of $27 in 1967 dollars ($1016 – $989 = $27).
3. In 1982 dollars, that represents $83 [($27)(306.1 ÷ 100) = $83].

Source: ICF, Inc. Presented to U.S. International Trade Commission, Investigation No. TA-201-47.

Economic Impact

Putting aside their statistical refutation of Harley's proposed tariff, the Japanese producers turned to an assessment of its economic impact. They looked in turn at "potential impacts" on motorcycle dealers (and indirectly, consumers), accessories producers, and workers throughout the industry.

(a) Dealers

If the $883 figure computed by Harley (see Exhibit 12) were applied to 700cc and larger Japanese-brand motorcycles, it would increase their average retail price by 23.3%, the brief asserted (see Exhibit 16). The Japanese producers' analysis assumed a 25% dealer markup on cost. The analysis also assumed that the tariff would apply to all Japanese motorcycles, whether imported or not.

Taking that estimated percentage price increase, the brief calculated the likely decline in sales of motorcycles subject to the tariff (see Exhibit 17). Assuming a demand for motorcycles that is moderately elastic ($\eta = 1$) with respect to price (on the rationale that cycles are non-essential and that their price represents a significant share of the average purchaser's annual income),

sales would decline by 45,293 units, from a base of 194,389. (The base figure—derived from Exhibit 13—equalled the average number of Japanese cycles shipped annually from 1977–81.) Assuming an even more elastic demand ($\eta = 1.5$), sales would fall by nearly 68,000 units. At an average dealer markup of $757 (25% of $3,026), this sales drop would reduce dealers' total net revenues by $34.2 to $51.4 million.

Of course, two effects could serve to offset those losses, the Japanese producers' analysis recognized: possible increases in sales of 650cc and smaller Japanese motorcycles and of Harley-Davidson motorcycles. Recognizing that "the vast majority of 700cc and larger motorcycle buyers are experienced riders who are either trading up from smaller machines or replacing heavyweight machines," the Japanese assumed that only 20% of those who would decline to buy 750cc and 850cc motorcycles would instead purchase a 650cc cycle. Offset sales of 650cc cycles would thus range from 4,710 to 7,065 units, depending on the elasticity of demand (throughout their brief, Japanese producers assumed that their customers' elasticity ranged from 1.0 to 1.5). At an average dealer profit of $500 per cycle,[4]

EXHIBIT 16   **Average Retail Price Increase for 700cc and Larger Japanese-Brand Motorcycles Implied by Harley-Davidson's Tariff Recommendations**

Average 1982 retail price*	$3,783
Average price increase to pass tariff cost on to consumers	$883
Percent retail price increase	23.3

*Based upon a dealer markup of 25 percent on cost, which is equal to the difference between listed dealer net prices for Japanese-brand machines and suggested retail prices.

Source: ICF, Inc. Presented to U.S. International Trade Commission, Investigation No. TA-201-47.

---

[4]That figure represented a 25% dealer markup on $2,000, the estimated average net cost for 550cc–650cc motorcycles.

EXHIBIT 17   **Decline in Sales of Japanese-Brand 700cc and Larger Motorcycles Associated with a 23.3 Percent Retail Price Increase**

	ELASTICITY OF 1.0	ELASTICITY OF 1.5
Base sales	194,389	194,389
Sales decline	45,293*	67,940†
Sales after price increase	149,096	126,449

*[(23.3 ÷ 100)(194,389)] = –45,293.
†[(23.3 ÷ 100)(–1.5)(194,389)] = –67,940.

Source: ICF, Inc. Presented to U.S. International Trade Commission, Investigation No. TA-201-47.

such sales would offset the decline in dealer revenues by $2.4 million–$3.6 million.

With respect to offset purchases of Harleys, the Japanese producers accepted, for the sake of argument, their opponent's view that "there is a significant cross-elasticity of demand relative to price between Harley products and 700cc and larger Japanese-brand machines.

. . . it will be assumed, to reflect Harley's point of view, that a tariff rate increase of 48 percent would be required [to restore Japanese brand prices to their 1979 level], and that the result of the tariff would be to increase Harley's sales to 42,500 units per year. (Harley claims that it needs to sell 40–45,000 units per year to make a satisfactory long-run profit.) Further reflecting Harley's point of view, sales of 42,500 units would reflect a sales gain of 6,200 units from a base sales level of 36,300 units. The base sales figure was derived by applying Harley's 15.2 percent market share [in 1982] of 700cc and larger motorcycles to a normal year's total sales of 239,000 units.

The Japanese producers calculated that with this sales gain of 6,200 cycles, Harley dealers' net revenue (profit) would rise

by $1,443—or $8.9 million. (The $1,443 figure represented 30% of Harley's net price to dealers during the first nine months of 1982 and was based on the difference between Harley's listed dealer prices and suggested retail prices for 1982.) The corresponding loss to Japanese-brand dealers, given an average profit of $757 per cycle, would be $4.7 million. Thus, tariff-induced sales of Harley cycles would offset the total decline in dealer revenues by $4.2 million ($8.9 million less $4.7 million). Taking both offsetting effects of the proposed tariff into account, then, the loss to dealers would range from $27.6 million to $43.6 million, the Japanese brief concluded (see Exhibit 18).

(b) Accessories producers

A sharp decline in motorcycle sales, argued Japanese producers, would stem the demand for related products, such as helmets, gloves, boots, mirrors, wind screens, and baggage carriers. "Assuming conservatively" that accessory purchases average $150 per new cycle sold, the loss of revenues to producers would amount to $6.1 million if elasticity of demand is low, $9.1 million if elasticity is high (see Exhibit 19).

EXHIBIT 18   **Effect of Proposed Tariff on Total Dealer Net Revenues (Million Dollars)**

	LOW	HIGH
Revenue lost due to decline in Japanese-brand 700cc and larger motorcycles	$ 34.2	$ 51.4
Revenues gained from sales of 650cc and smaller motorcycles	2.4	3.6
Revenues gained from increased Harley sales	4.2	4.2
Net revenue decline	$ 27.6	$ 43.6

Source: ICF, Inc. Presented to U.S. International Trade Commission, Investigation No. TA-201-47.

EXHIBIT 19   **Revenue Lost by Motorcycle Accessories Producers Due to Decline in Motorcycle Sales**

	LOW	HIGH
Decline in Japanese-brand sales (thousand units)[*]	46.8	67.0
Increase in Harley sales (thousand units)	6.2	6.2
Net sales decline (thousand units)	40.6	60.8
Revenue lost by accessories producers at $150 per unit (million dollars)	$ 6.1	$ 9.1

[*]Sales lost due to demand decline for 700cc and larger motorcycles + sales lost to Harley − increase in 650cc and smaller motorcycles = decline in Japanese-brand sales.

Source: ICF, Inc. Presented to U.S. International Trade Commission, Investigation No. TA-201-47.

(c) Workers

Workers throughout the motorcycle industry would be hurt by the proposed tariff, Japanese producers cautioned. For dealers, whose overhead costs are largely fixed, the losses indicated in exhibit 18 would lead to the layoff of from 1,910 to 3,028 workers, assuming an average annual wage rate of $14,400 (equal to the rate of non-supervisory employees in U.S. auto dealerships). For accessories producers, the lost revenue would translate into 359 to 535 layoffs, given an annual wage ($17,000) equal to that for all blue-collar manufacturing employees in the U.S. Honda and Kawasaki would also be forced to lay off U.S. workers—between 211 and 317 of them, assuming that (1) sales of U.S.-produced Japanese cycles drop at the same rate as sales of all Japanese cycles, and

EXHIBIT 20   **Potential Net Employment Effects of the Tariff Rate Increase Recommended by Harley-Davidson**

	LOW	HIGH
Assuming all Harley jobs at stake		
Other U.S. jobs lost*	2,500	3,900
Harley-Davidson jobs preserved†	(2,600)	(2,600)
Net jobs lost (preserved)	(100)	1,300
Assuming 500 Harley jobs at stake		
Other U.S. jobs lost*	2,500	3,900
Harley-Davidson jobs preserved†	(500)	(500)
Net jobs lost (preserved)	2,000	3,400

*Includes provision for gains in revenues and employment by Harley dealers.
†Direct employment at Harley-Davidson.

Source: ICF, Inc. Presented to U.S. International Trade Commission, Investigation No. TA-201-47.

(2) the decline in hours worked in U.S. plants is proportional to the decline in sales of U.S.-produced Japanese cycles. (The brief also noted that "Honda and Kawasaki [might] find continued domestic production to be uneconomical, thus putting all employment in the domestic production of [heavyweight] motorcycles in jeopardy.") In total, Japanese producers concluded, the proposed tariff would jeopardize 2,500–3,900 non-Harley jobs.

To determine employment effects on Harley, Japanese producers reasoned as follows: Harley produced at a rate of 32,000 units per year during 1982 with a labor force of 2,161 employees. An increase in annual production to 42,500 units (roughly the amount Harley claimed it would have to sell to make a satisfactory long-run profit) would raise output one-third. Assuming a proportional increase in employment, Harley would need roughly an additional 700 workers; but taking into account economies of scale, a reasonable estimate is that the proposed tariff would produce 500 new Harley jobs.

The Japanese producers acknowledge that were Harley to go out of business, all of the roughly 2,600 jobs involved might be lost. But they noted that Harley had been profitable in the late 1960s and early 1970s at a sales level of 15,000–35,000 cycles, and that a hard-core market of that size could sustain a reorganized and trimmed down company. In sum, even assuming all 2,600 Harley jobs were at stake, the proposed tariff would only preserve 100 domestic jobs overall. And under other assumptions, 3,400 U.S. jobs could be lost (see Exhibit 20). "The remedy proposed by Harley," the Japanese brief concluded, "is, therefore, far more likely to do serious damage during a period of desperately high unemployment than it is to produce even a temporary benefit."

Intangibles

While the ITC members were charged with assessing the narrow economic criteria contained in Section 201, it would be hard for them to ignore economic implications of the decision. Other U.S. industries lobbying hard against foreign imports—steel and machine-tools among them—waited and watched, as did those wary of an all-out trade war. The commissioners would also not be likely to ignore the special symbolism of Harley-Davidson: a peculiarly American product—loud, daring, and ruggedly individualistic—and the last true survivor of a once-prosperous U.S. industry.

Questions

1. Based on the information in this case, can we be reasonably sure that the United States has a comparative advantage in producing motorcycles? Why or why not?

2. If the United States no longer has a comparative advantage in producing motorcycles, should tariffs and quotas be imposed to ensure the survival of the U.S. motorcycle industry? Why or why not?

3. How important are exchange rates in determining whether Harley-Davidson can compete with its Japanese rivals? If they are important, why and in what way are they important?

4. Has there been a significant transfer of technology from Japan to the United States in the motorcycle industry? Have Japanese motorcycle makers established subsidiaries in the United States?

5. Was the harm to Harley-Davidson from motorcycle imports great enough to justify restricting such imports, based on the International Trade Commission's criteria?

6. Besides import competition, were there other possible reasons for Harley-Davidson's economic condition? Did Harley-Davidson measure reasonably precisely the effects of import competition and show that it was the principal cause of the firm's problems?

7. If the ITC's decision is to grant tariff relief to Harley-Davidson, what would be the effect on the well-being of (a) buyers of motorcycles, (b) motorcycle dealers, (c) Harley-Davidson stockholders, employees, and suppliers, and (d) Japanese motorcycle producers?

8. If you were an ITC member, would you vote in favor of Harley's requested tariff increase?